THE PRINCE CONSORT

H.R.H. THE PRINCE CONSORT

Reproduced by gracious permission of Her Majesty The Queen
from the painting by A. E. Penley at Windsor

The Prince Consort

A POLITICAL BIOGRAPHY

Frank Eyck

HOUGHTON MIFFLIN COMPANY, BOSTON
THE RIVERSIDE PRESS, CAMBRIDGE

K

To My Father and Teacher

CONTENTS

INTRODUCTION

THIS study arose from a conviction that the full historical importance of the Prince Consort could only be appreciated by linking his contribution to his new with that to his old country. There appeared to be a tendency for British writers to see the Prince only in the British setting and for German researchers to be primarily interested in the German angle. This has failed to do justice to his essentially Anglo-German and inter-European personality.

The largest collection of the Prince's correspondence is at Windsor and I have to acknowledge the gracious permission of Her Majesty the Queen to make use of material from the Royal Archives and to reproduce the portrait of Prince Albert by Penley. From 1954 onwards, I was privileged to be allowed to study the Prince's political papers on British and German affairs. I discovered that some of the most interesting remarks on British political life were written in German, just as light on his ideas about his native country was often cast by his correspondence with British ministers. Two trips to Coburg helped to show me the Prince in his native environment and thanks to the kindness of the Duchess and the Prince of Saxe-Coburg I was able to draw on the Ducal correspondence deposited in the local state archives. I also wish to express my appreciation of the Earl of Clarendon's permission to quote from the Clarendon papers. In addition, I used the British Foreign Office papers at the Public Record Office. My thanks are due to John Murray for allowing me to use extracts from the *Letters of Queen Victoria* and the *Letters of the Prince Consort*, edited by K. Jagow; to Longmans Green & Co. for permission to quote from the *Later Correspondence of Lord John Russell*, edited by G. P. Gooch; to the Oxford University Press for allowing me to use passages from *Early Victorian England*, edited by G. M. Young; and to Macmillan & Co. for authority to quote from the *Greville Memoirs*, edited by Lytton Strachey and Roger Fulford.

The Prince Consort did not look at the problems of England and Germany in isolation. After he had, with his methodical German mind, grasped and developed the theory and practice of the constitutional monarchy in Britain, he tried to ensure its application to Germany. The Prussian marriage of his daughter

9

was the culmination of this policy, which had far-reaching ideological and international implications. He wanted the new Germany to counter-balance Russian despotism and Bonapartism. The course of later history enhances the interest of these ideas if they are viewed sympathetically and not ironically. They represent a last attempt to utilise the old dynasticism to guide the new nationalism into safe channels.

I have refrained from dealing at length with parts of the Prince Consort's life which are already well known and have concentrated on those events on which I feel I can throw new light. Throughout I have tried to base my conclusions firmly on the sources and have, I hope, resisted the temptation of filling gaps with speculation.

A considerable portion of the quoted correspondence has been translated from the German. Everything marked *tr.* has been rendered from that language. Passages containing some English words in the original German have been shown as *mainly tr.* Many of the German constructions are so involved that some adaptation has been necessary to make them at all translatable and clear. But care has been taken to retain the essential flavour of style and thought.

Reference to books is made, after their first mention, by giving the author and a short title. Full titles will be found in the list of sources, which is arranged alphabetically by authors or editors. Page references in the footnotes are taken from the editions stated in the sources.

I owe much to the many who have helped me with the collection of material and the writing of the book. It is not possible to mention all of them here. I am particularly grateful for the assistance I received from the Queen's Librarian, Sir Owen Morshead, and his staff.

My researches were begun when I was still on the news staff of the British Broadcasting Corporation. Since October 1956 I have been fortunate enough to hold a Rockefeller Research Fellowship at St. Antony's College, Oxford. My thanks are due to the Warden and Fellows of the College for the encouragement and assistance they have given me.

As to my wife's help, all I can say is that without her sympathetic and yet critical co-operation this book would never have been written.

FRANK EYCK

Oxford, June 1958

PART ONE

The Setting

1819–1847

Chapter One

YOUTH

WHEN the twenty-year-old Prince Albert of Saxe-Coburg married his cousin Queen Victoria in February 1840, hardly anybody would have thought it possible that he would, within a short time, play an important part in British and European politics. The young Prince came from a minor German state about the size of a small English county, run—in spite of the Napoleonic upheaval—on the lines of eighteenth-century benevolent despotism. This type of dwarf state, immortalised in Thackeray's "Pumpernickel", did not pose any of the intricate constitutional problems which England faced at the time. Moreover, the position of a Consort to a Queen Regnant, under whatever title, was notoriously difficult. The precedents were hardly encouraging. In Portugal, Albert's Coburg cousin Ferdinand, though granted the title of King, had not always been able to make his influence felt over his wife, Queen Maria, who had all the traditional stubbornness of a Braganza. Was Albert going to find himself excluded from political influence by a young Queen of the headstrong temperament so characteristic of the Hanoverian dynasty, and to be another George of Denmark? Were British statesmen going to take kindly to foreign influence on the throne after the experience of Philip II of Spain and William III of Orange? Surely they were not likely to welcome a revival of German influence when the cumbersome tie of the British Crown with Hanover had just happily been severed, thanks to the different laws of succession prevailing in the two countries.

Prince Albert was born at Rosenau near Coburg on 26 August 1819. At birth his prospects could not be considered brilliant. He was the second son of Duke Ernest I of Saxe-Coburg and his wife Louise, the heiress of the slightly bigger Duchy of Gotha to the north of Coburg on the other side of the Thüringer Wald. The marriage of the young heiress of Gotha to the sixteen years older profligate Duke of Coburg was dictated purely by dynastic reasons. It fulfilled its purpose with the speedy birth of two sons, Ernest and Albert, who were in the line of succession to both Duchies. The Duke, however, neglected his lively and somewhat frivolous wife. The result was disastrous. The young mother sought distraction elsewhere and

eventually found in an officer at the Court, Baron von Hanstein,
later Count Poelzig, the love and sympathy which her husband had
denied her.[1] Thus far it is the story of the Princess of Ahlden,
George I's luckless wife, all over again, but now comes a nineteenth-
century variation. The Duke did not incarcerate his wife. He had
married her, as George I had wedded Sophia Dorothea, for her
inheritance. Ernest did not pretend to any indignation he could not
have possessed. Louise allowed the Gotha dominions to pass to
Coburg, although she might have played them as a card against her
husband. One has the impression that Louise was indifferent to
position and wealth and that she merely sought an elusive happiness.
A separation was arranged in 1824, soon followed by a divorce. The
Duke had achieved all he wanted. Gotha had been caught in the
Coburg net. Louise was not so fortunate. She retired with her para-
mour, whom she married, to the small Coburg possession of St. Wen-
del in the Saar. She was no longer allowed access to her children and
never got over their loss. She only saw them again once, when, in
the guise of a peasant woman, she caught a glimpse of them at
a festival.[2] She died of cancer in 1831, at the age of thirty, in
Paris.

The boys were the victims. The elder, Ernest, followed in his
father's footsteps and—except for some interest in politics—frittered
away his life in a series of love affairs.[3] Albert, a year younger, took
a different turn. The loss of his mother and the break-up of his home
when he was five years old had a profound influence on him. He
still remembered vividly many years later what a shock it had been
for him to have suddenly lost his mother,[4] for whom he always kept
an affection. Deep down, he had her warmth and sensitivity. He
was never on close terms with his father. When he reached adolescence, he reacted strongly against his father's immorality. For him,
after the experience of his childhood, looseness of morals acquired the
inevitable connotation of domestic unhappiness.

Indirectly, the disreputable father proved a blessing, as there were
forces at work which wanted to prevent Albert's contamination with
this polluted atmosphere. The Prince seems to have owed his

[1] The present writer is unimpressed by the doubts which have been voiced as
to Ernest I's paternity of Albert.
[2] Max Mueller, "Die Stammutter des englischen Königshauses hält Totenrast
. . ." 2 ff.
[3] For Ernest II's "famille ducale et demi-ducale" see A. Ponsonby, Henry
Ponsonby, 350.
[4] Florschütz to Queen Victoria, 7 January 1863 (Royal Archives Z.272.6).

removal from Coburg for long periods mainly to Baron Stockmar.[1] This remarkable man contributed considerably to the complete change of circumstances of the Coburg dynasty which was then taking place.

When Albert was born, the fortunes of the family were at a low ebb. Albert's uncle Leopold, his father's younger brother, seemed to be looking forward to a splendid position when he married the English Prince Regent's only child and heir, Princess Charlotte, in 1816. But the following year saw the complete destruction of his hopes with his wife's death in childbed. Still, the Coburgs never gave up, and 1818 saw Leopold's sister Victoria, the widowed Princess of Leiningen, installed as the wife of the Duke of Kent, a younger brother of the Prince Regent. Death, which had been so unkind to Leopold, was now kind to his sister by removing all those who stood between her daughter Victoria and the throne. The Princess Victoria was born a few weeks before Prince Albert and from an early age Leopold and Stockmar prepared the cousins for the idea of their eventual marriage.

In 1831, as Albert was beginning to approach his adolescence, Leopold became King of the Belgians. This event was to change Albert's life. Staying from time to time at his uncle's court at Brussels, he was initiated into the affairs of a state whose secession from the Netherlands had made a stir in Europe and had caused raised eyebrows in Vienna and St. Petersburg. He was beginning to learn about the inner workings of the diplomacy of the Powers, a subject which fascinated him right down to the end of his days. He saw how his uncle was applying to his new kingdom the experience of constitutional monarchy he had gained during his residence in Britain. He became firmly opposed to the autocratic system of the Holy Alliance powers, which at that period treated King Leopold as one of their worst enemies.

There was always a slight disproportion between the high aims of the Coburg political mission in Europe and the family's greed for power and wealth. Naturally, the spectacular rise of the family from insignificance in 1815 to a European position in the middle of the century invited envy. Among his fellow princes in Germany, Leopold was given the nick-name of "Monsieur Peu-à-peu", or "Marquis Tout-doucement".[2] It was perhaps an anachronism that

---

[1] Memorandum by Prince Albert's Private Secretary George Anson, 16 February 1841 (Royal Archives Y.54.15).
[2] See H. v. Treitschke, "Deutsche Geschichte", IV, 82 ff.

in an age of rising nationalism a dynasty could still be successful in the international royal marriage market to an extent reminiscent of the Habsburgs in centuries gone by.

It is curious that Leopold was assisted in building up the fortunes of his family by a man who was out of sympathy with many of his main assumptions. Stockmar, the physician from Coburg, remained a believer in the future of his German fatherland to which Leopold, with his international plans, was indifferent. Stockmar saw the futility of the separate existence of so many small German states. Leopold was a man of the world, who was ready to sacrifice moral principles at the altar of success, and who enjoyed the good things of life which went with position and wealth. Stockmar, on the other hand, remained abstemious, dour, moral and high-principled. Both men drove Albert hard during his adolescence and early manhood, Stockmar even harder than Leopold. The young Prince never resented Stockmar's imperiousness. It may be doubted, however, whether the Baron was wise in forcing his pupil to be for ever serious at an age when he should have had time to enjoy himself. The Baron's deadly earnestness was not a useful example for the Prince. It was a pity in some ways that Stockmar's influence was so much more predominant than Leopold's, for Albert might have profited by emulating some of his uncle's ease of manners. Stockmar's uncritical pro-Germanism also proved a hindrance to Albert in England. The Baron did not, however, shake his pupil's faith in the destiny of his family and in the importance of the small German states in general and of the Duchies of Coburg and Gotha in particular.

Albert's tutor, Florschütz, another Coburger, must also have been an unusual personality. Albert later always recognised his debt to him. In the eyes of some notables in the Duchies, Florschütz had a great defect. He was suspected of liberalism. One of the notables, a Herr von Wangenheim, considered it his duty "as a faithful Gothaner" to report officially to the Ministry at Coburg that

> his suspicion about the Prince having imbibed liberal principles had been justified.[1]

Wangenheim gathered that Florschütz was to be blamed for this development, even more than the influence of Brussels. One of Florschütz's crimes was that he encouraged his pupils to study philosophy, obviously an undertaking fraught with danger.[2]

---

[1] G. v. Wangenheim from Hanover, 11 April 1838 (Coburg Archives), tr.
[2] Ibid.

One dreads to think what would have become of Albert if the narrow-minded and reactionary Coburg officials—so typical of most contemporary German states—would have continued to run his life. Their power over him was, however, about to end. They could not prevent him from drinking at the poisoned wells of "liberalism" at his uncle's court at Brussels. All they could now endeavour to do was to select a university for him which was likely to put him politically on the right track. Through an intermediary the court officials consulted the famous conservative jurist Savigny at Berlin. The intermediary reported that he had confidentially informed Savigny of the dangers which were feared at Coburg. Savigny considered that for middle class students "the danger of seduction was perhaps less great in Berlin than at the smaller universities". But for princes there were too many distractions in Berlin, such as court balls, parades, etc., and therefore a quieter place might be better. For these reasons Savigny recommended the Prussian University of Bonn.[1]

The advice was followed, and the brothers studied law at Bonn from 1837 to 1838. One of their teachers, Moritz August von Bethmann-Hollweg, a grandfather of the Reich Chancellor, was a follower of Savigny and of the Historical Law School which was then coming to the fore. The School stressed the historical roots of representative institutions like the Estates in Germany. Bethmann-Hollweg was at that time ultra-conservative, but later dissociated himself from the reactionaries and became a Minister in the Prussian "New Era" government just before Bismarck's rise to the Premiership. Another professor, August Wilhelm Schlegel, provided a link with the Romantic movement. Albert was out of sympathy with the catholicising tendencies of some of the Romantics and he was not converted to its idealisation of the past. The most important effect the German Romantic movement had on him was to endow him with its strong faith in German unification.

Albert's time at Bonn University reinforced the strong hereditary Protestantism appropriate for a member of the Ernestine line of the House of Saxony. The Prince does not appear to have taken to the spirit of conciliation between the two denominations for which the university stood. To be fair to all sides, two theological faculties— a Catholic and a Protestant one—were created when the university was refounded by King Frederick William III of Prussia in 1818.

[1] Extract from an anonymous letter by a pupil of Savigny from Berlin, 9 January 1837 (Coburg Archives), tr.

Actually, while Prince Albert was at Bonn, the conciliatory con-
fessional policy of the Prussian government was running into trouble.
The Roman Catholic Archbishop of Cologne, Droste-Vischering,
clashed with the civil authorities over the question of mixed marriages
and was arrested.[1] Albert had no hesitation about siding with the
government against the Archbishop. He spoke of the prelate's "open
war against the Prussian government" and took seriously Catholic
threats to "chase the Prussians out of the country with flails".[2]

His dislike of Catholicism influenced his attitude to Italy which
he visited in 1837 and in 1839. During his stay in Rome on his second
trip, he was stirred for a moment when the Pope blessed the crowds,
but most of what he saw in the Holy City during Easter week smacked
of idolatry to him.[3] He was, however, pleased to be received by the
Pope, who discussed art with him. Generally he was disappointed
with Italy:

> In many, many respects the country is far behind what one had expected.
> In the climate, in the scenery, in the study of the arts, one feels most
> disagreeably disappointed.[4]

His reserved attitude to the country was to be of political importance
when the question of Italian unity became acute in the years from
1848 onwards. The trip was, however, a useful corrective to Romantic
artistic influences, for he wrote that he had "made his peace with
the Antique".[5]

One of his earliest expressions of opinion about public affairs dates
from the Italian journey. From Florence, he voiced his horror to his
tutor Florschütz that a death sentence had been carried out at Gotha.
He added characteristically:

> For the great mass, however, it is a spectacle, and I can well believe that
> many people poured in.[6]

The fickleness and the foolishness of the masses is a Leitmotiv in
Albert's view.

A further journey to Italy was the first which he undertook without his brother. But his brother's activities were never far from his

[1] The distinguished German historian Franz Schnabel, a Catholic, only puts up
a hesitant defence of the Archbishop in his "Deutsche Geschichte im 19. Jahrhundert" (IV, 133 ff.).
[2] To his father from Bonn, 24 November 1837 (C. Grey, "The Early Years of
the Prince Consort", pp. 159–60 and 408), tr.
[3] To his father from Rome, 31 March 1838 (Grey, pp. 200 and 416).
[4] To Prince William Löwenstein from Coburg, 30 June 1839 (Grey, pp. 206
and 418), tr.
[5] To Florschütz from Naples, 7 April 1839 (Royal Archives, Addl. Ms. A/6.20), tr.
[6] 5 March 1839 (Royal Archives Addl. Ms. A/6.17), tr.

mind, even after his marriage. He was horrified to discover that the father was being repeated in the son, that the younger Ernest was following the same path of unbridled immorality as the elder. This was a matter which touched Albert deeply. He still remembered their childhood and the unhappiness they had suffered. Here more unhappiness was being created. The danger of Coburg fickleness was a nightmare which haunted him all his life and accounts for some of the tension in his relations with his eldest son.

Albert's early maturity and goodness of heart is revealed in his personal correspondence with his brother after their parting. Thus, on New Year's Day 1841 Albert wrote to his brother, from Windsor:

> . . . I am deeply distressed and grieved by the news of your severe illness . . . I have to infer that it is a new outbreak of the same disease which you had here. If I should be wrong I shall thank God; but should I be right, I must advise you as a loving brother to give up all ideas of marriage for the next two years and to work earnestly for the restoration and consolidation of your health . . . to marry would be as immoral as dangerous . . . for you. If the worst should happen, you would deprive your wife of her health and honour, and should you have a family, you would give your children a life full of suffering . . . and your country a sick heir. At best your wife could not respect you and her love would thus not have any value for you; should you not have the strength to make her contented in married life (which demands its sacrifices), this would lead to domestic discord and unhappiness . . . For God's sake do not trifle with matters which are so sacred . . .[1]

These expressions of brotherly love and concern are not marred by any condescension or prudery. They impress by their simplicity and warmth. Albert also gave a warning to his brother that he could not criticise the father unless he set a good example. Altogether, this is a remarkable letter for a man of twenty-one.

Albert's outlook on morality is of profound importance in interpreting his attitude to politics. It is only too easy to dispose of it as prudery. Admittedly there was an element of that, and a strong one. The primary basis of his attitude to morality was a sense of responsibility born of an awareness of the consequences of irresponsibility which he had witnessed in his own family. In these matters he followed Stockmar and Florschütz. During his early manhood there was none of the Puritan perfectionism and intolerance which later on marred his approach, contrasting so strangely with the *via media* he adopted in so many questions.

[1] Prince Albert to his brother, 1 January 1841 (Coburg Archives), tr.

The story of Prince Albert's courtship with Queen Victoria has often been told. Mutual attraction smoothed the path of those who had for long planned the marriage. By the time of his wedding, Albert had easily outgrown the narrow particularism of the small Thuringian state. He had begun to form his own judgment on the affairs of Europe. He was quickly to find himself plunged into intricacies of British political affairs and constitutional conventions and to make his own contribution to the solution of a serious crisis.

Chapter Two

BEGINNINGS

IN 1840, the monarchy was, imperceptibly, in a stage of transition, at a parting of the ways. On the one hand, the personal influence of the Crown was still considerable, valued by any government. Thus the personal opening or prorogation of parliament by the Sovereign was a much appreciated sign of the support of the Crown. William IV in 1834 and Queen Victoria in 1839 had intervened decisively in government crises by allowing full rein to their personal views. When the question of the dissolution of parliament was discussed in May 1841, the Whig ministers pondered over the problem whether it was right to have a dissolution when a parliament might be "returned against the Crown". Melbourne proclaimed to the Queen the theory that the Crown had at any rate since the end of personal Stuart rule "always had a majority returned in favour of it" at general elections. But if the Whigs dissolved now, they were unlikely to obtain a majority. The conclusion he reached is interesting not so much for its historical accuracy as for the attitude to the Crown it reveals:

> I am afraid . . . that for the first time the Crown would have an opposition returned smack against it; and that would be an affront to which I am very unwilling to expose the Crown.[1]

The identification of the Crown with the government of the day was thus far more than a purely formal one, as it became later. On the other hand, there were already ominous signs of a decline in the power of the Crown. It was no longer so easy—as in the days before the great upheaval which began with the July Revolution of 1830 in Paris and ended with the Great Reform Act of 1832—for the Crown to secure the return of its government at election time. King William IV failed to get the Peel government confirmed in power at the general election of 1835. The Crown found itself in the dilemma of being expected to live up to the position of power associated with it in people's minds, without any longer being so influential.

In another way, too, Queen Victoria's reign had reached a critical

[1] Extract from the Queen's Journal, 15 May 1841 ("Letters of Queen Victoria", henceforth quoted as *Letters*).

stage at the time of her marriage. The original wave of popularity which had greeted the Queen had passed, and she had suffered a setback in 1839. Unwisely, she had allowed herself to become involved in the affair of Lady Flora Hastings and had given the impression that she believed the scandalous reports about her pregnancy which were proved so tragically wrong in the end with her early death from a malignant tumour. The Queen's apparent intervention was particularly unfortunate owing to Lady Flora's family connection with the Tories.

More important still was the Queen's course of action in the "Bedchamber Crisis" of 1839. The new Sovereign had completely identified herself with the Whig ministry in power at her accession and in particular with the Prime Minister, Lord Melbourne. The old statesman took a delight in explaining to the young Queen, in a homely way, the intricacies of British constitutional customs. He acted as Private Secretary to the Queen in addition to being Prime Minister. Listening attentively to the wisdom of old age, the Sovereign forgot that she might one day have to entrust the opposition with the task of government. Thus, when Lord Melbourne resigned in May 1839, the Queen allowed Peel's attempt to form a government to fail over her refusal to make *any* changes among the Whig Ladies of the Bedchamber.

King Leopold and Baron Stockmar had been determined from the first that Prince Albert should assist the Queen in her constitutional functions. King Leopold said in August 1840, when he was on a visit at Windsor:

> The Prince ought in business as in everything to be necessary to the Queen, he should be to her a walking dictionary for reference on any point which her own knowledge or education have not enabled her to answer. There should be no concealment from him on any subject . . .[1]

In general this was a sound view of the situation, though one might feel that the Prince, barely twenty-one and just married, was being driven rather too hard.

> With judgment, forethought and decision all will work well, but he must not sleep, he must studiously imbibe that information on every subject, which may enable him to be ready and fit to render advice under all circumstances . . .[2]

Early responsibility and the discipline imposed on him by Stockmar

---

[1] Memorandum by Anson, 15 August 1840 (Royal Archives Y.54.8).
[2] Ibid.

and Leopold no doubt partly accounts for Albert's excessive earnestness which proved a hindrance to him in his relations with the
outside world. His youthful tendencies to indolence and a harmless
light-heartedness were crushed. He was never allowed to be properly
young.

Twice a week, the Prince took lessons in British constitutional law
with "a famous jurist Mr. Selwyn",[1] as he reported to his brother.[2]
He said that he was very interested in the subject, to which he was
soon to make his contribution.

Melbourne's influence at first only received a slight check as a
result of the Queen's marriage. It was only towards the end of 1840,
as a consequence of the Queen's first pregnancy, that Prince Albert
was constituted a kind of Private Secretary to the Sovereign.
Melbourne did not actually hinder the Prince's progress, as he
generally believed in letting things work themselves out. But he
naturally did not do very much to enable the Prince to assume an
influence with the Queen which might limit his own. The greatest
obstacle to a harmonious political collaboration between husband
and wife was the former governess of the Queen, the German-born
Baroness Lehzen. King Leopold, Baron Stockmar and the Prince
were agreed that her influence on the Queen was bad. She was held
by them and by the Tories to have had a hand in the troubles of
1839. She seems to have encouraged the Queen to listen to gossip,
instead of forming her own opinion, as the Prince wished.

Prince Albert viewed the Queen's identification with the Whigs
with alarm. For this reason he had objected at the time of his marriage to the appointment of George Anson as his Private Secretary.
Anson, a member of a well-connected Whig family, on Lord Melbourne's staff, was at first supposed to combine his new duties for
the Prince with those for the Prime Minister, a typical example of
the merging of crown and government functions at this time. Prince
Albert succeeded in getting Anson for himself. The Prince had every
reason to be satisfied with the choice of his Private Secretary who
soon adapted himself to his new role at Court and ceased to be a
Whig partisan.

The Prince considered it essential that the Crown should remain
above party and should be scrupulously fair in its treatment of
political parties. The Crown should not descend into the political
arena, it should not take sides in the contest of parties, towards which

---

[1] William Selwyn (1775–1855), Treasurer of Lincoln's Inn.
[2] Prince Albert to his brother, 27 October 1840 (Coburg Archives), tr.

he had a sceptical attitude. As early as 15 April 1840—thus only
two months after his marriage—he had written:

> I do not think it is necessary to belong to any party. Composed as party
> is here of two extremes, both must be wrong. The exercise of an unbiased
> judgment may form a better and wiser creed by extracting the good from
> each.[1]

His opinion about the two major parties is interesting in the light
of the developments which were to take place during the two following decades:

> The Whigs seek to change *before change* is required. The love of change is
> their great failing. The Tories on the other hand *resist change* long after
> the feeling and temper of the times has loudly demanded it and at last
> make a virtue of necessity by an ungracious concession. My endeavour
> will be to form my opinions quite apart from politics and party, and I
> believe such an attempt may succeed.[2]

The Prince was thus adopting a line of conduct diametrically
opposed to that of the Queen. In January 1841, he began to explain
some of his political ideas to the Queen:

> The Prince . . . urged that her Majesty should by degrees regain possession
> of the privileges which through youth and inexperience she had been
> induced to yield up . . . The Prince said he could never feel satisfied till
> he saw her in the same position as when she ascended the throne.[3]

The Queen replied that the present was not the time to make
changes. At first sight, the Prince's attitude might look like an
attempt to "put the clock back". But it is more likely that the
Prince was indirectly criticising the Queen's identification with the
Whigs and also Melbourne's anomalous position which blurred the
line of division between acts of the Crown and acts of Government.
   Prince Albert saw that the Crown could not afford another
Bedchamber crisis or Flora Hastings affair. From the end of April
1841, when the Whig government was tottering, he worked cease-
lessly to remove all obstacles to a return of the Tories to power,
should the Whigs find it necessary to resign. The Prince's persistence
is all the more creditable as he was prepared to risk his wife's wrath.
The Queen still adhered strongly to the Whigs. She knew she could
rely on the Whigs, but was doubtful whether the Tories would ever
become her real friends. She did not want to exchange solid for
problematical assistance. The Prince rightly considered that the

---

[1] Memorandum by Prince Albert, 15 April 1840 (Royal Archives Y.54.3).
[2] Ibid.
[3] Memorandum by Anson, 2 January 1841 (Royal Archives Y.54.12).

Whig ministers were rather unscrupulous in squeezing the last ounce of support out of the Crown for their own purposes. Thus the Whig government insisted on the Queen personally proroguing parliament in June 1841.[1] Anson's previous remonstrance with Melbourne had proved of no avail. The Prime Minister had not hesitated to tell him:

> The Queen has committed herself too decidedly to hold back now and her opinions are well known to be with us.[2]

The immediate cause of the government crisis of May 1841 was the defeat of the Whigs in the House of Commons over the proposed reduction of the duty on foreign sugar. This commodity was political dynamite. Tampering with its protection stirred up powerful vested interests and evoked the slogan that sugar grown by free labour in the British colonies was being neglected in favour of that grown by slaves in foreign territories. On 18 May, the government found itself in a minority of thirty-six. Coming on top of a defeat on 29 April over the government's proposal to reduce the electoral property qualification in Ireland, and of the general weakness of their position, the Whig ministers had to consider whether to resign immediately or to dissolve parliament.

The crisis was a turning point in Prince Albert's career. He succeeded in overcoming the Queen's reluctance to consult him on affairs of state and established himself as her permanent political adviser. He was fast leaving behind the early political grounding which King Leopold and Baron Stockmar had given him, and making his own personal contribution to British political life and constitutional development in the light of his deepening knowledge of affairs. As appointments to the Queen's Household had proved the stumbling block in 1839, Prince Albert at the outset of the crisis formulated principles governing alterations in his own Household on a change of government. These were to be a model for the Queen's Household:

> . . . The Head of the Prince's Household should change with every Administration, thereby giving a sanction to the Queen's existing government . . .
>
> All other members of the House of Commons in His Royal Highness's Household should be required to give up their seats in parliament or to resign their offices.[3]

---

[1] Melbourne to Queen Victoria, 13 June 1841 (Royal Archives C.21.56).
[2] Memorandum by Anson, 13 June 1841 (Royal Archives Y.54.52).
[3] Memorandum by Anson, 5 May 1841 (Royal Archives Y.54.25).

The Prince saw that the era of the personal rule of monarchs was over in Britain. There could be no return to the second decade of George III's reign. The Crown must always be prepared to work with whatever party or party combination was strongest in the House of Commons. Albert felt that the Crown's position in the change-over from one party to another was needlessly complicated by its identification with one of them. The Sovereign should adopt certain general, objective and impartial rules in his relations with the political parties. It should be recognised that it was impossible to differentiate between the personal and political aspects of the Crown in affairs of state. The Royal Household could not be considered the purely personal affair of the Sovereign. Many appointments there had assumed a political significance and the way they were filled was considered a test of the co-operation of the Crown with the government of the day.

The negotiations with Peel, which were conducted with the utmost secrecy, began on 9 May 1841, while the Whig government was still in office, with the Queen's and Melbourne's approval. It was the Prince who pressed for a clarification of the situation at an early stage, while Melbourne characteristically would have preferred to follow events. The Queen soon grew restive and there was a serious danger of a breakdown of the negotiations. This would have put the monarchy in a difficult position.

On the part of the Court the conversations were conducted with great skill by Anson, who seems to have had the confidence of the Queen, as well as of Sir Robert Peel.[1] To deal with the immediate difficulty of the Whig Ladies of the Bedchamber, the Prince proposed having Peel informed that it would not be necessary for him to raise the question again. The Queen would simply tell the Tory leader at the first interview that the three Ladies closely connected with the outgoing administration had tendered their resignation.[2] Peel went as far as he could to meet the Queen's wishes, particularly over matters of procedure. Thus the Queen attached considerable importance to announcing personally to Ladies of the Bedchamber that she wished to appoint them. At first Peel was unwilling to concede this. After Anson had again consulted the Queen, a *modus vivendi* was found which allowed the Sovereign to retain this right, conceding at the same time that the Prime Minister should previously

---

[1] Some of Anson's memoranda on the negotiations are given in *Letters*.
[2] Peel was informed accordingly by Anson at their, second meeting (Memorandum by Anson, 10 May 1841, Royal Archives Y.54.29).

notify to the Ladies the Queen's desire to appoint them. The whole matter had been complicated by the fact that in the past Lord Melbourne had sometimes written to the Ladies to offer them posts at the Court, but he considered that he had done so not in the capacity of a minister but of a friend.[1]

Within a month, the Queen was beginning to regret the negotiations. Trouble was being caused by the Russell faction led by the restless Lord John Russell, then Colonial Secretary. Apparently Lord John got his brother, the Duke of Bedford, rather a likeable, if weak man, to draft a memorandum, nominally addressed to his wife—one of the Ladies of the Bedchamber—but in fact meant for the Queen's eye. The memorandum is a subtle mixture of persuasion and blackmail:

> John thinks that if you were to resign immediately on a change of government, an impression would be given to the public that we thought the Queen wrong in May 1839, that it would have the appearance of deserting Her Majesty. It sanctions the course taken by Sir Robert Peel at that time . . . John thinks . . . that your resigning, at such a moment, would imply that you are to be considered as his representative in the Household —the truth being that your appointment [is] one offered by the Queen, and accepted by you, not on political, but on personal grounds . . . I consider the course proposed . . . by Lord Melbourne . . . would have the appearance of giving a triumph to him [Sir Robert Peel], which he could not fairly ask for . . . The remarks do not apply to the Duchess of Sutherland or Lady Normanby [the other two Ladies involved].[2]

The Queen was swayed by this memorandum. She told her husband that she thought it better if the Duchess resigned gradually. The Prince cogently replied that this step would then all the more clearly be seen to be arising from a demand of Sir Robert Peel, that the resignation previous to a change of government was designed to remove the ground for any demands of this kind on the part of the new Prime Minister. The Queen was particularly struck by the passage in the Duke's letter referring to Sir Robert's triumph, for she said that, if the Duchess resigned soon, she "would feel vanquished and lowered before the world". The Queen added that she had been rushed and compromised by the Prince and by Lord Melbourne.

The Duke of Bedford and Lord John Russell knew that the

---

[1] Memorandum by Anson about his third interview with Peel, 11 May 1841, exchange of letters between Anson and Peel of the same date (Royal Archives Y.54.37–39).
[2] The Duke to the Duchess of Bedford, Windsor Castle, 11 June 1841 (Royal Archives C.21.53).

argument about the Duchess being there in a purely personal capacity at the invitation of the Sovereign would appeal to the Queen. But the Prince realised that this division between personal and political capacities was artificial and had become untenable. Independently of Peel, he had reached the same conclusion which the Conservative leader put succinctly in a conversation with Anson:

> He [Sir Robert Peel] could not separate the political and private character of the Queen.[1]

Peel used this argument in connection with the necessity of employing Court appointments to strengthen his position in parliament:

> It would be his duty to strengthen Her Majesty's Government (in its uphill and difficult course) by every means. He must therefore reserve himself upon this question of appointing Equerries in or out of Parliament. The place of Equerry was tenable with a seat in Parliament and he must keep himself disengaged to strengthen his Government by every legitimate means.[2]

Fortunately Prince Albert persevered and the Queen did not in fact disavow the negotiations, as she threatened to do at one stage. Prince Albert was aware through reports from Anson that a critical situation would arise for the Monarchy if Peel were again foiled over the Household appointments. Lord Ashley, better known as the seventh Earl of Shaftesbury, then a close collaborator of Peel, told Anson that it took the Tory leader a long time to get over his failure in 1839. Ashley doubted whether Peel would have been prepared to make another attempt at forming a government within a few months of the Bedchamber Crisis of 1839. The unwillingness of a major party to co-operate with the Crown in the carrying on of Her Majesty's government would have created a dangerous situation. Ashley thought that another "Bedchamber Crisis" or "Flora Hastings affair" would prove fatal to the Monarchy.

The Prince received valuable support during these critical weeks from King Leopold, who happened to be on a visit to the British Court. Later on, the paths of nephew and uncle were frequently to diverge, but at this stage the King of the Belgians proved a staunch ally. He could appreciate his nephew's difficulties, for he had nearly found himself in a similar position as consort to a Queen Regnant. He could also tender advice as to how a husband might best treat a strong-minded Hanoverian princess. On several occasions,

---

[1] Memorandum by Anson about his 5th secret interview with Peel, 13 May 1841 (Royal Archives Y.54.43).
[2] Ibid.

Queen Victoria was given homilies about the virtues of her late cousin Charlotte.[1] With Melbourne and Stockmar, King Leopold counselled the Prince to remain patient at a time when he was straining at the leash and was toying with the idea of provoking a rupture with the Baroness Lehzen.

King Leopold was very critical of the state which affairs had reached.

> He thought Politics never ought to have been brought to the position they are in . . . Great cause of offence had been given to the Tory Party . . .[2]

He had himself built up a constitutional monarchy in Belgium which made history on the continent. This personal experience in government, coupled with his knowledge of British institutions, enabled him to give a candid judgment on the situation which would not have pleased his niece:

> The Monarchy of this Country has its sole foundation in the will of the people. Without that will it cannot stand and from that will it derives every prerogative and power. The Commonwealth has shown that the Country can exist and flourish without a monarchy and the Sovereign should be reminded forcibly by this fact, that the Sovereign of a free people cannot be the Sovereign of a party.[3]

The King condemned the Whigs for insisting on a dissolution though they expected to lose the election.

> It was unfair towards the Queen for the Government, knowing and expecting as they did to lose by a Dissolution, to use the power of the Crown to weaken the authority of the Crown by impairing the strength of that Government which they knew the Queen would be reduced to resort to.[4]

Actually the incoming Conservative Government was not weakened by the election, which cleared the air. From the point of view of the Crown perhaps the strongest argument against granting a dissolution to a weak government likely to go out was that it was deprived of a considerable handle over its successor by no longer having this power in reserve.

The smooth coming into power of Sir Robert Peel in 1841, without any further serious difficulties over Household questions, established Prince Albert firmly as the Queen's political adviser, increasingly overshadowing Stockmar, whom the Queen continued to consult occasionally during his periods of residence in Britain.

---

[1] Thus, King Leopold to Queen Victoria, 21 May 1845 (*Letters*).
[2] Memorandum by Anson, 14 July 1841 (Royal Archives Y.54.55).
[3] Ibid.   [4] Ibid.

From now on the Prince was never absent when important
political matters were discussed. Ministers on the whole began to
appreciate the usefulness of a semi-formal link with the throne.
Except in the struggle with Palmerston—and even there to some
extent—the Prince used his influence to moderate and reconcile.
Of a more dispassionate outlook than his wife, he was able to mediate
where the Queen's strong temperament put an excessive strain on
the nice balance of constitutional forces. In general, he successfully
opposed an objective attitude to the Queen's personal rather
Hanoverian approach. He was always on the lookout for general rules
and customs to govern constitutional relationships and thus to
remove a large sphere of government from the area of personal
likes and dislikes. At times he was perhaps, with his methodical
German mind, with that curious blend of scholar and official,
inclined to systematise too much. But under his guidance, the Queen
on the whole began to be swayed less by personal feelings and to
take a more detached view of affairs. Generally the Crown during
the remainder of Albert's lifetime played its part smoothly and
efficiently, often in very difficult circumstances of party politics.

With the removal of Baroness Lehzen in 1842, the last irresponsible
royal favourite disappears from British history. The moral tone of
the Court was raised. It may be argued that Prince Albert converted
the Queen to a prudery which she initially disliked. Sometimes moral
judgments certainly went to excessive lengths in affairs of state.
Melbourne said:

> That d— morality seemed to be entirely [i.e. the only thing] thought of
> and would be the destruction of everything. The system . . . is horrible,
> and you might as well set up two public censors of morals to pass judgment
> on every man who was thought of [for office].[1]

But the immediate future did not lie with the wise old eighteenth-
century sceptic or with Greville, who complained that the Court was
rather dull.[2] Inevitably, the looseness of Regency morals brought
forth a reaction. Albert's "middle-class morality" may have been
rather dull, but it was triumphant in the decade dominated by Sir
Robert Peel.

[1] Memorandum by Anson, 6 September 1841 (Royal Archives Y.54.73).
[2] See C. Greville's Memoirs, 10 June 1844 (V, 178–9).

Chapter Three

CONSOLIDATION

WITH Peel's return to power, Prince Albert no longer had a Prime Minister as his rival for the position of Private Secretary to the Queen. He ceased to be faced by the partnership of Queen and Prime Minister which he had found on his marriage. The new Prime Minister was still making his way—not only politically, but also socially—and owed much to the Prince's support.

Peel represented as nearly as possible that brand of enlightened conservatism which suited Prince Albert. His views on morality, too, were much closer to those of the Prince than Melbourne's had been. Peel was prepared to fall in with Prince Albert's ideas and to keep out of court appointments men with dubious personal records, however much trouble this might cause with his political friends. He did this although it was an open secret that the Queen did not then attach so much importance to this aspect.[1] Peel led a model family life in the Midlands, at Drayton, which the Queen and the Prince soon came to inspect. Melbourne, twice cited—not entirely innocently—in matrimonial suits, would not have been a suitable moral "censor", even if he had believed in moral censorship.

In foreign affairs the Court found the new government easier to deal with than the last. Sir Robert Peel agreed to a request of the Queen that Sir Hamilton Seymour should be retained as Minister at her uncle's Court at Brussels. He also promised that care should be taken in looking out for a moderate man to be Minister to Portugal. It was noted at Court that

> thus more was achieved by a simple letter from the Queen making the request than would have been extorted from Lord Palmerston by every remonstrance.[2]

It should not, however, be inferred from this sigh of relief that Palmerston had left office on bad terms with the Court.

The new Foreign Secretary, Lord Aberdeen, was inclined to take a more kindly view of the activities of Queen Maria and King Ferdinand of Portugal than the Whigs. Even the mild Melbourne had spoken of the King's "Coburg foolishness" and had blamed him for

[1] See Greville, 6 and 7 September 1841 (IV, 413-14).
[2] Memorandum by Anson, 8 September 1841 (Royal Archives Y.54.75).

not paying sufficient respect to liberal principles. He had suggested that Prince Albert should be cautious not to be misled by his example.[1] However, already while Lord Aberdeen was at the Foreign Office there were present in mild form the very elements which were to cause friction between the Crown and a masterful Foreign Secretary later. No minister of the Crown was likely to be particularly pleased if the Sovereign had independent sources of information, especially if they tended to undermine the conclusions he had himself reached. For inevitably this led to a questioning by the Crown of the reliability of the reports and of the value to be attached to the advice of the official diplomatic agent abroad. The British Minister to Portugal, Lord Howard de Walden, had come to the conclusion that the Portuguese Crown was very badly advised by the King's former tutor from Coburg, Dietz. Lord Aberdeen had sent to Prince Albert a private letter from Lord Howard putting forward this opinion. Prince Albert expressed concern:

> I really do not know how one could manage to get rid of Mr. Dietz and to supply his place with an equally honest but more enlightened and sensible man. I have been corresponding much lately with King Ferdinand, and should you like it and have time for it, I would send you my whole correspondence, which shows that the King is not blind about things and has great qualities, but he is inactive and not penetrated with that intense interest for public affairs which is wanted in that country more than anywhere to bring about the necessary changes. . . .[2]

Actually, the Prince was later converted to the necessity of Dietz's removal. But irrespective of this particular point at issue, problems were, of course, bound to crop up constantly on which various views could be held. A clash between Crown and Foreign Secretary was more likely to arise if each had his own informants. The Crown was entitled to see all important dispatches, though not all private letters, from the diplomatic agents abroad, to the Foreign Office. Prince Albert would not in the future always be as forthcoming in putting his own personal correspondence at the disposal of the Foreign Office as he was with Lord Aberdeen over Portugal. Ideally, the availability of two separate sources of information, at the ministerial and the Court level, should have been an advantage. But in practice, this often worked out differently, particularly after Palmerston's return to the Foreign Office.

The Foreign Secretary might feel that Prince Albert's correspon-

---

[1] Memorandum by Anson, 15 April 1841 (Royal Archives Y.54.19).
[2] Prince Albert to Aberdeen, 24 March 1843 (Royal Archives M.51.111).

dence with crowned heads abroad was tending—for the best of motives—to give away rather more of the British position than he would have considered wise. A case in point arose in the summer of 1843 when the British government insisted that a new trade agreement with Portugal should be concluded on the basis of *ad valorem* duties, to which the Portuguese objected. Prince Albert, who had been in touch with the Portuguese Court, asked Peel to reconsider his decision. He thought the *ad valorem* principle would lead to perpetual rather unpleasant negotiations:

> . . . for after the percentage [of duty to be levied] has been settled, the actual value of every article must be decided by mutual agreement, which is not always easy. . . . it lies in the nature of things that if the weaker is treating with the stronger, he must either give way or expose himself to an unequal quarrel. . . . this system therefore would subject Portugal to a state of dependence repugnant to the feelings of the nation. . . .
>
> . . . I cannot take upon myself to judge whether the maintenance of the principle *ad valorem* is *absolutely* necessary for the protection of our commercial interests, but I think that if it were ever enforced, the feeling of animosity against England, and suspicion of her sincerity, would take from such an arrangement all the advantages of a closer alliance between the two countries expected from it, and very much counterbalance the material advantages which England may reap from such an arrangement.[1]

Peel rejected the Prince's appeal on the grounds that the British government had already gone to the very limit of its concessions.

The Prince kept his cousin in Portugal informed of the steps taken and revealed the disagreement in their counsels in Britain:

> I have . . . written a long epistle to Sir Robert Peel, in which I made myself your advocate, and even attacked him and the Board of Trade somewhat by agreeing with Lord Aberdeen who puts political considerations first, before commercial and financial ones, and who wishes for everything which may consolidate the unity of the two old allies. . . .

He then quoted from Peel's reply to himself.[2] He had earlier informed King Ferdinand of Lord Aberdeen's disagreement with the Board of Trade and the Treasury.[3] When there was a strong clash of principle between Crown and Foreign Office over the principles of foreign policy, Prince Albert's private correspondence with his relatives and other courts was bound to be fraught with dangers.

During most of the period of Peel's government, the emphasis was, however, on home affairs. Prince Albert used this time not only to

---

[1] Prince Albert to Peel, 14 August 1843 (Royal Archives A.82.48).
[2] Prince Albert to King Ferdinand, 18 August 1843 (Royal Archives M.48.22), tr.
[3] Prince Albert to King Ferdinand, 22 March 1843 (Royal Archives M.48.15).

deepen his knowledge of the British constitution, but also to get to know as much as possible about industrial development and about the progress of the working classes. The Prince was in close touch with the leading exponent of the campaign for the amelioration of the conditions of the industrial workers, Lord Ashley. Prince Albert wrote warmly to express his and the Queen's appreciation for the efforts he was then making to improve working conditions in the coal mines:

> I . . . have been highly gratified by your efforts, as well as horror stricken by the statement[s] which you have brought before the country. I know you do not wish for praise and I therefore withhold it, but God's best blessing will rest with you and support you in your arduous but glorious task. . . .
> I have no doubt that the whole Country must be with you, at all events I can assure you that the Queen is.[1]

Prince Albert was determined to see the state of affairs in the industrial towns for himself and would not allow himself to be put off by the cautious attitude of cabinet ministers for ever on the look-out for Chartist plots. Thus, when the Prince suggested that he would like to visit Birmingham from Drayton Manor during his stay with Sir Robert Peel, both the Prime Minister and the Home Secretary, Sir James Graham, were not at all pleased. Peel[2] told Anson

> that the difficulty arose from the Mayor of Birmingham being a Chartist, and all the Town Council participating in the same violent and dangerous opinions. . . . If the Prince went, it must be notified to the Mayor, and that involved a somewhat awkward communication with a Leader of the Chartists. It would also entail the reception of an address in the Town Hall. . . . He had no doubt that the address would be most respectful and loyal, and that the reception of the Prince would be very enthusiastic, but it would be accompanied by an immense . . . physical demonstration of the trained masses of the second Town in the country.[3]

Anson said the Prince was anxious to go, because he thought it right to see one of the greatest towns in the country and because he was anxious to have a look at the great manufactories.

Sir James Graham was called into the council and took a timid view of the situation. He admitted that the Prince was not likely to run any personal risk, but generally feared the violence of the Chartists.[4] Eventually, the government's objection to the visit was

---

[1] Prince Albert to Ashley, 23 June 1842 (Royal Archives M.51.74), see Hodder, Shaftesbury, I, 421.
[2] For Peel's relations with Birmingham, see C. Gill, "History of Birmingham", I, particularly 270-1.
[3] Memorandum by Anson, 22 November 1843 (Royal Archives Y.55.44).
[4] Ibid.

withdrawn and its success proved the pessimists wrong. Anson was able to report:

> The 280,000 population of Birmingham seemed entirely to have turned out on the occasion, the streets were literally jammed, but nothing could exceed the good humour and good feeling, and apparently excess of loyalty which pervaded the whole multitude. There was not a single instance to the contrary amidst these dense masses, all vied with each other to do honour to the Prince's visit which they have taken as the greatest compliment.[1]

The Mayor held striking language:

> He said that the visit had created the greatest enthusiasm, that it had brought into union and harmony opposite political parties who had shown the deepest hatred towards each other, and that it had been productive of the happiest results to Birmingham. He said that he would *vouch* for the *devoted loyalty* of the whole Chartist Body. The Queen had not more loyal subjects in her dominions.[2]

All the rest of the day was taken up with a succession of visits to the various manufactories, inspecting the production of glass, papier mâché, guns, and so forth.[3]

Prince Albert's interest in the new society which was being created as a result of the industrial revolution is one of the reasons why he was particularly popular with the lower and middle classes. Sir Denis Le Marchant, the Whig official, recorded in 1843 that among the middle and lower classes he never heard his name mentioned without commendation. Le Marchant thought that the Prince "perhaps gained more than his due share of credit for any proceeding of the Court which is much approved."[4] Things did not go so well with the old families:

> ... with the higher classes, ... especially those in the habit of frequenting the Court ... there certainly is not the same cordial feeling towards him. They complain of his reserve, and of his attaching undue importance to etiquette in everything relating to *himself* or rather of his exacting a degree of homage which they consider more than his right. ... they are a little out of humour with him, consequently these points are ... dwelt on with much exaggeration in the absence of real defects ...[5]

Le Marchant considered that the Prince was less popular among the Tories than among the Whigs.[6] This is interesting in view of the services he had rendered Sir Robert Peel.

---

[1] Memorandum by Anson, 29 November 1843 (Royal Archives Y.55.48).
[2] Ibid.   [3] Ibid.
[4] Le Marchant to Anson, 13 October 1843 (Royal Archives Y.55.38).
[5] Ibid.   [6] Ibid.

The difficulties which were to pursue the Prince throughout thus commenced early. The trouble was that he put a higher value on his own position and his contribution to British political life than the traditional court circles, at any rate, were prepared to give it. On the whole, the Prince was wise enough to work behind the scenes. If he insisted on what was considered an unwarranted degree of homage, this was because he—unlike the Queen—had to establish his position.

The Prince's reserve, sometimes criticised even more strongly as pride and haughtiness,[1] was unfortunate. It seems to have been the consequence of a strict code of self-denial which he imposed on himself on becoming the Queen's husband. Of this a memorandum he laid down for his conduct in March 1840 bears witness. It is headed "Necessity of caution in the extreme and discretion in the Society of a Court". He felt that one is

> constantly subject to the influence of petty intrigue and jealousy. The less the intercourse with all inmates, save with your principal [presumably with the Household officers] the better your chance of escaping difficulty . . . Avoid all in a general way as much as possible. [Be] always an attentive listener, but avoid giving an opinion as much as possible, and *never* volunteer it.[2]

Some circumspection was justified, but the Prince went to excessive lengths, which did him much harm. He hardly ever appeared relaxed. He seemed to be constantly on guard, always afraid that his actions might be misinterpreted, as they often unavoidably were.

Occasionally, however, the Prince would fling caution to the winds and come out strongly and openly in favour of a particular course of action. This happened over the Repeal of the Corn Laws by Peel. Prince Albert unreservedly accepted Peel's arguments and showed this publicly by attending in the gallery of the House of Commons on a day critical for the Prime Minister. The abandonment of Protection became an article of faith with him and the Queen. He was particularly impressed by the way in which Peel seemed to put nation above party. This was to him the mark of the true statesman. Perhaps the Prince underestimated the importance of parties for the healthy development of political life. With his efficiency and apparent detachment Peel was the Prince's ideal as Prime Minister. It was unlikely that the Prince ever revised his judgment on this point in the light of the achievements of Peel's successors, however much he liked or respected some of them.

---

[1] Memorandum by Anson, July 1843 (Royal Archives Y.55.21).
[2] Memorandum by Prince Albert, March 1840 (Royal Archives Y.54.2).

The Prince did his best to follow these breath-taking events. Through Baron Stockmar and the Private Secretaries he had access to opposition sources, but on the whole he tended to get information primarily from the government of the day. He was not very sympathetic to the Protectionists:

> ... They have no leader and one of their chief members admitted the other day ... that they were quite divided and very jealous of each other. There is a host of young men, who have never in their life paid any attention to public business, whose chief employment has been hunting and who now come down to the House of Commons as great statesmen, cheering each other and rendering it almost impossible for any business to be carried on. . . .[1]

Prince Albert regarded the Protectionist leader, Lord Stanley, as "extremely imprudent".[2] Perhaps he did not consider sufficiently the difficulty of Stanley's position. He was leading the Protectionists from the Lords and had little control over the more radical Bentinck and Disraeli in the Commons. Prince Albert based his judgment to some extent on what he heard privately from Ministers. Thus he was given Lord Aberdeen's report of a curious conversation with Lord Stanley, in which the Protectionist leader was alleged to have said regarding the Repeal of the Corn Laws, that Peel "must not throw the matter up and go out, he must first be beat". According to Lord Aberdeen, Lord Stanley had added how glad he was that the "absurd notion of a Protectionist Government" had been given up. Asked by Lord Aberdeen what would happen if the Protectionists overthrew the Government and were then unprepared to undertake the responsibility they had incurred, Lord Stanley is quoted as having replied that first Lord John would turn out Peel, that then the Tories would reunite and turn out Lord John.[3] On the basis of this information the Prince concluded:

> How Lord Stanley, who aspires to the name of a Statesman, can say such things? I begin to think that the Spectator is right, who said . . . Lord Stanley should be sent back to Eton again. He must not have studied Sir Robert's character much, to fancy, that he would make himself a party to such a profligate policy . . .[4]

The Prince was taken aback by the bitterness with which Peel was attacked by his former followers and does not seem to have appreciated that the Protectionist Rump considered itself to have

[1] Memorandum by Prince Albert, 14 March 1846 (Royal Archives C.24.1). Compare Peel's reference to the hunting men in his letter to Lord Hardinge, 24 September 1846 (C. S. Parker, Sir Robert Peel, III, 472–4).
[2] Ibid.   [3] Ibid.   [4] Ibid.

been betrayed by their former leader. The Prince took too dispassionate a view of the situation, considering merely the problem of government—of the action required once the Corn Laws had apparently proved themselves unworkable—without taking account of the intensity of feeling engendered by Peel's switch. It is curious that somebody as deeply concerned with political principle as the Prince overlooked what seems a betrayal of principle in Peel. But to the Prince the national interest appears to have been sufficient to excuse any moral lapses on the party level. In any case Peel had resigned in December 1845, but the Whigs had failed to form a government to repeal the Corn Laws. Thus Peel hardly had an alternative but to carry on and to act.

Prince Albert was beginning to appreciate increasingly the strain imposed on the whole party system by the Tory split. Late in March 1846 he recorded after an interview with Sir Robert Peel:

> ... All parties are in a perfect state of dissolution, the great Conservative majority is broken up, the Protectionists are only kept together by their opposition to the commercial measures of the Government and their feeling of revenge against Sir Robert Peel, they have not one man of reputation or experience amongst them, and it is difficult to see what is to be their basis when protection has absolutely been swept away. The Government have only 112 followers. The Liberals are in a most disorganised state, Lord Palmerston is dreaded from a fear of a rupture of peace, Lord Grey goes to all extremities and carries the whole of the Radicals with him, Lord John Russell seems to have little authority over the Whigs . . .[1]

The Prince recognised that in the long run a party group consisting only of one sixth of the House of Commons could not continue in power. He was, however, sceptical as to how a new government could be formed out of the various opposition groups.[2]

To the Prince the gravest threat lay in the way the Protectionists and the Irish combined to prevent the House of Commons from working properly:

> Sir Robert begins to look with great uneasiness upon the state of things. Parliament sits . . . since January and not a single public Bill has passed, not a vote in supply has been taken, in fact nothing has been done whilst trade is stagnating, Ireland desolated by famine, disease and crime. Yet Irish members and now the Protectionists in compact with them mean to delay all further business. What is to be done . . .? Is the Irish Bill[3] to be given up in deference to this unconstitutional proceeding? This would establish a dreadfully dangerous precedent enabling any set of desperate

---

[1] Undated memorandum by Prince Albert, obviously of late March 1846 (Royal Archives C.24.20).
[2] Ibid.   [3] An Irish Coercion Bill.

men to defy the Crown, the House of Lords and the great majority of
the Commons and to defeat a measure sanctioned by the three branches
of the Legislature by the mere abuse of their privileges as members of
the House of Commons.[1]

The Prince rejected as a solution the resignation of the Government,
for this would put into the hands of a small minority the power of
turning out any ministry possessing the confidence of the Crown and
of a large majority in both Houses of Parliament. The dissolution
of Parliament would not be a remedy either, for the same methods
were likely to be used in the new House of Commons. In any case
it was wrong to "hand over to a small faction the power of forcing
the Crown to . . . exercise . . . its highest prerogative." [2]

The Queen, the Prince and the Prime Minister realised, however,
that there was not much to be done "except patiently to sit it out".
In the Prince's view the character of the House of Commons was
decidedly going to suffer.[3]

The Prince was full of admiration for the leader of the Anti-Corn
Law League, Richard Cobden, although he generally did not approve of political "agitation":

Cobden is a most remarkable man and has hitherto shown the greatest
disregard to party or party connexion, constantly employed at the same
thing, professing to have no ulterior object, possessing great talent and
certainly knowing the state of public feeling better than any man in the
country. . . .[4]

Like everyone else, the Prince was puzzled over the reasons which
made Peel pay his great tribute to Cobden in his parting speech as
Prime Minister:

My own belief is that it was the expression of a sincere feeling of admiration for Mr. Cobden's great talents, integrity and energy, and of gratitude
for the great services he has rendered to Sir Robert in keeping the League
so entirely quiet during the whole discussion and the Whigs in such awe,
that they dared not endanger the measure by becoming factious.
. . . In order not to disgust his own party and to deprive himself of their
cordial support, he was obliged to keep secret from everybody, that he
used Cobden to keep his heterogeneous majority together; but knowing
what this man had been doing and with what complete disinterestedness,
whilst almost everybody around him had a *personal* motive which prompted
him and acted only under the mask of patriotism, Sir Robert thought it
generous and just at the risk of himself being again violently assailed, to
mark publicly, that it was to Cobden chiefly that the success was owing.[5]

[1] Memorandum by Prince Albert, ? 25 April 1846 (Royal Archives C.24.30).
[2] Ibid.   [3] Ibid.
[4] Memorandum by Prince Albert, 14 March 1846 (Royal Archives C.24.1).
[5] Memorandum by Prince Albert, 4 July 1846 (Royal Archives C.25.35).

The Prince gives the interesting information that Peel had been converted by Cobden two years before. It will be recalled that as early as March 1845, Peel asked Sidney Herbert to reply to Cobden in a debate. He told Herbert: "You must answer this for me, for I cannot." The Prince felt, however, that it would have been better if Peel had not said what he did. The utterance created a barrier to the return of some of his former followers who might have joined him again.[1]

On the whole, the Prince took Peel's fall quietly enough. He noted on 26 June 1846:

> The Corn Bill and the Customs Duties Bill have both been read a third time in the House of Lords after some angry discussion, but without any further division being taken upon them. Today the Queen has signed the Commission for giving the Royal Assent and so these two great measures have been made the Law of the Land. Sir Robert and his Cabinet however have been upset on the very night on which these two measures were adopted by the Peers. The Whigs are prepared to take office and are unseemingly [sic] distributing places amongst themselves. . . .[2]

The Crown could never look back, it always had to look ahead. For its support was necessary for the carrying on of the Queen's government, whatever the personal views of the Court.

[1] Memorandum by Prince Albert, 4 July 1846 (Royal Archives C.25.35).
[2] Memorandum by Prince Albert, 26 June 1846 (Royal Archives C.24.100).

Chapter Four

CO-OPERATION WITH PALMERSTON

PALMERSTON's return to the Foreign Office in the summer of 1846 coincided with Prince Albert's increasing interest in international affairs. During the Corn Law crisis, domestic affairs had overshadowed everything else. Now that the Free Trade issue had been settled, it was possible for the Prince to devote more attention to affairs abroad. Prince Albert was wise to make himself thoroughly acquainted with the intricacies of British politics before he plunged into the secrets of European diplomacy. An understanding of the domestic situation was essential for an appreciation of the possibilities—and limitations—of British foreign policy. There was at this time a particularly close link between Britain's domestic political institutions and her position abroad. Britain's prestige on the continent was partly due to her reputation as the cradle of constitutional monarchy. How far was constitutional government an article for export? Controversy arose as to the extent to which the British government was justified in supporting liberal movements abroad against the lawfully constituted authorities of other countries. In the increasing internal and international tension which heralded the revolutionary year of 1848, answers to these questions could not be evaded. Was Prince Albert going to accept Palmerston's interventionist views?

When it came to foreign affairs, Prince Albert did not, as in domestic affairs, have the same disadvantage of starting with hardly any direct acquaintance. The Queen was—initially—better informed about the political situation at home than he was. It was different with European affairs. The Prince had the advantage over the Queen and over the ministers of having lived on the Continent. He was thus able to establish an even more complete ascendancy over the Queen in the field of foreign affairs than in that of domestic politics.

This extension of the Prince's influence did not pass unchallenged and there was a constant rumbling of criticism. The constitution did not know anything of a Prince Consort—or King Consort—to a Queen Regnant. The Queen and the Prince sometimes argued that the Prince's position had been regularised by his becoming a Privy Councillor. But, unlike the majority of Privy Councillors, he could never have been called to account by Parliament. The strongest argument for allowing the Prince to become the *alter ego* of the Queen was that the burden was too much for a woman who during seventeen years gave birth to nine children and who was bound to be occupied to a considerable extent—and not only for private reasons—with her family responsibilities. The advice of the Prince was merely of importance to the extent that it was accepted by the Queen. It left her constitutional prerogatives intact. It is a different matter whether the Prince's views were always such as to make it advisable for the Queen to follow them.

Prince Albert was determined from the beginning to recover for the Crown any rightful prerogatives which had been allowed to fall into disuse. This applied particularly to the control of foreign affairs by the Crown. The Queen had during the first years of her reign lacked the knowledge to oppose the ideas of an experienced and determined Foreign Secretary like Lord Palmerston. During the Peel administration foreign affairs had, on the whole, been over-shadowed by happenings at home. The change of government in 1846 and the ending of the domestic crisis seemed to be a good opportunity for paying more attention to the supervision of foreign affairs by the Crown.

The Crown was entitled to be consulted over the general lines of foreign policy and its approval was necessary for the sending of Foreign Office instructions to diplomatic representatives abroad, at least whenever time allowed. In case of any disagreement with the Foreign Secretary, the matter would be referred to the Prime Minister, who exercised a general supervision over foreign affairs. If the Queen considered the outcome unsatisfactory, she could appeal to the Cabinet by asking the Prime Minister to put her views to it. The Crown could insist on its constitutional right to be consulted wherever possible, but it could not enforce its views if the Cabinet rejected them. Thus the Crown was dependent on persuading the Prime Minister directly or the majority of the Cabinet indirectly. It was also able to act as a trustee of a Cabinet majority overawed by a dictatorial Foreign Secretary.

Owing to Prince Albert's advice to the Queen, Lord Palmerston had to accept a far closer supervision of foreign policy by the Crown than during his earlier period of office in her reign. Europe was then beginning to go through a period of disturbance which culminated in the revolutionary outbreaks of 1848. There was not only the perennial instability of government in Spain and Portugal with all the dangers of foreign intervention this implied. Within a few months, the Eastern Powers were to deal the remnants of Polish nationalism another blow by the Austrian annexation of the independent Galician republic of Cracow. Civil war in Switzerland brought Europe to the brink of a war of intervention. Finally, the settlement imposed on Italy by the Congress of Vienna was being seriously threatened.

From August 1846 onwards, Lord Palmerston's drafts on Spain and Portugal were criticised by the Court and amendments secured. The conduct of diplomatic representatives was called in question by the Crown. This did not interfere with the good relations between the Court and the Foreign Secretary. As the Prince recorded later, Lord Palmerston

> was rather a favourite of the Queen during the first years of her reign and was treated with particular confidence by us both on his return to Office in 1846.[1]

It must be recalled, however, that the Queen in 1845 had

> some apprehension that his return to the Foreign Office might cause great alarm in other countries . . .[2]

Queen Victoria had been on friendly terms with Lady Cowper, who married Lord Palmerston in 1839. The Prince at first joined in this friendly atmosphere. In the summer of 1841, the Queen and the Prince stayed with the Palmerstons and Cowpers at Panshanger. Here the Prince seems to have found time to indulge his musical interests. Prince Albert's charming and relaxed note to the younger Lady Cowper after the visit certainly goes beyond a purely formal letter of thanks:

> I hasten to fulfil my promise in sending you the songs of my composition, begging you not to consider them as the work of an artist, but as the results of a leisure hour's occupation. I was so much pleased with your eldest boy's verses that I felt tempted to put them to music, and I venture to add this song to the rest.[3]

Another reflection of Palmerston's special position at Court in 1841 was the accession to his request that a baronetcy should be granted to Mr. Easthope, the proprietor of the *Morning Chronicle*.

[1] Prince Albert's memorandum on Palmerston's foreign policy, 14 July 1852 (Royal Archives A.81.32).
[2] Memorandum by Prince Albert, 20 December 1845 (*Letters*).
[3] Prince Albert to Lady Cowper, 1 August 1841 (Royal Archives M.51.32).

The Queen had rather disliked giving this honoured rank to a "nouveau riche" of "extreme views" who was, to crown all evil, connected with the Press. Apparently Melbourne did not specially like Easthope, but as Palmerston—whose connection with the *Morning Chronicle* was a particularly close one—asked for the honour as a personal favour, the Queen granted it.[1] The *Morning Chronicle* had been a regular supporter of Palmerston's policy.

By 1847 the Crown had clearly re-established its control over foreign policy. There was not yet a generally strained atmosphere between the Court and Lord Palmerston, though there were signs of the Foreign Secretary not always attaching sufficient weight to the opinion of the Sovereign or of his own colleagues. At first the relations between Prince Albert and Lord Palmerston were good. The Foreign Secretary seems to have had a friendly disposition to advice coming from the Prince. The area of agreement between them was still larger than that of disagreement, a position which was slowly being reversed.

Court and Foreign Secretary were one in their condemnation of the behaviour of the French over the "Spanish Marriages". For years, the British government had tried to prevent the marriage of the Queen of Spain's younger sister to a son of Louis Philippe before the occupant of the throne had borne a child. The matter had been discussed with the King of the French who had, in the opinion of the Foreign Secretaries of both parties, accepted the British thesis. British diplomacy thus suffered a severe defeat when a double betrothal was announced in Madrid in August 1846. Queen Isabella married her cousin Don Francisco and her younger sister the Duke of Montpensier. Prince Albert wrote indignantly to the King of Prussia:

> through the perfidy of France, the Entente Cordiale has been smashed with one blow. We English regard this as a great misfortune, as that Entente . . . made it possible for the moral weight of England to chain the restless spirit of France to the maintenance of treaties . . .[2]

The Queen noted, however, that Palmerston, who had only just returned to the Foreign Office, had mismanaged the affair at Madrid by forcing his candidate Don Enrique for the hand of the Queen.[3] Incidentally this criticism indicates one of the Court's main objec-

---

[1] Memorandum by Anson, 25 August 1841 (Royal Archives Y.54.64).
[2] Prince Albert to the King of Prussia, 11 December 1846 (Royal Archives H.49.5), tr.
[3] Prince Albert to King Leopold, 14 September 1846 (*Letters*).

tions to Palmerston's policy, to his "meddling" in the internal affairs of other countries.

Like Palmerston, Prince Albert condemned the annexation of the independent Polish Republic of Cracow by Austria in November 1846, which involved a breach of the Treaty of Vienna. Russia and Prussia had consented, but neither of the other co-signatories, France and Britain, had been consulted in advance. The Prince was primarily concerned about the legal and moral aspects and consequences of the annexation. He wanted the distinguished political journalist Henry Reeve to write a pamphlet on the issues involved. An incident, slight in itself, showed that Prince Albert did not see quite eye to eye with the Foreign Secretary on this question. When Reeve, before complying with the Prince's request, asked for permission to consult Lord Palmerston, Albert replied that he did not see any necessity for referring the matter to the Foreign Secretary, though he had no objection to Mr. Reeve asking the Prime Minister.[1] He thereupon actually himself wrote a note to Lord John Russell:

> The affair of Cracow and the shock which has been given by it to the security of a *legal* state in Europe much engross my mind. I think it is of the greatest importance that the public of England as well as that of the continent should arrive at a just appreciation of the present crisis and should not take the impression which violent party statements in the newspapers written in an offhand style are apt to give.[2]

The Prince said he had selected Mr. Reeve for the task of writing a pamphlet on the Cracow affair as "a person . . . versed in public and international law and well acquainted with the political state of Europe". Having taken Mr. Reeve's point about the necessity of consulting the government, the Prince added:

> Not wishing . . . to do anything which might not be in accordance with the views of the government, I thought it best to send Mr. Reeve direct to you . . .[3]

Actually Reeve offered an article to the *Edinburgh Review*, but the editor was already committed and the whole project came to nothing.

Besides acting as Private Secretary and intimate adviser to the Queen, the Prince conducted an extensive private correspondence with statesmen abroad in his personal capacity. While his expressions of views here did not carry any official weight, not having received

[1] Walpole, Russell, II, 8.
[2] Prince Albert to Russell, 6 January 1847 (Royal Archives C.16.8).
[3] Ibid.

the sanction of the government, there was a danger that the distinction between a public and a private correspondence might not always be clearly understood abroad. Actually, as long as the Prince was in sympathy with the policy of the government, a confidential correspondence between him and other princes was quite useful. It was a different matter when he found himself in disagreement with the principles of the government's foreign policy.

One of the Prince's most frequent correspondents at this time was the gifted, if unreliable, King of Prussia, Frederick William IV. He told the King:

> Through the unfortunate step of Austria concerning Cracow the basis of the treaties on which the whole structure of peace and the European Balance of Power has rested since the last war . . . has now been undermined by those from whom one would have expected it least. The door . . . has been opened to anyone with a long nourished wish to the fulfilment of which those treaties alone stood in the way.[1]

The Prince feared the complete annihilation of Poland, though this did not actually happen. He thought the effect on the German Confederation of the growing power of Russia in the East and of France in the West would be disastrous.[2]

Prince Albert knew that Prussia had been the least happy of the Eastern Powers about the annexation of Cracow. He therefore thought it worth while to recur to the subject in another letter to the King of Prussia and pointed out the danger to Europe arising from treaty violations of this kind. He tried to frighten the King by putting forward the dubious theory that the legal validity of the whole of the Vienna Treaty settlement had been called in question by the violation of one clause. As a result, Prussia's claim to the Rhineland, acquired in 1815, had become merely a *de facto* one![3]

The letter contained a strong appeal to leave the Holy Alliance:

> The common policy of the three powers has, since the Peace, had the most disadvantageous consequences for the healthy development of German and Prussian strength. . . . Prussia has been forced to submit to the colossal pressure of a truly Russian policy . . . and to the misleading influence of the many-headed Austrian statecraft. . . . Prussia has thus been prevented from finding and adopting its correct position towards Europe and particularly towards Germany . . .
> As long as I see the true German interests of Prussia and of my Fatherland

---

[1] Prince Albert to the King of Prussia, 11 December 1846 (Royal Archives H.49.5), tr.
[2] Ibid.
[3] Prince Albert to the King of Prussia, 21 December 1846 (Royal Archives H.49.21), tr. This is almost certainly the letter Sir Theodor Martin could not find (see Martin, II, 52).

subordinated in the first instance to the spirit of solidarity of the three powers and in the second to the *un-German tutelage of the Viennese Cabinet,* I shall have to continue to believe not only that the present and future true welfare of Germany and Prussia will remain endangered, but that European tension will increase . . .[1]

The Prince also paid a striking and perhaps rather unexpected tribute to the power of public opinion:

The idea that the European governments of our day are obliged to guide the destiny of their peoples according to the principles of true law and justice *has penetrated deeply into the consciousness of all the peoples of Europe.* . . . This consciousness of the peoples will take into consideration the causes of each new war and will determine the degree of warmth and energy of the common sympathy with which they will take part. I must therefore fear that in a war for the defence of the policy which annihilated Cracow the strongest of all supports, "the belief of peoples in the justice of their cause", will be lacking . . . Without this belief some of the peoples, at any rate, would be conscious or become conscious that they are meant to fight for political maxims which conflict violently with the achievements of contemporary European civilisation. The peoples will, even if they in the beginning lend their hands willingly, deny their hearts and in the course of the struggle they will obey the great moral law which governs this earth more than their governments.—The German Powers would repent too late that they, forgetful of the greatest of all goods, gave up the blessing of justice and based themselves entirely on brute force.[2]

This is not merely a noteworthy programme of the principles on which governments should base their policies. It is also a far-sighted forecast of some of the developments during the following century. The Revolution of 1848 was still more than a year distant. It confirmed some of the Prince's warnings. But the full extent of his prescience was only revealed in the twentieth century.

Palmerston took the Cracow incident in his stride. He does not seem to have been worried much about the moral and legal aspects involved. He considered a purely nominal reservation sufficient whereas Lord John Russell insisted on a public protest. Palmerston was more concerned with giving France a "tit for tat" for the Spanish marriages.[3] He thus did not have time for the Prince's fine moral feelings. The practical diplomat had to take the situation as he found it. He could not always go back to first principles. The Prince was later to object to this lack of principle on Palmerston's part.

Palmerston in fact did not want to overemphasise existing rights.

---

[1] Ibid.   [2] Ibid.
[3] See Gooch, Russell, I, 127–8; Walpole, Russell, II, 8; Bell, Palmerston, I, 389–90.

He needed some fluidity for the success of his policy. In Cracow it happened to have been the reactionary powers which broke existing treaties. But next time it would more likely be some liberal revolutionary movement which would overturn existing rights. A small ruler might challenge the legal title of a Great Power to territory it had earlier conquered, and this ruler—like the King of Sardinia in his struggle with Austria over Lombardy—might be a potential ally for Britain. The philosophy of existing rights could too easily strengthen the legitimist camp against liberal movements. It could be used to justify the cold brutality of despotic monarchs against their internal political enemies, as in Portugal.

Prince Albert conducted a lively correspondence with his cousin King Ferdinand of Portugal, and Queen Victoria occasionally exchanged letters with Donna Maria. The British Court made use of these independent sources of information and was thus able to challenge the conclusions of the accredited representatives at Lisbon. The Secretary of Legation, Southern, came in for considerable royal criticism. The Court was sure to find out quickly if the Foreign Secretary deviated in any way from the directives which had been agreed between Crown and Cabinet.

Portugal was then going through a period of civil war, with the danger of international complications arising from it. Once the strong hand of Costa Cabral, who had governed dictatorially from 1842 to May 1846, had been removed as the result of a rising, there had been constant government changes punctuated by more insurrections. Queen Maria had not distinguished herself in this difficult situation either by her openness or by her leniency. Instead she had resorted to ill faith, intrigue and cruelty, paying little regard to constitutional processes and playing off one faction against the other. She had failed to rally the country by a straightforward, and moderate policy. The Queen was in danger of losing her throne owing to the constant attacks made on her by the rival monarchist faction, the Miguelites, on the right, and by the radical Septemberists on the left. The Queen's strongest asset in Britain was that any alternative to her was considered even worse. England could hardly admit the reactionary Miguelites—allied to Metternich—or the "democrats" to the government of her oldest ally.

At first, the Court and Palmerston seemed to see eye to eye on Portugal, for the Queen thanked Palmerston "for his zeal about Portugal" in the middle of July 1846.[1] But differences of approach

[1] The Queen to Palmerston, 16 July 1846 (*Letters*).

soon came to light and some of them were fundamental. Prince Albert was always concerned with the rights of small countries, to which Palmerston was largely indifferent. While Palmerston tended to ignore the difficulties of the Portuguese Crown, Prince Albert saw them very clearly, particularly the gulf which separated the political conditions of England and Portugal:

> One of the great dangers to *her* [the Queen of Portugal] lies in the total absence of constitutional education and feeling on the part of the statesmen and politicians in Portugal who (to whatever party they may belong) will not carry their weight of *constitutional responsibility* and in all matters of difficulty throw it upon the Queen. It appears that even in refusing applications for places, which they cannot or will not grant, they always say: "The *Queen* won't do it, the *Queen* cannot be prevailed upon. . . ."[1]

Where Palmerston overrated the possibilities of constitutional government, the Prince underrated them. Thus the opposition appeared to Palmerston in the guise of heroes, who were to be pitied for the persecution they were enduring, whereas to the Prince they were merely rebels against lawful authority, to whose sufferings he was indifferent. Some of the "liberal" groups backed by Palmerston were in Prince Albert's opinion little better than their opponents.

Prince Albert was fundamentally opposed to the entire principle of intervention. He denied the right of the British government, which Palmerston assumed, of supporting particular political parties in other countries. Palmerston maintained that as the shaky throne of Donna Maria depended in the last resort on the help of the British fleet, "strings" should be attached to any help given. But the British Foreign Secretary did not merely want to insist on the Portuguese government putting its own house in order, he wanted to dictate to the Portuguese Crown the composition of its own cabinet.

Intervention set off an endless chain reaction. All too often, as the Prince later pointed out,

> the fact that the English Minister takes part in the internal party feuds in a country induces the French, the Russian, the Austrian Minister to do the same. They attach themselves likewise to a party, but take perhaps generally the opposite side from your own. The contest becomes now one of foreign powers fought on the ground of the internal government of the country to which their Ministers are accredited. . . . The English advice itself becomes still more biased, for it is now given with a view even of damaging the French or Austrian policy.[2]

---

[1] Prince Albert to Russell, 2 August 1847 (Royal Archives C.16.12).
[2] Prince Albert's memorandum on Palmerston's foreign policy, 14 July 1852 (Royal Archives A.81.32).

Prince Albert did not approve of Palmerston's use of British pressure to make the Queen of Portugal adopt political measures she disliked. He had a faith in his relatives which Palmerston could not share:

> . . . in the whole country the only persons who have the real good of it alone at heart are the Queen and the King, and all who can ought to do their utmost to *assist* these two persons in their most arduous tasks instead of running them down.[1]

At the same time, the Prince and the Queen went to the limit in trying to persuade their Portuguese relations to use constitutional methods, as far as was possible in the circumstances.[2] Prince Albert sent a long letter to King Ferdinand's former German tutor, Dietz, the "Eminence Grise" at the Portuguese Court, appealing to him to leave the country. The letter contained a long catalogue of Dietz's crimes in the eyes of public opinion, which blamed him for the mistakes of the Portuguese Court.[3] It was backed by a simultaneous communication from Queen Victoria to her sister of Portugal.[4] Prince Albert had been taken aback by the poor reception given to their cousin Count Alexander Mensdorff (the later Austrian Foreign Minister) at the Portuguese Court in the winter of 1846–7. Mensdorff was supposed to give useful advice, but—as he reported to Albert—Donna Maria did not want to listen.[5] Prince Albert now concluded that Dietz was an obstacle to wiser counsels prevailing at the Portuguese Court.

By the end of November 1846, Palmerston's Portuguese policy was coming under fire from the Court. The Queen told Palmerston that one of his drafts to the Legation at Lisbon gave the impression that Britain was on the side of the Portuguese rebels:

> Lord Palmerston . . . takes the nation and the opposition to be one and the same thing. What we must insist upon is a return to constitutional government. And what we may advise is a compromise with the opposition. What Ministry is to be formed ought to be left to the Portuguese themselves. . . .[6]

The Queen mildly reprimanded her Foreign Secretary for "putting

---

[1] Prince Albert to Palmerston, 9 August 1846 (Royal Archives C.25.74).
[2] Thus Prince Albert to King Ferdinand, 16 March 1847 (Royal Archives J.57.11).
[3] Prince Albert to Dietz, 26 January 1847 (Royal Archives J.56.31).
[4] Queen Victoria to Donna Maria, 26 January 1847 (Royal Archives J.56.32).
[5] Mensdorff to Prince Albert, 26 February 1847 (Royal Archives J.57.1).
[6] The Queen to Palmerston, 28 November 1846 (*Letters*).

it out of her power to state her opinion in good time", for she presumed the despatch had already gone off.[1]

The Prince did not hide the British Court's dissatisfaction with Palmerston's policy from the King of Portugal:

> We disapproved of the last instructions from here (but they had already gone). My principle is: Send honest, decent and intelligent people to the spot, who can find out about the state of affairs, and do not give instructions for specific acts, which may be out of date by the time of arrival.[2]

In the Prince's opinion it was best merely to state "universal true maxims" and to leave their application to the agent on the spot.[3] This was a characteristic sentiment, but not practicable. Albert's frequent criticism of the actions of diplomatic agents shows how difficult that kind of system would have been to operate. This very letter to the King of Portugal contained criticism of the Chargé d'Affaires at Lisbon, Southern. The Prince called him "by nature a *party man*", though it defended him against the charge of ill-will against the Portuguese Sovereigns.[4] Actually the only way to avoid constant bickerings with the diplomatic agents abroad was to give them clear instructions.

The task which Prince Albert set himself was to get all concerned —not only the British Foreign Secretary, but also the Portuguese Court—to steer a middle course. It goes without saying that he did not make himself popular with anybody in the process. It could certainly not be inferred from the official backing he gave to the Portuguese Court in London that he was entirely happy about the conduct of his Portuguese relations. He saw little appreciation of the help the British fleet was giving to steady the situation in Portugal, rent by internal disruption. Colonel Wylde, sent on a confidential mission with the full support of the British Court, had—like Mensdorff—been cold-shouldered. Prince Albert tried to make it clear to his cousin that he only wished to help him and his wife. He did his best to "sell" Wylde to the Portuguese Court:

> Wylde . . . considers himself as your *personal* servant, as his attachment to Victoria and me dictates, that he also enjoys Lord Palmerston's confidence from former times is a great discovery.[5]

Palmerston, who was shown some of the King of Portugal's letters

---

[1] Ibid.
[2] Prince Albert to King Ferdinand, 15 December 1846 (Royal Archives M.48.55), tr.
[3] Ibid.   [4] Ibid.   [5] Ibid.

by the British Court, was quick to remark to Lord John Russell
on King Ferdinand's dislike of Wylde, although—as the Foreign
Secretary pointed out—he had been "sent from the Court itself
more than by the Government here".[1]

By the end of January 1847, a strong difference of opinion had
certainly arisen between Prince Albert and Lord Palmerston, but
there was not yet any sign of personal asperity. The Prince felt the
British government was interfering too much in the internal affairs
of Portugal by instructing Colonel Wylde to assure the insurgents
at Oporto that the Queen of Portugal would restore constitutional
government. Palmerston persevered in his view. He wrote to Lord
John Russell in no uncertain terms:

> . . . I think the Prince takes a somewhat strained view of mine [my letter]
> to Wylde. . . . What the Portuguese Court and Government want is
> that we should make to the [Revolutionary] Junta a declaration in the
> Austrian or Prussian fashion that we disapprove of their proceedings and
> bid them surrender. Now this . . . would be to erect ourselves into judges
> between the Queen and her people . . .[2]

The reference to Prussian methods was clearly aimed at Prince
Albert, with his favourable attitude to Prussia. It need hardly be
added that this was not what he wanted. A week after the initial
submission of the draft, the Queen was still not quite satisfied and
Palmerston made some alterations.

Early in February 1847, the Queen had asked Lord John Russell
for a definite undertaking by Britain to support the Portuguese
throne in the event of a full-scale Miguelite rebellion.[3] A few days
later the Queen and Prince Albert in a joint memorandum drawn
up for the government asked that the Secretary of Legation at
Lisbon, Southern, should be reprimanded for intervening on behalf
of captured insurgent officers due to be deported to Africa:

> . . . According to Colonel Wylde's . . . showing, this step produced so
> direct an effect upon the Portuguese Government that its ministers found
> themselves compelled to declare that they would resign if the destination
> of the prisoners was altered. . . . A step strong enough to dislodge a
> Ministry in so critical a moment must make the world believe at the time,
> when the English government refuses to lend the Queen of Portugal any
> assistance, it approves at the same time of steps taken in favour of the
> insurgents, quite strong enough to break down an existing Ministry and

---

[1] Palmerston to Russell, 12 December 1846 (Gooch, Russell, I, 139).
[2] Gooch, Russell, I, 140.
[3] The Queen to Russell, 2 February 1847 (Royal Archives J.56.38).

thereby increasing infinitely the existing difficulties and perplexities of Donna Maria.[1]

Prince Albert approved of the joint Anglo-French-Spanish intervention in Portugal in the summer of 1847 in accordance with the London Protocol. But he criticised Palmerston's attempt to turn the intervention to the advantage of the liberal party. He later recorded—probably with more bitterness than he would have felt at the time—his criticism of Palmerston's aims and methods:

> As France and Spain supported the reactionary party and Donna Maria's favourite and despotic minister Costa Cabral, and Spain supplied the Army which was called into Portugal by the London Protocol, Lord Palmerston could bring no counter poise except that which he always declares to be stronger than any material force, "*the public opinion of England*". He had to create this opinion, however, and could not do this without incessantly blackening the character of the Court of Portugal and its advisers, in support of which his own Protocol had bound him to intervene. This naturally recoiled upon himself; the Queen of Portugal, who is an obstinate Braganza, would not be bullied by Lord Palmerston's violent abuse, the less so as she had the Spanish army by her side. England did lose her influence, the liberal party was put down and Lord Palmerston excused himself at the expense of his own Sovereign![2]

The Prince did not show sufficient appreciation of the dangers Lord Palmerston averted, such as an exclusive Franco-Spanish intervention. Without his diplomacy, the situation probably would have been worse.

The difference of opinion between Prince Albert and the Foreign Secretary focuses attention on the neuralgic point, the attitude to revolutionary movements. The closer Europe moved to the major revolutionary outbreaks of 1848, the more intensive these differences of outlook were bound to become. With the increasing nervousness of monarchs for their crowns, to which Palmerston with his British insularity seems to have been strangely impervious, the dispassionate discussion of opposing principles took on the heat of a personal conflict. But in 1847, this still lay hidden in the future.

In September, Palmerston was certainly by no means *persona non grata* when he was Minister in Attendance while the Court was in Scotland, at Ardverikie. He had full discussions with the Prince about the problems of Europe and replied to long memoranda of Albert's at the same length. Dispatches to the British ministers

---

[1] Memorandum by the Queen and Prince Albert, 9 February 1847 (Royal Archives C.16.10).
[2] Prince Albert's memorandum on Palmerston's foreign policy, 14 July 1852 (Royal Archives A.81.32).

abroad were discussed orally in a relaxed atmosphere. The Prince might disagree with the Foreign Secretary, but both were still prepared to thrash out their differences. As the Prince wrote to Stockmar from Ardverikie in September:

> Lord Palmerston acts less upon principle; still, obstinate although he is, he always gives in when driven into a corner by argument.[1]

While the Prince might perhaps flatter himself too much about his superior powers of argumentation, the Foreign Secretary was clever enough to practise diplomacy at his own Court.

Fruitful co-operation was thus still possible when Palmerston suggested that the Lord Privy Seal, Lord Minto, should undertake a mission to Italy. Lord Minto was father-in-law to both the Prime Minister, Lord John Russell, and to the Minister at Turin, Ralph Abercromby. The idea of the mission was to strengthen the constitutionalist inclinations of the Italian sovereigns, and particularly of Pope Pius IX, against Austrian intervention. The Pope then still toyed with the idea of political reform and the Austrians had sent a military force to Ferrara to discourage him. Prince Albert was at first "startled by the suddenness of the proposition" about Lord Minto[2] and wrote a memorandum on the implications of the mission:

> ... sending a mission to Rome with the avowed or apparent object of supporting and encouraging the Pope in those measures of political reform which Austria has reason to dread so much is *a most hostile step* towards our old and natural ally.[3]

In saying that, the Prince was merely drawing an obvious inference from the situation and not expressing his opinions as to the desirability of a particular policy. How far the Prince was from being a diehard pro-Austrian is clear from a passage in a letter to Lord John Russell about the Minto mission a week later:

> "The conduct of Austria can only be explained in one way: that it is one of the convulsions of a dying man". Her system is rotten, and conscious of her own disease and weakness, she struggles in despair.[4]

The Prince then listed all her offences during the past year, including the annexation of Cracow and her backing for Louis Philippe's Spanish policy. In Germany, Austria was indicted for "leaguing herself with Russia against the liberal policy of Prussia

---

[1] Prince Albert to Stockmar, 11 September 1847 (Martin, I, 427), tr.
[2] Prince Albert to Russell, 5 September 1847 (Martin, I, 432).
[3] Memorandum by Prince Albert, 29 August 1847 (Martin, I, 429).
[4] Prince Albert to Russell, 5 September 1847 (Royal Archives C.16.17).

and Germany to which she belongs". In Italy she was charged with "setting herself openly against the Pope (the head of her Church)" and "threatening the independence of her neighbours and friends". After this long indictment the final *"coup de grâce"* was hardly necessary:

> ... *All* this is done by the *paternal* government of a *Catholic* and *Conservative* state.[1]

The Prince could be as scathing about "heretical" conservatives as he could about "infidel" revolutionaries.

Prince Albert wanted Britain to proclaim a doctrine declaring as an act of aggression any intervention by an outside power to stop constitutional reform where a "sovereign and people in a state are united in their determination to introduce" it. Acts of intervention of this kind should be considered as affecting the signatories of the Treaty of Vienna.

> The bold declaration of England for the right of independent states to manage their own internal affairs according to their own views, will make her most popular all over the Continent, and particularly in Germany, where the same national improvements are arrested or impeded by the same interference on the part of Austria. It will likewise serve as a basis to our policy with respect to Switzerland,[2]

where the Eastern Powers were threatening to intervene on behalf of the Sonderbund.

The Prince thought that the proclamation of the new doctrine would be all the more effective for being communicated to the Powers, and particularly to Austria, to which the Government agreed. But he uttered a warning to dissociate himself clearly from any Palmerstonian interventionism:

> Let her [England's] mode of acting ... be that of fostering and protecting every effort made by a state to advance in that direction, but not of pressing upon any state an advance which is not the result of its own impulse. Civilisation and liberal institutions must be of organic growth, and of national development, if they are to prosper and lead to the happiness of a people. Any stage in that development missed, any jump made in it, is sure to lead to confusion, and to retard that very development which we desire. . . .[3]

There had been a deviation from these principles in Greece, Spain and Portugal.

[1] Prince Albert to Russell, 5 September 1847 (Royal Archives C.16.17).
[2] Memorandum by Prince Albert, 29 August 1847 (Martin, I, 430).
[3] Prince Albert to Russell, 5 September 1847 (Martin, I, 433).

The instructions which were eventually agreed upon were quite moderate and could hardly offend Austria.[1] Furthermore, by the time Lord Minto reached the Vatican, the Austrians had evacuated Ferrara and indeed the entire political situation had changed. Soon the mission was overtaken by the revolutionary events of 1848, in which the Lord Privy Seal found himself more actively involved than had been anticipated. In January 1848, the Sicilians revolted against the tyrannous rule of the King of Naples. Lord Minto attempted, with little success, to mediate between the rebellious subjects and their ruler. He was handicapped by the refusal of Lord Palmerston to guarantee the Sicilian constitutional settlement,[2] and by the objection of the British Crown to the use of the fleet to help the Sicilians.[3] In any case, revolution did not appeal to Minto's Whiggism and the Foreign Secretary's advice to the rebels to abstain from force[4] can hardly have appealed to them.

Later the Prince felt that the Minto mission had carried England too far along the line of interventionism:

> The mission of Lord Minto arose . . . out of his desire to see his daughter Lady Mary Abercromby, sister to Lady John Russell, and who was going to be confined, at Turin without having to pay for the journey. Lord Palmerston was delighted by the proposal as it gave him as his agent the Lord Privy Seal and father-in-law to Lord John and therefore insured to him the support of Lord John and the Cabinet if he thoroughly compromised him. The subsequent facts proved the shrewdness of this calculation, for the Cabinet were bound to support his whole later foreign policy towards Italy even to its most extreme extravagances and immoralities.[5]

The Prince became increasingly pro-Austrian in Italy under the pressure of the events of 1848.

On his way to Italy, Lord Minto stopped at Berne for talks with the Swiss federal authorities on the crisis which had arisen over the "Sonderbund". The formation of a separate association of conservative Catholic cantons was not only endangering the unity of Switzerland, but also threatening the peace of Europe. The Eastern Powers wanted to intervene on the side of the "Sonderbund". France was considering joining them and only England was without any strong attachment to the Sonderbund.

---

[1] Viscount Palmerston to the Earl of Minto No. 7, 18 September 1847 (Public Record Office FO/44/1).

[2] Palmerston to Minto No. 2, 16 January 1848 (Public Record Office FO/44/3).

[3] Prince Albert to Russell, 1 February 1848 (Royal Archives C.16.43).

[4] Palmerston to Minto No. 18, 12 February 1848 (Public Record Office FO/44/3).

[5] Memorandum by Prince Albert on Palmerston's foreign policy, 14 July 1852 (Royal Archives A.81.32).

Palmerston's sympathies were with the Protestant federal authorities and the Prince on the whole agreed with him. He wrote frankly to the Prussian Minister in London, Chevalier Bunsen, whose King was violently pro-Sonderbund:

> . . . We have frequently discussed the Swiss affair with Lord Palmerston and are agreed that we should help to prevent a civil war. There has not yet been any decision about the *method* to be followed. . . . This will in any case have to be different from the French note in which Lord Palmerston rightly finds a similarity with the *Cracow Manifesto*, even the same terms.[1]

The increasing hold of the Jesuits over the Catholic cantons was one of the grievances of the Swiss Federal authorities. The Prince thought that the withdrawal of the Jesuits was quite necessary.

> It would be setting the fox to keep the geese [den Bock zum Gärtner machen] if one left the decision about the Jesuits to the Pope.[2]

When civil war seemed inevitable, the Prince was in favour of a conference of the Powers to bring the war to an early close:

> The treatment and settlement of the Swiss question by a conference and concurrence of the five powers will tend to restore to the public some degree of confidence with respect to the dislocated state of European politics. . . . we cannot refuse to consider the means of pacifying Switzerland and must make an attempt to come to some agreement with the other powers and to check the outbreak in Switzerland.

The aim should be to obtain the withdrawal of the Jesuits, the dissolution of the Sonderbund, the renouncing of any act of aggression on the part of the radical cantons, the disarming of the volunteers and the maintenance of the Federal compact.[3] Lord John Russell, who was the recipient of the Prince's views, agreed with the objectives stated in the memorandum, but did not show any enthusiasm for entering into a concert with the Great Powers of Europe respecting Switzerland.

> . . . Recent circumstances—the Montpensier marriage . . . , the seizure of Cracow . . .—must make us very cautious in our proceedings.[4]

As was his habit, Lord John saw all sides of the question, almost so well as to impede any programme of action. The Prime Minister drew attention to the Scylla of reactionary aggression—for instance

---

[1] Prince Albert to Bunsen, 10 November 1847 (Royal Archives I.102.28), tr.
[2] Ibid.
[3] Memorandum by Prince Albert, 10 November 1847 (Royal Archives C.16.25).
[4] Memorandum by Russell, 11 November 1847 (Royal Archives C.16.26).

on the part of Austria in Cracow—and the Charybdis of "democracy".

> . . . the force of democracy has greatly increased, and may become dangerous in Germany and France. It should be the part of England to temper these conflicting elements, so that the peace of Europe may be preserved.[1]

Palmerston paid lip-service to the idea of concerted action by the powers, but delayed any definite steps until the Sonderbund had been crushed. The Prince was highly satisfied with the result and in 1850 called the handling of the Sonderbund crisis Palmerston's only success.[2]

But in spite of this harmony over Switzerland, it is apparent that the relations between Prince and Foreign Secretary took a decided turn for the worse at this time. At the end of September, Prince Albert had still been defending Palmerston to a regular correspondent with whom he was in the habit of conducting a frank exchange of views, the Prussian minister, Bunsen. He congratulated Bunsen on having given a clear analysis of the underlying factors of British foreign policy to the Prussian Foreign Minister:

> Your reply to Herr von Canitz gives . . . a clear . . . idea of the *necessity* which impels the policy here, so that a continental statesman cannot for an instant be in any doubt as to what he can expect from here in every European question. On the continent, too much weight and influence is attributed to the individual personalities of English statesmen, it is believed that one is dealing with their *caprices* and that therefore their opinions can be easily modified by representations; then one is surprised about their obstinacy . . . when they do not seem to consider the representations (in Lord Palmerston's case this comes out most clearly and is looked for most).[3]

While the Prince was still supporting Palmerston to Bunsen at the end of September 1847, he appealed for his help against Palmerston in December. The King of Prussia had sent another of his verbose and bombastic letters to Queen Victoria. He was half out of his mind about the Radical danger in Switzerland, not unmindful at the same time of his important Swiss interests as "sovereign" of the tiny Neuchâtel (Neuenburg).[4] Prince Albert, a few days later, condemned the King's letter:

> . . . It is very much to be regretted that the King of Prussia should be

---

[1] Memorandum by Russell, 11 November 1847 (Royal Archives C.16.26).
[2] Prince Albert to Russell, 2 April 1850 (Royal Archives C.17.55).
[3] Prince Albert to Bunsen, 28 September 1847 (Royal Archives J.1.41), tr.
[4] The King of Prussia to Queen Victoria, 25 November 1847 (*Letters*).

carried away by his feelings to take so violent a part in the Swiss affairs and that he should hastily have plunged into the quarrel respecting Neuchâtel.[1]

The Prince realised that Lord Palmerston was touchy about diplomatic correspondence carried on direct between sovereigns. He returned the letter of the King of Prussia to Bunsen.

> . . . I advise you to inform Lord Palmerston of your mission and to ask him to take Her Majesty's pleasure on the subject. This covers you completely with Lord Palmerston and with your Master. . . . Should Lord Palmerston be concerned about this method, this will give you a very good opportunity to discuss with him altogether the right of a constitutional monarch to have an opinion and to be allowed to correspond with other crowned heads. . . .[2]

By December, Prince Albert had thus lost the easy assurance he had in September about his dealings with Palmerston. He was now afraid of him and had begun to try and curb him through third parties, later mainly through the Prime Minister. The correspondence the Prince had in mind and about which he was very sensitive was the unofficial one he conducted with German princes on political subjects.

Bunsen's "Memoirs" record Palmerston's reaction to the letter of the King of Prussia:

> As an abstract Whig he said "it was unheard of, quite unusual, that a foreign Sovereign should write to the Sovereign of England on *politics*".

When Bunsen replied that Palmerston had only recently praised Prince Albert for an excellent political letter to the Queen of Portugal, the Foreign Secretary retorted that this was between relations.[3]

A cautious approach was adopted by Queen Victoria to get the Foreign Secretary to consult the Crown about the letter and to enable Bunsen to present it personally:

> . . . As Lord Westmorland's dispatch [from Berlin] shows that the King of Prussia's letter contains, besides his thanks for the Prince of Wales's portrait, political matters, the Queen wishes Lord Palmerston to bring Chevalier Bunsen down here [to Osborne] that he may deliver the letter according to the King's wish and that the Queen may communicate its contents to Lord Palmerston.[4]

This was done, and eventually a non-committal reply was sent to

[1] Prince Albert to Russell, 6 December 1847 (Royal Archives I.103.32a).
[2] Prince Albert to Bunsen, 1 December 1847 (Royal Archives I.103.6), mainly tr.
[3] Frances Baroness Bunsen, "A Memoir of Baron Bunsen", II, 354 ff.
[4] The Queen to Palmerston, 2 December 1847 (Royal Archives I.103.18).

the King of Prussia, the possibility of any intervention having been ruled out by the defeat of the Sonderbund.

A proper clash between the Court and Palmerston only occurred from 1848, after the outbreak of the February and March revolutions. Palmerston's autocratic methods, which he had already adopted earlier, were not sufficient in themselves to create a complete impasse. But when a major and irreconcilable clash of views was added to dissatisfaction about methods, a critical phase was reached. The revolutionary era about to open provided the necessary combustible material.

PART TWO

Years of Decision

1848–1852

Chapter Five

REVOLUTION

THE revolutionary year of 1848 opened a period of unique influence for Prince Albert. He followed with close attention the unfolding of events which were to change the political map of Europe, at any rate for a time. The Sicilian insurrection in January proved to be the forerunner of a massive movement of revolution which shook the whole of Europe and had repercussions as far to the West as Ireland and as far to the East as Poland. Paris, which had played a decisive part in 1830, did so again. In February, the restricted monarchy which had survived the first onslaught in 1830, was discarded and France returned to the republican tradition of the French Revolution. Soon nearly the whole continent was ablaze. Revolutionary outbreaks shook Vienna and Berlin, as well as many other German capitals, in March. Metternich had to flee, and in Berlin, the heir of Frederick the Great had to bare his head to the insurgents his own troops had killed. Germany and Italy were clamouring for the fulfilment of their national aspirations which the régime of the reaction had so long frustrated. A new epoch had opened in Europe.

More than any other year, 1848 marks the transition from the dynastic to the national age in Europe. It proved a turning point in Prince Albert's life who now utilised his position as a link between England and Germany, which he owed to the old international monarchical society, to try and guide the German national movement into safe channels for the future good of Europe. It is noteworthy that at this time the leaders of the German national movement were delighted to co-operate with men like Prince Albert and Baron Stockmar who had been receptive to foreign influences. Indeed, Prince Albert's prestige in Germany was enhanced by his status as the husband of the Queen of England and by his experience of British constitutional government.

Prince Albert saw developments, whether they took place in England or on the continent, as part of the general European situation. He had great faith in the ability of human beings to shape things and to influence the course of events:

It . . . all depends on throwing in the right yeast while the brew is fermenting . . .[1]

With his wide interests in other subjects besides politics, he went to the social and economic roots of the political malaise of the age. It is characteristic that in 1849, while the war in Italy was raging and when Chartist pressure was still a vivid memory, he conceived the idea of an international exhibition, the first of its kind, in London.

The Prince disapproved, almost with equal emphasis, of the two extremes which Europe was facing at this time, the radical republican tradition of France and the autocracy of Russia and Austria. He blamed Metternich for the temporary success of the "democrats", by having systematically stifled all criticism, relying merely on the use of force and oppression:

> The reason for the futility [Nichtigkeit] of the governments lies in the fact that their *physical* power has been broken in the various revolutions (particularly in Vienna and Berlin) and they have never had a *moral* one.[2]

He hoped that the removal of the Metternich system would make possible the solution of many urgent problems which had for too long been ignored:

> However terrible such a disruption of a system, which has long been under tension, may be, and however much one may have to tremble [in fear] of excesses, yet I see in this event the deliverance of Germany and also of Italy.[3]

The Prince realised that something had to be done to satisfy the national aspirations of peoples which did not yet have their own states. But their fulfilment should not conflict with the requirements of the balance of power in Europe. They were only admissible to the extent that they helped to strengthen Europe's defence against the "red republicanism" of France and the reactionary despotism of Russia. To the Prince, German unity satisfied the essential requirements. He visualised a united Germany as a bulwark against France and an ally of England. As the march of events became clearer in 1848, however, he rejected Italian unity as incompatible with the maintenance of an Austria sufficiently strong to act as a counterweight to Russia. He also thought that an independent Italy would be too much under the sway of France.

Immediately after the revolution in Vienna, the Prince still be-

---

[1] Prince Albert to his brother, 13 April 1848 (Royal Archives I.3.59), tr.
[2] Prince Albert to King Leopold, 28 April 1848 (Royal Archives I.3.113), tr.
[3] Prince Albert to King Leopold, 21 March 1848 (Coburg Archives), tr.

lieved that a federal solution could save the Austrian empire. He advocated:

> Austrian provincial estates in Bohemia, Moravia, Tirol, Austria, Carniola, Styria, Venetia, Lombardy; United Diet in Vienna on the Prussian model. Formal modern constitution in Hungary. Popularly organised German Confederation with German Estates, with the Vicarship alternating between Austria and Prussia.[1]

Eventually there might be a German and an Italian customs union. The rights of the princes in Germany and Italy were to be preserved. Constitutional government should only be granted in moderate doses, depending on the political condition of the people concerned. There was to be nothing like government by the people, "democracy", or the establishment of republics. Court diplomacy should be maintained. England ought to respect the right of individual governments, and thus of their princes, to look after their own internal and external affairs. It should refrain from imposing constitutions on other countries which did not want them.

It will readily be seen that the Prince found himself at odds with Palmerston over almost every point at issue. The relationship with Palmerston dominated Prince Albert's whole existence during the following years, as the differences between Court and Foreign Secretary over foreign policy had repercussions on the confused domestic political situation. The party system had not yet recovered from the shock it had suffered owing to the Corn Law controversy. It was thrown into even greater confusion by the tension in the religious sphere generated by the new fervour in the Church of England and the Church of Rome.

The challenge of the revolutionary era found the Prince generally advocating a middle course, shying away from autocracy as much as from "democracy", advising a mixture of firmness and reform. On many subjects, he was remarkably open to new ideas. Once he had adopted a plan for making changes, he adhered to it singlemindedly. More than other statesmen of his day, in Britain or Germany, he had faith in the "right yeast". He wanted to have it applied in the first instance to help his native country.

[1] Prince Albert to King Leopold, 21 March 1848 (Coburg Archives), tr.

Chapter Six

GERMANY'S NEW ROLE IN EUROPE

(i)

A^N appreciation of his attitude to the country of his birth is essential for a true understanding of Prince Albert. The fulfilment of German national aspirations remained one of his dearest wishes, in spite of the new allegiance to his country of adoption. The Prince Consort's historical reputation has certainly suffered from the anti-German reaction with which his eldest son, King Edward VII, is so prominently associated. Queen Victoria herself, in her attempt at a posthumous justification of her husband, unwittingly seemed to supply chapter and verse for the violent pro-Germanism[1] with which he had been charged. But what the Queen after her husband's death put forward, with her usual determination, as his views was often only a part of them, deprived of the qualifications with which Albert hedged his opinions. Quoting a dead man as one's witness is always a dubious undertaking. There is certainly no evidence that Albert would have viewed the Bismarckian solution of the German problem with the same sympathy which his widow displayed in obedience to what she thought had been his views.

There were no strong political differences between England and Germany before the Schleswig-Holstein question complicated matters from 1848 onwards. In September 1847, when Lord Palmerston was Minister-in-Attendance while the Court was in Scotland, the Prince and the Foreign Secretary had many leisurely discussions on the problems of Europe. Palmerston then drew up for the Prince a memorandum on the relationship between England and Germany. It comes down without hesitation on the side of an intimate political understanding of the two countries and of support for German national aspirations:

> There can be no doubt that it is greatly for the interest of England to cultivate a close political connection and alliance with Germany, as it is also the manifest interest of Germany to ally itself politically with England. The great interests of the two are the same. Germany and England are

---

[1] Thus Greville on 15 September 1849: ". . . Aberdeen . . . said the Prince's views were generally sound and wise, with one exception, which was his violent and incorrigible German unionism. He goes all lengths with Prussia . . ." (V, 257).

as regards the state of territorial possession in Europe the two great conservative powers. Geographical reasons prevent England, and ethnical reasons prevent Germany from aiming at territorial aggrandisement: neither therefore can wish to subjugate any neighbours but both have a common interest in preventing any neighbour from subjugating them. Both England and Germany are threatened by the same danger . . . [,] an attack from Russia or from France separately, or . . . united. . . . England and Germany . . . have mutually a direct interest in assisting each other to become rich, united and strong. . . .[1]

These sentiments are remarkable coming from a statesman who was not pro-German. They cannot be dismissed as the utterances of a courtier, echoing what he knows to be the pet views of his master, even if it is assumed that the Foreign Secretary considered it essential at the time to humour the Court. For the same memorandum contains a strong attack on the high duties of the German customs union, the Zollverein:

> . . . as long as the Zollverein continues to act upon its protective system and imposes high duties on British commodities for the express purpose of either excluding them altogether, or of restricting the quantity of them to be imported, so long will the Public in England look upon the Zollverein as a League founded in Hostility to England . . .[2]

The Foreign Secretary's memorandum was in answer to one by the Prince emphasising the strong yearning in his native country for the establishment of popular forms of government and for the construction of a united Germany. The Prince thus recognised even before the revolutionary outbreaks of 1848 the twin aims of the German movement, liberty and unity. He saw the main obstacles to the attainment of unity in the mutual jealousy of the nearly forty different governments making up the German Confederation as well as in Austrian opposition to it.

In 1815 the Powers at the Congress of Vienna had appreciated the impossibility of restoring the Holy Roman Empire, which had proved quite incapable of dealing with the problems of Germany in modern conditions. At the same time, no adequate provision was made in the peace settlement to satisfy popular aspirations for the foundation of a proper German state and for the establishment of constitutional forms of government. Instead of a single state, a loose association of nearly forty "sovereign" princes, the German Confederation, was set up with its headquarters at Frankfurt-on-the-Main. The very terms of its constitution decreed almost perpetual

---

[1] Memorandum by Lord Palmerston, 15 September 1847 (Royal Archives I.1.43). See also Martin, I, 447 ff.
[2] Ibid.

immobility. The permanent presidency of the Confederation was in the hands of a power by no means exclusively German, Austria. Under the Austrian minister, Prince Metternich, the German Confederation became a bulwark of reaction, in which the policy of the Holy Alliance of Russia, Austria and Prussia reigned supreme. The conservative—or ultra-conservative—rulers in Vienna, Berlin and Frankfurt ruthlessly stamped out such pernicious heresies inherited from the French Revolution, as the belief in the rights of nationalities and in popular liberty.

Prince Albert had been infected with enthusiasm for German unity while he was a student at Bonn. Baron Stockmar's influence pointed in the same direction. The Prince favoured a moderate dose of constitutional government for Germany, particularly after seeing ministerial responsibility to Parliament functioning in Britain. He realised the intimate connection between the prospects for unity and those for constitutional government in Germany. The strongest opponents of German unification were the very powers which trampled on popular liberty, Austria and Russia. The only hope for the achievement of German unity lay in finding a state in Germany proper which was prepared to risk the wrath of Austria and Russia by following a national and liberal policy.

From the time of the annexation of Cracow, Prince Albert strained every nerve to bring nearer the establishment of German unity on a constitutional basis. The attainment of this objective was the main purpose of his extensive correspondence with the Prussian King, Frederick William IV. Prussia was the leading preponderantly German state and Prince Albert therefore turned to it. The other kingdoms, like Bavaria, were too weak individually to be able to brave Austria single-handed. Prince Albert realised that Prussia could never undertake the leadership of Germany unless it became a constitutional state. On this vital question he came up, early on, against the extreme legitimist attitude of the King of Prussia.

Frederick William IV, the elder brother of the later German Emperor William I, was one of the most gifted rulers of the house of Hohenzollern. He had wide artistic and literary interests and befriended many of the day's leading scholars, such as the historian Ranke and the scientist Alexander von Humboldt. Well educated and pacifically minded, he was a rarity among the rulers of his house. Unfortunately, there were some fatal flaws in his intellectual make-up. He did not know his own mind and proved completely incapable of dealing with the exceptional strain of the times in which he was fated to find himself on the Prussian throne. He sought an escape from the problems of government in the more extreme forms of the Romantic Movement. One of his main interests was the establishment of the Protestant bishopric in Jerusalem, a task in which he was assisted by the only slightly more practical humanist and theologian, the Chevalier Bunsen, whom he sent to London as Prussian Minister.

The King at heart realised that it would be impossible to preserve intact the ultra-conservative régime he had inherited from his father. But he was not prepared to draw the necessary conclusions. Too cultured for systematic repression, he was completely unsuited to the role of a ruthless despot. On the other hand he abhorred the idea of parting with any of his prerogatives and thus paving the way for more constitutional forms of government. Instead, he sought refuge in historical romanticism, longing for a return to the feudal forms of the Middle Ages. He toyed with the notion of a revival of the Holy Roman Empire under Austrian leadership.

Frederick William's attachment to the Holy Alliance with Austria and Russia had for some time been a target of Prince Albert's criticism. In the Prince's opinion, the alliance of the three Eastern Powers resulted in the constant subordination of German interests to those of Russia and Austria. These powers imposed a strangle-hold on the Diet of the German Confederation at Frankfurt which had to be broken before any progress could be made with German unity. While Austria could legitimately claim some influence as the Presidential Power of the Confederation, Russia was not even a member. It had merely been one of the signatories of the general Vienna settlement of 1815, in which the Act setting up the Confederation had been embodied. Yet the accredited Russian diplomatic representatives actually led the reactionary party at many German courts, including those of Berlin and Stuttgart. Thus, when Baron von Meyendorff, a Baltic German, was appointed Russian Minister at Stuttgart, he received terse instructions about his mission there to the effect that the King of Württemberg should be made to co-operate with the Eastern Powers internationally and internally. The King was expected in particular "to be firm against the revolutionaries" and to show complete obedience to the decrees of the German Diet at Frankfurt.[1] When von Meyendorff was later transferred to the Legation at Berlin, he on his own showing flattered the Prussian Foreign Minister, von Canitz, as a "conservative

[1] Peter v. Meyendorff, "Briefwechsel", I, 21, tr.

statesman" as long as the Prussian followed his advice. But he became unpleasant as soon as the Prussians wanted to carry out a policy of their own, without consulting Russia and Austria. "These people must not engage in grande politique because they do not understand it." [1] Diplomacy and ideology were thus closely interconnected in Germany, as Prince Albert appreciated. The King of Prussia could not carry out any constitutional reforms, as long as he was swayed by the two major Holy Alliance Powers.

Frederick William had a great respect and liking for England, which he visited early in his reign in 1842. But the England of his imagination hardly corresponded to reality. He mistook the traditional forms of the constitution for its substance and spirit. In his preoccupation with medieval remnants, he missed the decisive strides which had been made and were being made in the creation of a modern British state. Prince Albert did his best to acquaint the nearly a quarter of a century older King by correspondence with such really important features of the British constitution as might usefully be adopted by Prussia and by a united Germany.

The correspondence, which assumed political significance with the rape of Cracow, was unusually outspoken for royal personages. It thus encountered some criticism on the part of the King's ministers. Von Canitz commented in April 1847:

> The old formula "mon chancelier vous dira le reste" cannot be applied to these communications; I should like to get to know the Minister charged with making supplementary commentaries to the words of our master. Well might many a chancellor warn, however, not to say so much and to leave far more unsaid. The letters of the Prince are of a sincerity which is seldom matched in the cabinet correspondence of our day . . .[2]

Prince Albert's advice may well have contributed to Frederick William's decision in February 1847 to issue a patent establishing one United Diet for the whole of Prussia. Previously there had been only separate provincial diets in the various parts of the far flung Prussian monarchy, such as in East Prussia and Silesia to the East and in the Rhineland to the West. The patent was Frederick William's way of fulfilling the promise given by his father in 1820, towards the end of Hardenberg's ministry, that loans should only be floated by the state with the consent of National Estates (*National-stände*). These National Estates still had to be formed. The King was

---

[1] Meyendorff, II, 37; I, 376, tr. from French.
[2] Veit Valentin, "Geschichte der deutschen Revolution von 1848-49", I, 577-8, tr.

careful not to have them elected by the people and therefore decreed
that the existing provincial diets should meet jointly in Berlin. The
provincial diets consisted of representatives of the nobility, the towns
and the peasantry. The King added an Upper House (*Herrenhaus*)
for the princes of the blood and the higher nobility, in imitation of
the British House of Lords. The immediate cause for the calling of
the Diet was the necessity of floating a loan for the construction
of the Berlin-Königsberg railway.

The patent did not satisfy anybody. It was an attempt to have the
best of all worlds, to make a show of fulfilling the constitutional
promises of Frederick William III without granting a genuine constitution. Metternich thought that the convening of the Diet would
set a precedent from which there would be no retreat, and that any
attempt to withhold real powers from it would be useless. The
liberal elements in Prussia, on the other hand, were disappointed
with the failure of the King to create a proper parliament and
impatient at the limitations imposed on the activities of the Diet.
The liberal leaders decided, however, to co-operate, at the same
time protesting against the Government's failure to fulfil all its
promises.

Prince Albert condemned the speech with which the King opened
the Diet. The King made a solemn declaration that "no power on
earth" would ever succeed in getting him "to convert the natural
relationship between prince and people into a conventional, constitutional one".[1] The Prince wrote to Stockmar:

> What confusion of ideas, and what boldness in a king to speak extempore;
> and at such a moment and at such length, not only to touch on topics
> so terrible and difficult, but to dispose of them in that slapdash way, to
> call God to witness, to promise, to threaten, to pledge his word. . . .[2]

He also criticised the King's subjectivity, which made any clear-cut
argumentation with him impossible. He thought the King was basing
himself too much on narrow Hohenzollern ideas.[3]

Frederick William sensed Albert's critical attitude to his policy
and attempted an elaborate defence in the usual high-flowing
terms.[4] Prince Albert tried to encourage the King to continue
further on the path he had taken. He endeavoured to use the

---

[1] A. Stern, "Geschichte Europas", VI, 266, tr.
[2] Prince Albert to Stockmar, 15 April 1847. See the correspondence of the Prince
Consort from the Hohenzollern Archives edited by K. Jagow (henceforth quoted
as *Jagow*), tr.
[3] Prince Albert to Stockmar, 17 April 1847 (*Jagow*), tr.
[4] Thus his letter to Prince Albert of 13 April 1847 (Royal Archives H.49.74).

establishment of the Diet to weaken Prussia's ties with the Holy Alliance:

> The *most important* and *most dangerous* of all the ties which chained Prussia to Russia and Austria, the assumed agreement of these Powers over the principle "that outside officialdom nobody . . . is entitled to a regular participation in the administration of the life of the national community" at last seems to have been severed.[1]

Like Metternich, but from completely different premises, Albert came to the conclusion that the King's experiment would of necessity lead him further:

> One cannot marvel sufficiently how so much truly parliamentary eloquence and skill, so much fatherlandish and patriotic ability and sincerity *could have been buried so long* in the German and Prussian people, and yet to have been ready suddenly to spring to life . . . The complete *novelty* of these phenomena elucidates the *extent of difference* between provincial estates and *united estates* which Your Majesty had doubted . . .[2]

The Prince remonstrated against the King's conjuring up the past:

> . . . it is awkward if one expects one's nation . . . to preserve a gradual and slow development . . . as if it still found itself in the Middle Ages.[3]

The correspondence with the King of Prussia was only one method of influencing developments in Germany. Prince Albert also frequently exchanged views with the Chevalier Bunsen, the Prussian Minister at the Court of St. James's. A scholar, Bunsen did not take easily to the conventionality of diplomatic life and his numerous and lengthy memoranda on the most intricate questions of legal and constitutional importance bear witness to his overriding academic interests. The Chevalier, who had a British wife, née Waddington, was a fervent propagator of Anglo-German friendship. Prince Albert turned to him when he heard about Prussian proposals for tightening up press censorship. The lack of co-ordination between the censorship authorities of the individual German states had allowed many a publication to slip through the net. The Prussian scheme would have plugged all the loopholes. Curiously enough, the Prussian proposals were not put into effect because Metternich considered they did not go far enough. The Prince pointed out the discrepancy between what the draft law contained

---

[1] Prince Albert to the King of Prussia, 2 May 1847 (Royal Archives H.49.77), tr. Jagow wrongly dates this letter 2 April, which cannot be correct as it contains a reference to later events that month.
[2] Ibid.
[3] Ibid.

and what Germany expected of the King. He made a passionate appeal for the rule of law in the affairs of the press:

> There is . . . to be appointed for the whole of Germany an omnipotent federal police, which can *arbitrarily* prohibit even the writings allowed through by the police of the state concerned, as well as those which have been the subject of court action and have been duly cleared; it can, in addition, inflict punishments not only on the originators of writings, but even on the government of the state in which the writing has been published, allowed and recognised as lawful in court. . . . There is to be a very severe repressive system and . . . a court of inquisition which can act arbitrarily outside all laws . . .[1]

When Frederick William in November 1847 referred to his fears of radicalism and to the consequent need to abstain from constitutional experiments, the Prince contradicted him:

> The only way to deal with this onrush threatening destruction is to bind that part of the people which has means and intelligence (i.e. the real people) to the government by trustfully admitting it to participation in the administration of its own life. For as long as this people is kept separated from the government, it will have neither the interest nor the ability to assist the latter in its unequal struggle. In fact, it will hardly be able to help rejoicing secretly about any defeats suffered by the bureaucracy, which it hates (because it sees itself excluded by the bureaucracy from its due activity and from direct intercourse with its Prince) and thus lending its support to the radicals' plans of destruction.[2]

As a student at Bonn, Prince Albert had been deeply influenced by the teachings of the Historical School of German Law which, helped by the researches of the Romantics, was trying to uncover the roots of German constitutional development before the advent of the absolutism imported from France in the seventeenth and eighteenth century. He was thus able to turn the tables on Frederick William IV's historical arguments. Referring to the threat of the Elector of Hesse, Frederick William I, that he would abrogate the Hessian constitution and once more exclude the people completely from any participation in the government, the Prince wrote to the King of Prussia:

> This is certainly an ill chosen moment for reminding the German people once more after some previous incidents that it was not the German people, but the princes, who started subverting the existing order and that the origin of the *present* allegedly legitimist and historically German monarchical principle is in fact nothing else than an imitation of the *French absolutism*, as developed by Richelieu and Mazarin and displayed by Louis XIV, on

---

[1] Prince Albert to Bunsen, 14 June 1847 (Royal Archives I.1.36), tr.
[2] Prince Albert to the King of Prussia, 12 December 1847 (Coburg Archives), tr.

the ruins of the traditional rights of the Estates and of the people . . .
A demand on the part of the German people to regain these rights and,
where they have been regranted, a courageous adherence to them, I
cannot view as *French and radical*, but I must consider as truly *German and
conservative*.[1]

The Prince maintained that if each new sovereign could start afresh
constitutionally, this would undermine the monarchical principle
altogether, and lead to the degeneration of states to the level of the
"unhappy elective monarchy in Poland".[2] The Elector of Hesse was
now threatening to follow the precedent set by Queen Victoria's
uncle Ernest Augustus who revoked the Hanoverian constitution on
ascending the Guelph throne in 1837. In certain circumstances, a
people might even, as Prince Albert put it, be forced into making
what he called a "lawful rising" to resist the removal of constitutional privileges which had already been granted to them.[3] Prince
Albert was thus out of sympathy with the authoritarian trend which
became so important an element of the Bismarckian Empire. He
would not have had any doubt where right and wrong lay in those
terrible struggles of conscience which plagued those who resisted
the dictatorial state during the Nazi régime.

Events moved too fast for the Elector of Hesse. The implementa-
tion of his intentions was overtaken by the Revolution. When the
Revolution came, nobody could accuse Prince Albert of not having
foreseen the danger or of having kept silent.

(ii)

Prince Albert received the news of the revolution in Germany with
mixed feelings. As the holder of an annuity from Coburg and as the
guardian of the rights of his second son, who was heir presumptive
to the Duchy, he did not wish to see the existing order overthrown
altogether. He was certainly firmly opposed to the radicals who
wanted to abolish the monarchy and nobility. But at the same time
he welcomed the opportunity which now presented itself of bringing
about the unification of Germany. In sponsoring German unity, he
was not afraid of any undue curtailment of his own rights, because
he did not see any conflict between the interests of the whole and
those of the parts. In fact, he felt that Germany drew strength from
its regional variations and would suffer from any attempt to impose
excessive uniformity on it. As the representative of one of the smallest

---

[1] Prince Albert to the King of Prussia, 12 December 1847 (Coburg Archives), tr.
[2] Ibid.   [3] Ibid.

dynasties in the country, he certainly could not have any ambition of giving his family a leading position in the new Germany. The utmost for which he could hope was to save the Duchy of Coburg from amalgamation with a bigger grouping of Thuringian or Saxon states.

However much the Prince desired German unification, he was not an uncritical admirer of the German character. He wrote to his uncle about his efforts to interest the British government in the German question:

> I endeavour to plead the necessity [of a German nationality] and prophesy that the German nationality will be as uncomfortable to us [in] England and will have to be treated by us with as much caution, as the French and American . . . , up to now the only ones which besides ours have definite expression. The kind of reasoning which has to be applied with France and America and which we claim for ourselves will now also have to be applied to Germany: [i.e.] There are certain things, which admit of no reasoning, it is the popular feeling, the national feeling, etc. etc., and this must be respected. No government could struggle against it etc. etc.—This will be uncomfortable, but it is already so in Schleswig.[1]

The Prince realised how difficult it was for British statesmen, with their completely different historical background, to come to grips with the intricacies of the German problem:

> You also ask me what does the English government think about the German state of affairs? I should like to answer: *Nothing*, for it does not know what to think. Our diplomacy in Germany[2] is not brilliant and the English will find it difficult to absorb a German nationality in their way of thinking, which is a closed entity.[3]

King Leopold replied that "the English cabinet should gradually get some ideas about Germany".[4]

The German problem was so complicated that it did not offer any obvious solution. During 1848 in particular, while the general European situation was still fluid, there were thus unlimited opportunities for plans, suggestions and constitutional schemes, of which Prince Albert took full advantage. He aimed at applying to Germany the constitutional benefits which he had observed in England. His German proposals are eloquent testimony for his admiration of the political institutions of his new country. A letter he wrote to his

---

[1] Prince Albert to King Leopold, 28 April 1848 (Royal Archives I.3.113), mainly tr.
[2] See p. 120 ff.
[3] Prince Albert to King Leopold, 28 April 1848 (Royal Archives I.3.113), tr.
[4] King Leopold to Prince Albert, 2 May 1848 (Royal Archives I.4.9), tr.

brother on 17 March 1848, before the full extent of the revolutionary outbreak was known, is typical of this admiration:

> I feel sorry for you and the whole state of affairs in Germany . . . but I hope that you will not lose courage: for besides the first explosion there is also a good sentiment in what is going on in Germany. I expect a great blessing for all parts of Germany from the spiritual, material and political popular activity which has now been secured. The most important thing is the free press: it must be the lever to move the education of peoples and to secure their confidence in developments. Ask your best men now to write, not official articles, which look down with bureaucratic authority on the "uncomprehending, uninitiated public", but those which use popular arguments and talk common sense. That is now more important than all government files. It is an extraordinary gain that from now on wisdom of state will no longer belong to *one caste*, ex-officio. Beware of officials who do not recognise or do not want to recognise this change, or who even believe that they can . . . bring about a reaction. If you want to be strong now, find out who enjoys the greatest public confidence and call him to your councils without any further ado, without worrying about the etiquette of special advancements. Public jurisdiction and jury are great advances: they give the people confidence in the courts and develop its sense of justice.[1]

The Prince then developed one of his favourite themes, that freedom and justice are in their roots rather German than French. He said that public court proceedings and the jury system were considered too much from the point of view of how they work in France.

> On Gallic soil these free institutions do not flourish. In spite of his liberté, égalité, fraternité, the Frenchman is and remains a despot, and seeks freedom less in raising himself than in suppressing others. Of true freedom the German races [Stämme] are worthy. Jury and public proceedings are just as much rooted in the German past as they are of a piece with the German character, and they were only supplanted in Germany by the Roman [Welsch] law.[2]

The Prince recurred to the subject of constitutional government in another letter to his brother on 19 March 1848. He wrote that the essence of constitutional government—"taking as one's ministers the favourites, for the time being, of the public"—was not easily carried into practice in Germany. This was particularly so in the smaller states, owing to considerations of seniority, pensions, etc., for the state servants.

> But a new leaf *has to be* turned over and there *must* be government with the majority (which is the essence of the thing).[3]

---

[1] Prince Albert to his brother, 17 March 1848 (Royal Archives I.2.52), tr.
[2] Ibid.
[3] Prince Albert to his brother, 19 March 1848 (Royal Archives I.2.58), tr.

The Prince wrote that to overcome the difficulties a clear distinction had to be made—as in England—between permanent civil servants and changing ministers. He therefore proposed that there should be irremovable civil servants on the lower and middle levels, but that at the top there should be removable ministers:

> . . . the ministry should be formed . . . according to the majority in the Estates and should be changed by you *with this* majority, like an old coat. Reduce the ministry in numbers and do not award any pensions. Do not worry about such pedantry, as that it has to consist of *ordained bureaucrats.* Advocates, landowners, the military, scholars, citizens, and merchants are just as good and better if they are intelligent people. I wished that this happened throughout Germany, it is the only hope. Set the *example* and show the other sovereigns how it is to be done.[1]

The German question in 1848 differentiates Prince Albert much more than before from his teachers, King Leopold and Baron Stockmar, as well as from his brother-in-law, Prince Leiningen. Most of the Coburg "circle", including Albert's brother Ernest II, the reigning Duke, played a prominent part in German affairs at this stage. Stockmar went to Frankfurt as the representative of the Duchy of Coburg at the Diet and was at one time thought of as a possible Foreign Minister of the new German Central Power. Prince Leiningen actually made history, if only for a fleeting moment, as the first Minister-President of the new Central Power. Only King Leopold did not play a prominent part in this. He had lost touch with his Fatherland. As the Prince of Prussia wrote to him, he had "found a haven" elsewhere.[2]

Prince Albert occupied an intermediate position between King Leopold on the one hand, and Stockmar and Leiningen on the other. Ernest's usefulness lay mainly in being his brother's mouthpiece. King Leopold, so unorthodox in 1830, had himself become a "vested interest" and did not want to be reminded too much of the origin of his power, particularly after Austria and Russia had admitted him to their "salon". Prince Albert thought that his uncle had become too conservative by 1848. On the other hand, he considered Baron Stockmar and Prince Leiningen too extreme on some points. Stockmar did not have any scruples about sacrificing the rights of the small princes on the altar of German unity. Leiningen went even further and advocated thorough-going changes in the whole structure of society, to the consternation of Queen Victoria and Prince Albert.

---

[1] Ibid.
[2] The Prince of Prussia to King Leopold, 5 July 1848 (Royal Archives I.6.12), tr.

The question of German unification posed the most intricate problems of nationality, diplomacy and ideology. The survival of the Habsburg Monarchy into the age of nationalism bedevilled the whole issue at the outset. The Austrian Empire neither belonged completely to Germany nor could it easily be excluded from it. Legally, Austria with some of its possessions belonged to the German Confederation. On the other hand, endless complications could be caused for a modern German state, to which another power belonged with only part of its territories. The inclusion of the whole of the Habsburg Monarchy in the new Germany was not feasible, as it would have created a monster state in the centre of Europe which the other Powers would not have tolerated. At first completely baffled by this Austrian problem, the German liberal leaders of 1848 made some remarks about the position of non-German nationalities which later acquired an unfortunate flavour in the light of National Socialist doctrines.[1]

The controversy as to whether the new Germany should be formed with Austria, or whether Austria should be excluded, impeded a rapid solution of the question of German unity. The position of the nearly forty "sovereign" princes was another. Opinions were divided about the extent to which their rights should be respected. All these problems came before the German National Assembly which met in Frankfurt in May. It had been elected, generally by universal suffrage, in the territories of the German Confederation and even in some parts of the Austrian Empire which were only partly German. The Assembly seemed to dominate the scene right to the end of 1848 at least, but in 1849 its total lack of power became patent for all the world to see. In endless discussions about procedure and about the most involved constitutional issues[2] it missed the psychological moment for imposing its solution on the existing governments in Germany, which alone commanded the necessary power to implement changes. Once Austria and Prussia had begun to set their houses in order, the inflated bubble of the self-importance of the National Assembly was pricked.

The relations between the National Assembly and the state governments were never happy. The most trying—yet the most important—of these governments was that of Prussia. Once Austria

---

[1] See Sir Lewis Namier, "The Revolution of the Intellectuals", e.g. pp. 207, 212 etc.

[2] See the Stenographic Reports: Stenographischer Bericht über die Verhandlungen der deutschen konstituierenden Nationalversammlung zu Frankfurt am Main, 9 vols., particularly I.

had been excluded, as eventually became inevitable, the Prussian monarchy was left as the leading power in Germany. Any progress with German unification was out of the question as long as Prussia refused to co-operate. Unfortunately Frederick William's whole outlook rebelled against what the Frankfurt National Assembly was trying to do. He abhorred the self-appointed representatives of the people who pretended to a wisdom which only princes possessed. He objected to accepting the imperial crown at the hands of the people. He did not wish to see Austria excluded from what he considered her rightful place, hallowed by the tradition of the Holy Roman Empire. Particularly after experiencing street-fighting in Berlin, he did not want to be deprived of the support of Austria and Russia against the dreaded revolutionaries.

(iii)

As a curious by-product of the turmoil in March 1848, Prince Albert secured a strong ally close to the Prussian throne in the person of the Prince of Prussia, the later King and Emperor William I. The Prussian prince had to flee from Berlin soon after the March rising, as he was known as the advocate of firm resistance to the outbreak. There was some opposition in the British cabinet to Prince William taking up residence in Britain. This appears from a communication Lord Palmerston made to Prince Albert:

> . . . having on my return to the Cabinet mentioned to Lord Lansdowne [then Lord President of the Council] the opinion which I had expressed to Your Royal Highness that there could be no objection to the Prince of Prussia taking up his residence at once in England, instead of going in the first place for a short time to Madeira, I found that Lord Lansdowne was disposed to take a different view of the matter, and to think it would be better that the Prince of Prussia should not at once be mixed up with . . . the other exiles who arrived here under similar circumstances. I had not an opportunity of ascertaining the opinion of Lord John Russell.[1]

Prince Albert succeeded, however, in overcoming all obstacles to the Prince of Prussia's reception in England.[2] He made use of Prince William's presence to begin a sustained attempt to win over the Prussian Crown to constitutionalism and to its German mission. The friendship of the thirty-year-old Prince Albert with the heir of the Prussian throne who was nearly twice his age, helped by the regular correspondence of their wives, provided the background for the marriage of their eldest children. Their union was designed to

---

[1] Palmerston to Prince Albert, 25 March 1848 (Royal Archives I.2.94).
[2] Palmerston to Prince Albert, 27 March 1848 (Royal Archives I.2.105).

do politically what human foresight could do to help the spread of liberal ideas and international understanding in Germany.

William impressed Albert by the manly courage and lack of vindictiveness he showed in adversity. Prince Albert wrote to King Leopold within a few days of the new refugee's arrival:

> Yesterday I received the poor Prince of Prussia who is extraordinarily affected by all that has passed in Berlin. He fell as a victim of the fury against the troops, although he by no means gave the order to shoot or had any command, as is generally believed in Berlin . . . I hope that the misunderstanding will soon clear itself up. Men like him Germany certainly cannot do without now and it would be sad if a stigma remained on the heir of the Prussian throne.[1]

He set about the task of opening the older man's eyes to new ideas and of convincing him that an attachment to the old order did not require a rigid adherence to every tradition. Drawing on his intimate experience of English political life gained during eight years, he showed the Prince of Prussia how England had been able to adapt itself to inevitable changes without any weakening in the loyalty to the Crown and in the respect of the historical past represented by the monarchy. The workmanlike exposition by the husband of the Queen of England pointed to a lesson which the Prussian Prince was about to draw from the course of events. It was underlined by the calm and efficient manner in which the British authorities dealt with the Chartist threat on 10 April 1848. This showed him that autocratic discipline was perhaps not the best way to preserve order.

Prince Albert encouraged his friend to show that he was prepared to co-operate with the constitutional government which his brother, the King of Prussia, had been compelled to install:

> Would it not be a good thing if you had yourself elected as a member of the [Prussian] constituent assembly? This would give you a natural right to take part in the debates, it would be the clearest proof that you wish the new state of affairs well. It would give you the means of speaking out personally and it would be a proof of the confidence of the people in your person.[2]

The Prince then voiced a sentiment which frequently occurs in his correspondence:

> . . . It is very much to be desired that persons of rank should take part in the Assembly, so that the important task does not fall entirely into the hands of advocates, professors and journalists. The whole tone of the debates would thus be raised. Germany is not really represented without

---

[1] Prince Albert to King Leopold, 28 March 1848 (Royal Archives I.2.111), tr.
[2] Prince Albert to the Prince of Prussia, 16 April 1848 (Royal Archives I.3.66), tr.

the highest classes. Naturally you must not expose yourself to a rebuff and your election would have to be assured; but I should imagine that this could be achieved in a quieter part of the Monarchy, for instance in Pomerania.[1]

The Prince of Prussia eventually followed the suggestion, but had to go as far East as the province of Posen to find a constituency. Prince Albert made similar approaches to princes of other royal families in Germany, including that of Saxony. He also asked King Leopold to get the Austrian archdukes to put themselves up for election.[2]

The favourable impression the British system of government made on William strengthened his wife's political influence on him. The Princess of Prussia, Augusta, was a granddaughter of that Grand-Duke Charles Augustus of Saxe-Weimar who had been the patron of Goethe and the sponsor of constitutional rights in the period of reaction after the Congress of Vienna. For many years the Princess had tried to interest her husband in the importance of constitutional concessions; she was considerably influenced by what was happening in England, where she had visited Queen Victoria. In vain she had pleaded with her husband to adopt a conciliatory attitude to the United Prussian Diet in 1847. She had then written to him:

> Look at England and generally at the parliamentary history of all countries, in order to apply the right standard to our situation. Remember that it is the main task of politics to find a conciliatory way out, even where a rupture seems to be unavoidable.[3]

To this Augusta added a moving personal appeal:

> I have so far spoken to your intellect; now I turn to your heart and I am encouraged in this partly by a sense of duty as your faithful wife, partly by a consciousness that I have no other aim in mind than your welfare and the welfare of the dynasty, the welfare of the dear German Fatherland which can at this moment either be put into danger or be made safe.[4]

Considering that William was not the most faithful of husbands, Augusta's behaviour excites even more admiration.

Princess Augusta deeply appreciated the hospitality which Queen Victoria and Prince Albert extended to her husband in 1848. She opened her heart to the Queen about the things she had gone through during his absence:

> You are right, beloved cousin, it has been a terrible time for me. I had to

---

[1] Ibid.

[2] Prince Albert to King Leopold, 28 April 1848 (Royal Archives I.3.113).

[3] June 1847, quoted in Bailleu & Schuster, "Aus dem literarischen Nachlass der Kaiserin Augusta", Vol. I, 353-5, tr.

[4] Ibid.

represent and guard here the rights of my husband, I thus *had to* stay, although without protection against the most violent attacks and insults of all kinds. I had the saddest insight into human nature and found out the futility of earthly goods during the sudden passage from an advantageous position to a depressed one, for which God alone could give the necessary strength.[1]

The Princess may here well be referring to the intrigues of Prince Charles, the reactionary younger brother of the King and the Prince of Prussia, to stage a counter-revolution in the days after the Berlin outbreak. The plan was that Frederick William IV should abdicate and be succeeded by his young nephew Frederick William (the later Emperor Frederick III), passing over his absent father, the Prince of Prussia. Prince Charles reckoned on wielding the real power, at any rate initially. This episode is all the more interesting, as Bismarck, then one of the leaders of the ultra-conservatives, apparently went to see the Princess Augusta, on behalf of Prince Charles, on 23 March. By a strange twist of fate, Bismarck later served for a quarter of a century as the chief minister of this same Prince William whom he wanted to disinherit during his absence in 1848. How eager Bismarck was to let the world forget about his earlier attitude to his venerated master is shown by the distorted account he gives of the interview in his memoirs. He tried to make out that the suggestion for a change in the succession came from the Princess, which is a grave libel on a faithful wife and a complete perversion of the truth. The way he exposed himself at the interview contributed to the Iron Chancellor's hatred for Augusta.[2] In any case, Bismarck disapproved of her political outlook and of her influence over her husband. He realised that she stood in the way of his plans as a minister and immediately after his appointment systematically set about excluding her from her husband's councils, in which he succeeded only too well.

(iv)

The European importance of Britain as the model constitutional monarchy of the day and the influence of Prince Albert as its advocate are well illustrated by a four-cornered correspondence between the King of Prussia, the Chevalier Bunsen, Prince Albert and the Duke of Wellington, at the turn of May to June in 1848. On

---

[1] The Princess of Prussia to the Queen, 15 June 1848 (Royal Archives I.5.36), tr.
[2] Erich Eyck, "Bismarck", I, 87 ff.

3 June Bunsen received a request from the King of Prussia for speedy and precise information on a number of questions concerning the division of control over the British Army between the civil and the military authorities. Bunsen at once turned to Prince Albert for advice. The King had asked the following questions:

> How does the *"responsibility"* of the Secretary of War as a Minister fit in with the exclusive command of the Sovereign over the armies? Is he merely a financial administrator for the army? Can the Secretary or the Ministry as a whole issue orders to the Commander-in-Chief? Can the Ministry . . . force the Commander-in-Chief to employ or dismiss this or that person . . . under political pretexts? . . . Do the English principles permit the government of Her Majesty to make a *Cabinet question* out of the refused employment or dismissal of a General on the part of the Sovereign or the Commander-in-Chief?[1]

The King did not explain why he so particularly wanted all this information. Bunsen guessed that a conflict had arisen between the King and his liberal ministry over the constitutional position regarding the army.[2] Light on these differences is thrown by the Memoirs of General Leopold von Gerlach, Aide-de-Camp General to the King of Prussia and one of the leaders of the reactionary "Camarilla" at Court. In the entry in his diary on 5 June, Gerlach says:

> . . . The King . . . read me a letter to the Ministry, in which he refused with determination the retirement of General Colomb [the Prussian Commander in the Province of Posen], although Camphausen [the Prime Minister] had declared that Hansemann [the Finance Minister] and Auerswald [another Minister] had made it a condition for their remaining in the Ministry. I said to the King: "Let them go, the one is a traitor and the other is completely incapable." The letter was refined and determined; . . . The Ministers should consider that even a constitutional King, for example that of England, which was surely for us the only model, disposed freely over the army, but that this was a condition of vital importance for a King of Prussia, and that he would, as a human being, as a Prussian and as a King have to protest severely against being expected to do anything which separated him from the army. He put it to the patriotism of the Ministers to consider this, for he would prefer abdication to a separation from his army.[3]

The future of General Colomb was a question of first-rate importance, for here the Ministry was fighting on an issue with the widest possible ramifications. General Colomb, as the local commander, had done everything in his power to frustrate his fellow general von

---

[1] Frederick William IV to Bunsen, 30 May 1848 (Royal Archives I.5.12), mainly tr.

[2] Bunsen to Prince Albert, 3 June 1848 (Royal Archives I.5.11).

[3] L. v. Gerlach, "Denkwürdigkeiten", I, 151 ff. (particularly 163–4), tr.

Willisen, who had been sent by the Ministry in Berlin to end the Polish rising in Posen by a grand reconciliation between Germans and Poles. What was at stake, beyond the important constitutional issue of the power of the civil government over the army, was the very future of Prussian policy both internal and external, for in Posen home and foreign policy overlapped. A conciliation between Germans and Poles, which was anathema to extreme conservatives like von Gerlach, was also bound to widen the gulf between Prussia and that power which was the bitterest enemy of Polish nationalism and the leader of European reaction, Russia. Willisen had a plan for forming a Polish Free Corps, but this was turned down in Berlin, though—according to Gerlach—some of the Ministers were favourably inclined towards it. Tsar Nicholas, who was in any case very displeased with the weak attitude of his Prussian brother-in-law towards the revolution in Berlin, would have been even more enraged if a Polish Free Corps had been formed on Prussian territory. The Prussian policy in Posen was the touchstone of the entire future trend of the country. This was realised as much by the moderate constitutional "March" Ministry of Camphausen as by the "Camarilla" and by the King. The Ministry of War formed a key plank in the plans of the Camarilla. As Gerlach wrote in an entry in his diary on 21 April, he

> believed that the King could through the Ministry of War save the foreign policy and the army from the claws of the revolution and of constitutionalism, and raise himself up on it again when the occasion arose.[1]

The King was thus already contemplating going back on the promises of constitutional government he had given in March.

In London, Prince Albert set to work immediately on receipt of Bunsen's communication. He turned to the greatest expert on the relations between the civil and the military in Britain, the Duke of Wellington, who had held the highest offices in both spheres and was then Commander-in-Chief. The Duke had but a few weeks previously been in command of the troops in London on the day of the Chartist monster demonstration. He explained in detail how at every stage he was compelled by law to get the consent of the civil government. He instanced that he could not have closed the London park gates, had he not succeeded in obtaining authorisation from the Home Secretary.[2]

---

[1] L. v. Gerlach, I, 152, tr.

[2] The Duke of Wellington to Prince Albert, 3 June 1848 (Royal Archives I.5.12a).

Prince Albert informed Bunsen of the result of his researches, and enclosed the Duke's memorandum:

> . . . the whole thing is indeed very involved, but still, if one looks at it more closely, it is very reasonable. For Prussia the most opportune adaptation of our principles would seem to me for the King to have a Commander-in-Chief who would at the same time also be in charge of ordnance . . . , if the King further has a *civilian* Minister of War who looked after the finances of the army and would be responsible for these, and that the Prime Minister were also the Secretary of State through whom the King issued his orders and to whom the primary responsibility for them fell. . . . Thus promotion and all affairs of personnel would remain in the hands of the King, the *military authorities would not be responsible constitutionally*, only the *Minister* who issues the King's orders to them . . .[1]

The particular crisis which had made the King of Prussia seek information in London in the first instance no longer seemed to have been in the forefront of affairs in Berlin by the time Bunsen's reply arrived. Colomb was not recalled and the two ministers who had apparently threatened to resign remained at their posts. The King is not likely, in this instance, to have paid much attention to Prince Albert's advice. He continued to listen to the whisperings of the "Camarilla" who were determined to prevent the establishment of parliamentary control over the army. The problem of constitutional supervision was not solved under Frederick William IV.

(v)

Prince Albert had for some time before the revolution been corresponding with the King of Prussia about German unity. His views underwent a considerable development after September 1847, when he drew up his first plan. Before the revolution, he considered that a federation of states would provide a sufficient framework. By the end of March 1848 he had accepted the idea of a single German state, though it was to be a federal one. Until the latter part of 1848, he opposed the exclusion of Austria from a united Germany. Later, in November 1848, he agreed with this exclusion. He then adopted the concept of Heinrich von Gagern, perhaps the most prominent statesman of the Frankfurt National Assembly, that Germany and Austria should form two separate states, by treaty indissolubly linked in union. There were, however, some fixed points in his views, such as the advocacy of Prussian leadership and of an elective—as opposed to a hereditary—emperorship, as

[1] Prince Albert to Bunsen, 5 June 1848 (Royal Archives I.5.17), tr.

well as his emphasis on the maintenance of the special position of the individual sovereigns.

In his first post-revolutionary plan at the end of March 1848,[1] the Prince conceded that a confederation of states was no longer adequate for Germany and that a single state was a necessity. He now recognised that the task was to convert Germany from a confederation of comparatively independent states into one federal state. He wanted the individuality of the different parts and peoples of Germany to be maintained as far as possible and rejected a "shallow centralisation of the same stamp". He identified the special character of the different parts with their "crowns and dynasties" and inferred that the existing rights of the princes should be preserved. No concessions were made to the clamour for a directly elected German parliament. The Lower House of the Reich was to be elected indirectly by the Estates of the various kingdoms and principalities. Its decisions could be vetoed by a Diet of Princes (*Fürstentag*). An Emperor was to be elected, for a period of years, by the Diet of Princes. The accountability of the Reich ministers to parliament was to be strictly limited.

The plan certainly did not go far enough. Its strongest point was the emphasis on the co-operation of the princes. Without it, not even the Frankfurter National Assembly could impose its will. It has, however, been maintained that there was an insuperable dilemma, that the support of the princes could only be purchased with concessions which would have vitiated German unity.[2]

The reception accorded to the plan varied. King Leopold was enthusiastic. The King of Prussia was so impressed that he sent the Prince's memorandum to his fellow monarchs with his own annotations. He did not, however, agree with the proposal for an elected emperorship and suggested the revival of the Roman Imperial Crown vested in the Habsburgs.[3] Duke Ernest did not think much of his brother's plan or of the suggestions of the King of Prussia. As he said tersely in his Memoirs:

> The conception of the King of Prussia . . . rivalled the draft of my brother . . . in the doctrinaire statement of improbabilities and impossibilities.[4]

The Duke also thought his brother was wrong in insisting on an elective Emperorship.[5]

Stockmar and Prince Albert did not see eye to eye on the German

---

[1] See Ernst II, "Aus meinem Leben", I, 273 ff.
[2] K. Binding, "Zum Werden und Leben der Staaten", 18.
[3] Ernst, I, 273 ff.   [4] Ernst, I, 275, tr.   [5] Ibid.

question at this time. The basic cause of their difference of outlook
was that Stockmar did not share the Prince's enthusiasm for the
survival of that very dynastic particularism which he had so faith-
fully served for many years, but which he now considered harmful.
This led him to the conception of a centralised German state, as
opposed to the Prince's federal idea. The Germany visualised by
Stockmar was less dynastic and more parliamentary than the
Prince's. Both, however, were agreed in their belief in Prussian
leadership for Germany, though neither wanted to see Germany
become Prussianised. Stockmar's idea was that Prussia should merge
in Germany, the one concession with the Hohenzollern dynasty was
not prepared to make in any circumstances. Prince Albert was more
realistic in proposing a federal solution, quite apart from the possibly unfortunate national and international implications of German
centralism.

Like Prince Albert, Stockmar blamed Austrian policy for the
early success of the revolution in Germany. But he disagreed with
his pupil about the usefulness of the small states. He wrote later:

> The main feature of the present condition in Germany is the development
> and spread of democratic feeling in the masses to excess. Our division into
> so many, and partly such small states, gives the democratic element
> increased strength and increased danger.[1]

He also went much further than Prince Albert in insisting on the
necessity of popular participation in government:

> To me the correct answer on which nearly everything depends is whether
> it is possible for Germany in future to be governed without allowing the
> popular element a lawful participation in the government? I do not
> think that it would be possible to exclude it once more from what is
> called self-government. But if it cannot be excluded, something has to be
> invented so that one can govern alongside and with it, and [so that] the
> executive of the federation, as well as of the individual states can be
> made strong enough to compress the expansion of the democratic element
> so that a proper order for the state may become possible. . . . Only two
> forms of government will be possible in the near future: Absolute military
> rule or constitutional monarchy on the broadest democratic basis. Only
> the former—up to now improbable—makes it possible for Austria to
> have again an overwhelming position in Germany. The latter points . . .
> to Prussia. It is only by Prussia that all the true German spiritual and
> material interests can be represented and appreciated . . . Now it is a
> matter not only of determining the constitution, but also of protecting

---

[1] Stockmar to King Leopold, 20 April 1849. Copy to Prince Albert (Royal
Archives I.13.70), tr.

it against the crazy plans and desires of our numerous democrats and anarchists . . .[1]

Prince Albert again intervened when the "Seventeen Men of Confidence" appointed by the Frankfurt Diet published their constitutional proposals. The draft plan envisaged a hereditary emperorship, by implication held by the King of Prussia, and seemed to suggest the exclusion of Austria from Germany. It provided for a federal state on a constitutional basis, with a Reich Ministry responsible to a Reichstag. The Reichstag was to consist of two houses. The Upper House was to be made up of the Sovereigns and their representatives, as well as of over a hundred Councillors elected by the Estates and governments of the individual states. The Lower House was to be elected by universal and equal suffrage. The Prince objected to the hereditary emperorship, to the presence of sovereigns in the Upper House and to the stipulations about the Reich Councillors. He correctly forecast the gradual exclusion of the individual sovereigns from major affairs of state under a hereditary emperorship, as occurred during the Bismarckian Empire. He also realised how easily the hereditary emperor might by his blunders involve the whole of the monarchical principle in ruin, a feat achieved by his own grandson, the Emperor William II:

. . . The danger resulting from possible revolutions is reduced in the case of the elected emperor by the circumstance that movements which are directed against him always only attack the individual person, whereas those which are directed against a hereditary emperor attack the monarchical principle itself.[2]

Furthermore, the chance that the emperorship might "fall *into unsuitable hands*" was greater if it became attached to a particular dynasty.[3]

He was acutely conscious of the danger of Germany becoming Prussianised, of the Prussian military becoming the prototype for the whole of the country. He agreed with Stockmar that Prussia should, if it took over the leadership in Germany, merge in Germany rather than that Germany should become Prussianised. But he did not share Stockmar's optimism that this Prussianisation of Germany would be prevented in a centralised state:

If I also consider the influence which the future German emperor will from time to time exercise on the development of our future German

---

[1] Stockmar to King Leopold, 20 April 1849. Copy to Prince Albert (Royal Archives I.13.70), tr.
[2] Memorandum by Prince Albert, 6 May 1848 (Royal Archives I.4.20), tr.
[3] Ibid.

history, I cannot . . . help fearing that the indissoluble tying of the dignity of emperor to a single dynasty and country must force a certain unnatural one-sidedness on the development of our whole national life.[1]

As Prussia was the only power ever seriously considered for the hereditary emperorship during this period, it is safe to assume that the Prince was critical of an excessive Prussian influence over the future of Germany.

Furthermore, he thought it absurd that the sovereigns should be Reich Peers:

> The constitutional monarch, who *may* not voice any other public political will than that which he has formed, with the advice of a responsible ministry, in accordance with the proclaimed majority of the popular representatives of his state and who is supposed to be in every one of his words the total expression of the opinion *of his* state—how can he be put in a position of having to record his voice in an advisory chamber in accordance with his own individual judgment?[2]

The political philosopher and historian Dahlmann, who was one of the authors of the proposals, himself later admitted that this plan for an Upper House was rather unfortunate.[3] Prince Albert also would have liked to have seen a provision that some, at any rate, of the Reich councillors should be drawn from the ranks of the landowners and the hereditary nobility. In this he had the English example in mind.

King Leopold was—like the King of Prussia and the Duke of Coburg—among the recipients of the Prince's memorandum. He thought that a centralised Germany, as advocated by Dahlmann, would lead to a "Prussian super-nation":

> An efficient Germany can come of it, only it would in a kind of way be a Germany subordinated to Prussia.[4]

Prince Albert welcomed the appointment of the Austrian Archduke John as Vicar of the Empire by the Frankfurt National Assembly, however little he was pleased by the manner in which the election had taken place. He felt that it had been wrong to exclude the German princes from this important act establishing a Provisional Central Power for Germany. He encouraged the Archduke to take up his new appointment.[5]

---

[1] Ibid.
[2] Ibid.
[3] Valentin, I, 518–19.
[4] King Leopold to Prince Albert, 13 May 1848 (Royal Archives I.4.43), tr.
[5] Prince Albert to Archduke John, 1 July 1848 (Royal Archives I.6.2).

(vi)

In his defence of the rights of the German sovereigns, Prince
Albert met the fierce counter-argument of his brother-in-law who
was playing an important part at Frankfurt. Leiningen wrote:

> By the election of the Vicar of the Empire a step for the better has . . .
> been taken . . . As for your observation that while you are pleased about
> the event itself, you are not pleased about the method of the election, and
> indeed on grounds of principle, allow me to say that one has, in Germany,
> been thrown from the path of lawful reform on to that of revolution
> mainly in consequence of the former system, only as a result of the mistakes
> of the governments . . .[1]

Leiningen thought it was useless to speak of principles and rights in
the prevailing situation. The first necessity in his view was the ending of the revolution by establishing a Central Power. Himself the
heir of a mediatised, formerly "sovereign" principality, he thought
most of the remaining princes would now go the same way.

Leiningen became President of the first completed Reich Ministry
set up by the Central Power at the beginning of August 1848. He
considered the individual states to be mere executors of the wishes
of the Central Power. He failed to grasp the impotence of the Reich
Ministry acting on its own, as the only real power remained in the
hands of the individual states.

Prince Albert gave a qualified welcome to his brother-in-law's
appointment, though he had not endeared himself to him with his
views. As he wrote to his brother, he had thought for some time that
Leiningen wanted to get into the government, in view of the radical
opinions he had been expressing in the press:

> On the other hand it is very important that a man of rank should be at
> the head of the Ministry and Charles has a talent for foreign policy.
> Whether he will have the necessary stamina remains to be seen—Stockmar
> will probably prompt a little.[2]

Stockmar, who remained at Frankfurt, without becoming a member
of the National Assembly, certainly had more experience of foreign
affairs than Leiningen, with whom he agreed in advocating a
centralised Germany under Prussian leadership. Prince Albert did
not misjudge the situation when he sounded a warning about his
brother-in-law's stamina, for Leiningen only held his post for a few
weeks. It should, however, be emphasised that he resigned on grounds

---

[1] Leiningen to Prince Albert, 21 July 1848 (Royal Archives I.6.44), tr.
[2] Prince Albert to his brother, 9 August 1848 (Coburg Archives), tr.

of principle, over the Schleswig-Holstein question. After that he just faded away.

Prince Albert was particularly sensitive about Leiningen's radicalism in view of his cherished political and property rights in Coburg. He was horrified to hear in April 1848 that Leiningen was proposing to surrender the special seigniorial position (as *Standesherr*) which his family had retained. He wrote to his brother-in-law:

> That you want to renounce your birth, tradition, position and nature, and to part company with your peers, I consider a *moral* as well as a *political* mistake, . . . You have enjoyed all the advantages of this estate for over forty years and thus you have no right to leave it at the very moment when it is atttacked . . . and to cast stones at it. This is treason against oneself. Thus far the moral mistake. The *political* mistake is that you consider the thing at all possible . . . Even now you feel . . . that you do not escape the mistrust *from above* and *from below*. You incur the enmity of your peers as a republican and the democrats look at you askance as a hidden reactionary . . .[1]

Albert ended by reminding his brother-in-law of the fate of the Duke Philippe "Égalité" of Orléans in the French Revolution:

> He [the Duke of Orléans] foreswore his estate, abandoned everything to the people, became Citoyen Égalité, himself voted for the death of the King to show his sincerity towards the people, and afterwards mounted the scaffold . . .[2]

Prince Albert's arguments carried so little weight with Leiningen, that Queen Victoria eventually made a strong appeal to her half-brother:

> . . . when I hear that . . . *you go* so far as to propose and *urge* that the Sovereigns should *voluntarily* give *up their sacred charge*, and *abdicate* for the sake of *low pecuniary* advantages, I *cannot* remain silent, but must express to you *my indignation* and *my astonishment*. You injure by this proceeding your own Family, and your *own name*, and I fear that you will injure *yourself seriously*. *Painful* as it is for me to write thus to you, my *own Brother*, whom I have *ever dearly loved*, I must here positively declare that if *you persist* in this course, we can no longer be on the same terms that we have been on before, and that this *must* make a separation between us. Pause before you plunge yourself and many others in inextricable ruin, pause before it is too late and before you tear yourself from your dearest and nearest relations and friends.
>
> I have written this with the anxious love of a *truly* affectionate sister, and pray that it may not be too late. . . .[3]

---

[1] Prince Albert to Leiningen, 29 April 1848 (Royal Archives I.3.121), tr.
[2] Ibid.
[3] The Queen to Leiningen, 19 October 1848 (Royal Archives I.8.53).

The letter is signed:

> Your affectionate and deeply grieved sister.[1]

As was Prince Albert's wont, he did not hesitate to dig into the past to provide himself with further arguments, once the battle with Leiningen had been joined. He now accused him of having intrigued with Sir John Conroy against Queen Victoria before her accession. Conroy had been Controller of the Household of the Duchess of Kent, the mother of Queen Victoria and of Prince Leiningen, and was believed to have been the Duchess' lover. Prince Albert also charged Leiningen with intrigues against King Louis I of Bavaria in March 1848. The King's position had, in any case, become untenable, largely as a result of his association with Lola Montez, and he would have been forced to abdicate, even if Leiningen had had nothing to do with it. Prince Albert continued:

> Concerning your belief that someone has maligned you as a Jacobin, I need only say that the *public* preaching by a Prince of the right of revolution, of the sovereignty of the people, of the abolition of the nobility, of the entails [Fideicommisse] and now also of the sovereignties, is *pure* Jacobinism. Cutting off heads [das Kopfabhauen] does not necessarily belong to it; and you have described even civil war as something unfortunate, though perhaps unavoidable. . . .[2]

Leiningen's conclusion that the position of the smaller sovereigns had become untenable and that they would be well advised to cut their losses was also reached by an authority far removed from his radical outlook. Lord Cowley, the British Minister at Frankfurt, reported to Lord Palmerston in the late autumn that the existence of the smaller sovereigns was considered incompatible with a united Germany.[3] Cowley could not be accused of revolutionary tendencies. He was the son of the Duke of Wellington's youngest brother and, like his father, ended his diplomatic career as Ambassador to France. He was an excellent observer, trusted by the ministers and parliamentarians at Frankfurt who were delighted at the intelligence, integrity and culture of this distinguished member of a distinguished family. Cowley's reports do not contain a hint of that insularity which is so frequently a barrier to British understanding of the European continent.

Cowley realised the delicacy of this question in view of Prince

---

[1] The Queen to Leiningen, 19 October 1848 (Royal Archives I.8.53).
[2] Prince Albert to Leiningen, 8 November 1848 (Royal Archives I.9.19), tr.
[3] Cowley to Palmerston, 15 October 1848, Despatch No. 182 (Royal Archives I.8.41).

Albert's special position with regard to Germany and he had there-fore to tread warily. In the public despatch, which he knew would be circulated to the Queen and the Prince, he expressed his view that the German princes in the North were more popular than those in the South and thus had a greater chance of surviving. Presumably he had in mind the outbreaks in Baden and Württemberg which could only be crushed with outside help. It was proved later, how-ever, that the major dynasties in the South were to become particu-larly popular. Like Prince Leiningen, Lord Cowley thought that the sovereigns ought to settle while they could still get reasonable terms:

> To replace Germany as it was at the beginning of the year I look upon as an impossibility. There may be districts in which the necessity of amal-gamation is less felt than in others. It might indeed be possible to keep the whole machine moving as it is for some time longer, but the word has gone forth that the existence of the smaller states is incompatible with German unity and Central Government, and unless it pleases Divine Providence to overrule human speculations that word will become the fiat of the people.[1]

Lord Cowley accompanied his official despatch with a private letter to the Foreign Secretary:

> It is exceedingly difficult with the relations in which the Queen and Prince Albert stand to Germany to say all that I think ought to be said concerning the amalgamation of the smaller with the larger states. Mr. Meyer, Prince Albert's Secretary, has lately been here and had visited Coburg and Gotha. He says that those two countries are well disposed towards the Duke, and that sooner than lose him they would agree to continue to pay the expenses of the Court. The Central Govern-ment has accounts of a very different nature. What I conceive would be the most prudent course would be for everything Saxon to offer to unite itself to the Crown of Saxony, for the Hesses to endeavour to make an arrangement of the same kind and so on . . .[2]

Actually, Lord Palmerston forwarded Lord Cowley's letter to Prince Albert,[3] who had already seen the despatch. The Prince countered by arguing that the strength of monarchical feeling in Germany consisted in "the remains of attachment of the people to their sovereigns" and that this loyalty could not be transferred:

> The destruction of social and political ties in Germany has already been so dreadful, and one should have thought that the Central Power would feel the advantage of respecting the little that remains. I believe it has

[1] Ibid.
[2] Cowley to Palmerston, 16 October 1848 (Royal Archives I.8.61).
[3] Palmerston to Prince Albert, 21 October 1848 (Royal Archives I.8.60).

been the idea of some of the politicians at Frankfurt to buy the consent of the various Kingdoms to the omnipotence of the Central Power by the sacrifice to them of the smaller states.[1]

He emphasised that no sovereign was entitled to abdicate his power into the hands of another prince in the absence of a clearly expressed wish of the people that he should do so.[2]

Lord Palmerston sent Prince Albert's reply to Lord Cowley who suggested that the Prince "laboured under a fatal error" in supposing that any attachment of the people to their sovereigns remained in Germany. Lord Cowley did not accept Prince Albert's thesis that the weakness of the governments in the South-West of Germany was the consequence of the extensive mediatisation of small possessions which had been carried out in these parts. He thought the unrest had been mainly due to the influence of the "French and Swiss Proletaires". He then quoted the evidence of a strong witness, to whose opinion he knew the Queen and her husband to attach considerable importance. Baron Stockmar had called on him en route from Coburg to England:

> Stockmar . . . is convinced that Coburg cannot be saved. He says that . . . if at this moment you were to canvass the towns of Coburg and Gotha, they would say, let us have our Duke by all means, because those two towns derive some benefit from the Court residing in them, but he adds that even they are not to be trusted . . . and that the day will come when they will be the first to cry out for a change.[3]

Prince Albert, who was shown this letter, agreed that it was "certainly best to hear everything and everybody". But he dismissed Cowley's arguments as being curiously similar to those of a Weimar politician, Wiedenbruck, who wanted to unite the whole of Thuringia under his Grand Duke.[4] The suspicion of the rulers of Coburg and Weimar was mutual. The Weimar dynasty thought there was British support for the aggrandisement of Coburg, possibly at their expense. At this very time, the Prince of Prussia was asked by his wife's Weimar relatives to intervene at Frankfurt against these designs. William complied and the Prussian representative at Frankfurt, Camphausen, apparently received satisfactory assurances from the Central Power. He asked his wife's relatives not to reveal the undertakings, because it would not do for them to become known at Frankfurt. Otherwise Camphausen might be compromised.[5]

---

[1] Prince Albert to Palmerston, ? 22 October 1848 (Royal Archives I.8.62).
[2] Ibid.
[3] Cowley to Palmerston, 11 November 1848 (Royal Archives I.9.53).
[4] Prince Albert to Palmerston, 24 November 1848 (Royal Archives I.9.56).
[5] See "Die Briefe Kaiser Wilhelm I. Weimarer Briefe", I, 186. Edited J. Schultze.

If mediatisation became inevitable, Prince Albert preferred that it should be carried out by the King of Saxony rather than the Grand-Duke of Weimar. At the same time, he welcomed schemes for a Thuringian Federation:

> One is surprised that the revolution of 1848 was needed to bring about so obvious and necessary an understanding. The governments and the bureaucrats really have much to answer for.[1]

Actually, it was not only the authorities who had been the stumbling block to rational organisation. Even the citizens of Coburg and Gotha, though united under one duke, had refused to allow themselves to be welded into a single state system. Particularism was thus deeply rooted in the feelings of the people.

In assessing Prince Albert's views about the advisability of preserving Coburg, his property rights there should be taken into account. The Prince, however, did not take a narrow and exclusively financial view of these rights:

> We have received the property from the [i.e. our] fathers, but at the same time also their *faults* and debts; let us do our duty in the conviction that however much evil we may have to bear because of them, yet the good which they have passed on predominates.[2]

On the other hand it should not be assumed from this that the Prince was oblivious of the importance of money. He was furious with his brother for having gone further in his concessions to popular financial demands than he thought necessary. Like his fellow princes in Germany, the Duke found himself hard pressed and had little option. This did not deter the other members of the Coburg dynasty from officially protesting to the Duke about the violation of their rights.[3] When the beneficiary from an annuity paid by Prince Albert in Coburg had his grant stopped, the Prince made a strong complaint to his brother:

> I must protest energetically against this. It is my private fortune to which the Kammer [the Ducal finance administration] is not entitled in any way. If it is bankrupt, it has to declare this, for one would then be entitled to liquidation. You must tackle the question . . . I have allotted about fifteen thousand fl. yearly in pensions, foundations and subscriptions, the money for which I really cannot afford to loan out [to somebody else] . . .[4]

---

[1] Prince Albert to his brother, 9 August 1848 (Coburg Archives), tr.
[2] Prince Albert to his brother, 17 March 1848 (Royal Archives I.2.52), tr.
[3] Thus Prince Albert and King Leopold, 27 February 1850 (Royal Archives I.18.52).
[4] Prince Albert to his brother, 9 August 1848 (Coburg Archives), tr.

In viewing the situation at Coburg and Gotha, Albert's mind was influenced by a mixture of interested and disinterested motives. If his faith in the loyalty of the subjects of Coburg and Gotha for their dynasty was rather too unqualified, Stockmar's and Cowley's point of view has not been borne out by later developments. Dynasticism was often blamed for a particularism for which it was by no means solely responsible. Particularism outlived the dynasties and some of its most harmful manifestations belonged to the era of the Weimar Republic.

(vii)

If the first impulse of the German movement failed to translate itself into terms of reality, this was not mainly due to the particularism of the small states, but to the deficient leadership provided by Prussia. However much Prince Albert regretted that no firm steps had been taken towards German unification, he approved of Frederick William's reluctance to accept the Imperial German crown at the hands of the National Assembly without the prior agreement of the individual sovereigns; he wrote to King Leopold:

> Although Gagern will have tried once more in Berlin to get the King of Prussia to help himself now to the Imperial German crown and thus put himself in the debt of the revolution and the omnipotence of the Frankfurt democrats . . . , the King will . . . be too honest . . . to allow himself to fall into the snare, and will not, without the co-operation and *legal* agreement of the other states and crowns, want to usurp any supremacy over them. Thus one will have to do what should have happened from the very beginning and against which Charles [Leiningen] warned as shameful and disgraceful, that is to *negotiate with the existing governments* about the position which one wants to allot to them in the Reich.[1]

If the King of Prussia had been really determined, a beginning with unification could have been made in the North of Germany, in much more favourable circumstances than when the Prussian Government swung round to this policy in the following two years.

Prince Albert wanted the German princes to assemble at Frankfurt and to come to terms with the National Assembly:

> The Vicar of the Empire . . . could depose his power into the hands of a Council of Princes . . . By such an act, he would restore the power granted to him by way of revolution to that authority from which he should really have received it . . . Time presses for the immediate carrying out of such a measure.[2]

---

[1] Prince Albert to King Leopold, 6 December 1848 (Royal Archives I.10.15), tr.
[2] Memorandum by Prince Albert, 6 December 1848 (Royal Archives I.10.17), tr.

He criticised the King of Prussia for taking the line that "everything depended on gaining time". He thought this waiting attitude was playing into the hands of all those, on the right and on the left, who were trying to sabotage the task of unification. He was as severe in his condemnation of the strict particularism of the King of Bavaria as of the attitude of the Left wing at Frankfurt. Indeed, he thought the intrigues of the princes, particularly of the King of Bavaria, were playing straight into the hands of the radicals in the National Assembly who would be able to seize the initiative.[1] The Prince was increasingly out of humour with the acts of the National Assembly which seemed to fall more and more under the sway of the extremists. He considered the "Basic Rights" of the citizen which the Assembly had voted as excessive and disposed of them as "silly".[2] He was doubtless put off by the clause decreeing the abolition of the nobility as an Estate.[3] He looked on those Basic Rights as potential means for the annihilation of the smaller states:

> The democrats are pleased if unity fails, for with the Basic Rights they have achieved everything to which they attach importance and with them they can destroy singly all the smaller states such as Baden, Württemberg, Hesse and Saxony (not to speak of the smallest ones), like so many isolated units of troops, and thus achieve individual republics. Germany under one supreme constitutional head in charge of *one* army offers them very little chance.[4]

It is not surprising that Prince Albert opposed co-operation with the radicals on the Left. On the other hand there was no possibility of working with the men of the Right who, with their legitimist outlook, objected to any modification of the German Confederation. Prince Albert failed to see that the rejection of so many groups because they were either too extreme or too conservative left the German movement with rather a narrow basis. Everything thus became too dependent on the King of Prussia, who, with his legitimist outlook, could not be trusted by the Frankfurt National Assembly.

In his eagerness to see the sovereigns take the initiative out of the hands of the parliamentarians, the Prince may have misjudged the situation in Prussia. He congratulated Frederick William on getting rid of his Constituent Assembly.[5] Under the influence of the unofficial advice of the Court "Camarilla" and of Bismarck, the King

[1] Ibid.
[2] Prince Albert to King Leopold, 19 January 1849 (Royal Archives I.11.38), tr.
[3] Basic Rights, § 137.
[4] Prince Albert to King Leopold, 19 January 1849 (Royal Archives I.11.38), tr.
[5] Prince Albert to the King of Prussia, 13 December 1848 (Royal Archives I.10.48), tr.

had dissolved the Prussian National Assembly elected in May, before it had completed its draft of the Prussian constitution. The King had at the same time granted (*oktroyiert*) a constitution of his own free will, without any discussion with the Assembly. This Constitution corresponded in many respects to the draft of the Assembly's Constitutional Committee, though with some autocratic additions. But universal suffrage for the second (popular) Chamber, for instance, had been retained. The Prince thought that the King's

> ... gift of a Constitution ... so *completely* secures for Prussia the *achievements of March* that hardly any honest democrat can be dissatisfied with it except for his regret that *he* has not made it.[1]

Perhaps he was rather hasty in his judgment in agreeing with the King. He did not realise sufficiently that this was only a further step in Frederick William's abandonment of the position he had been forced to take up in March. Even one of Frederick William's closest advisers, Josef Maria von Radowitz, the main advocate of German unity at the Prussian Court, felt that the Crown should have remained true to its constitutional obligations and that it should have persisted in trying to come to an agreement with Parliament, however difficult this might be.[2]

There were special considerations involved. The Prussian National Assembly had, indeed, throughout been more radical than its German counterpart at Frankfurt. The atmosphere in Berlin became tense as the extreme left wing at Frankfurt had, after the crushing of the abortive September rising there, decided to move its centre of operations to Berlin. There had been a resumption of sporadic street fighting in the Prussian capital and there seemed to be a danger of further collisions. In addition some of the politicians at Frankfurt saw in Prussian progress on the road to constitution making a potential threat to a united Germany. Thus Heinrich von Gagern, who had taken over control of the Reich Ministry at Frankfurt, was only prepared to accept the imposed constitution of December 1848 in the hope that it would give way to a more comprehensive—and no doubt not so advanced—constitution for the whole of Germany.

In October 1848, Gagern had put forward to the National Assembly at Frankfurt his plan that Germany and Austria should form two separate states linked in permanent and indissoluble union.

---

[1] Prince Albert to the King of Prussia, 13 December 1848 (Royal Archives I.10.48), tr.
[2] F. Meinecke, Radowitz, 180 ff.

Prince Albert agreed with Gagern in principle, though he did not like all the details of his proposals. The Prince wanted a defensive and offensive alliance (*Schutz- und Trutzbündnis*) and a customs union between the two states, as well as equality of civic rights and free movement. All nationalities should have equal rights in Austria, and thus in Germany too.[1] He thought this solution would be to the advantage of both states, leading to the rejuvenation of each:

> Every day that Austria continues its present policy of only half doing things . . . and to waver between its real Austrian and its imaginary German advantages . . . is a new obstacle to the development of both Empires.[2]

The Prince was not slow to put the main responsibility for the initial failure of the German unity movement squarely on the shoulders of Prussia and even more of Austria. He wrote to the Archduke John, the Vicar of the Empire, in June 1849:

> When the revolution of last year overthrew the old state of law in Germany and Austria and created conditions of general confusion and anarchy, it was certainly at first mainly a matter of *founding as quickly as possible a new state of law*, in order to be able to restore order and peace . . . It must have been clear to every statesman of insight that the old relationship of Austria and Prussia to Germany and to each other, which involved— by keeping each other in balance—*condemning* Germany to an *eternal lack of movement*, could not be restored. It therefore became the most urgent duty of all the statesmen of Austria and of Prussia to devote all their energy . . . to finding . . . the most effective relationship . . . between Austria, Prussia and Germany. But instead of making this attempt with sincerity and eagerness, the governments of both states have done *the very opposite* and . . . have, driven by mutual misunderstanding and jealousy, *not only left this principal question undetermined*, but have *deliberately put it in the background* . . . while they permitted the National Assembly to complete the new Constitution down to the *smallest detail*, well knowing that *without previous* solution of this . . . question the Constitution would of necessity be a chimera and that it could *not* be solved by the National Assembly, but *only* by the governments of Austria and Prussia . . .[3]

Prince Albert's indictment was directed primarily against Austria. He seems to have put in the references to Prussia for good measure, so as to appear fair to his Austrian correspondent. The Prince had approved of Frederick William's refusal of the offer of the Imperial Crown at the hands of the Frankfurt National Assembly in the

[1] Prince Albert to Leiningen, 8 November 1848 (Royal Archives I.9.19), tr.
[2] Memorandum by Prince Albert, 30 December 1848 (Royal Archives I.10.89), tr.
[3] Prince Albert to Archduke John, 8 June 1849 (Royal Archives I.15.20), tr.

spring of 1849, which dealt a death blow to this body. He was pleased about the initiative passing to Prussia. The letter to the Archduke John is thus mainly a strong criticism of Austria. The Prince's rejection of Austria's policy in Germany contrasts with his support for the Habsburgs in Italy which was one of the points at issue in the conflict between the Court and the Foreign Secretary, Viscount Palmerston.

Chapter Seven

THE CLASH WITH PALMERSTON—I

(i)

THE trial of strength with Palmerston was the most critical political problem Prince Albert had to face after he had established himself as the Queen's permanent adviser in affairs of state. The issue at stake was not simply whether this or that course should be followed in foreign policy, important though this was. Crown criticism of the handling of foreign policy by the responsible minister was found to involve, sooner or later, questions of constitutional machinery and of propriety. The Prime Minister could not stand aloof, when the Crown appealed to him against the Foreign Secretary. Whenever the Prime Minister failed to settle the dispute, the Cabinet also became involved, as an arbiter between the Foreign Secretary and the Crown. Knowing that his policy was disliked at Court, the Foreign Secretary attempted to evade Crown control by sending off despatches without authority. The Crown naturally countered by putting beyond dispute its right to the supervision of despatches. This, in turn, evoked murmurs of excessive royal interference, embittering the atmosphere even further. Each side reacted characteristically. Palmerston continued, apparently unperturbed, to his fall, though this did not prove to be his anticipated final doom. As for Prince Albert, the whole question never ceased to exercise his mind from May 1848, when it first arose in critical form. Starting by having differences of opinion with Palmerston, he soon saw the problem in moral terms, and began to look on Palmerston's influence as evil. Here Palmerston's earlier gay private life seemed to him to clinch the argument. Whilst the Prince's approach remained basically one of intellectual reasoning, that of the Queen was first and foremost instinctive and emotional, affecting her whole person and well-being even more than was the case with her husband.

In disagreeing with Palmerston, the royal couple was encountering the most powerful member of the government. As Lord John Russell realised, Palmerston—and not he himself—was the government's main strength. Palmerston was the last Foreign Secretary who was a great popular national figure. Right to the end of his days, long after he had left the Foreign Office, it was his foreign policy which was his strength in the country. This was unpalatable to the Court. Foreign policy was taken out of the atmosphere of confidential discussion, in which the Crown could make its influence felt, and transferred to a forum in which the Sovereign had to remain silent. With some justification, the Prince also felt that the settlement of international difficulties might not be helped if public passion were aroused.

Particularly after the death of Sir Robert Peel in July 1850, Palmerston was the dominant political figure of his day, courted by both the major parties. While he never returned to the Foreign Office after his dismissal in December 1851, he was only rarely out of power, rising to the supreme ministerial office in 1855. Thus, from July 1846 onwards, the Prince normally had to deal with Palmerston in some important official capacity.

The sporadic disagreement between the Foreign Secretary and the Court developed into an explosive situation in May and June 1848. It began with Schleswig-Holstein and within a few weeks took in the affairs of the Iberian Peninsula and of Italy. The differences of opinion which emerged were so decisive and the Foreign Secretary's apparent indifference to royal criticism so galling to the Court, that the personal relations between the royal couple and the minister did not recover even reasonable harmony for many years.

Prince Albert's belief in the justice of German national aspirations at the beginning of May 1848 led to the first serious disagreement with Lord Palmerston. It concerned the Schleswig-Holstein question, which became a burning international problem with the rebellion of the German population of the Duchies in March 1848.

The position of the Duchies of Schleswig and Holstein was anomalous. While the King of Denmark was Duke of both, only Holstein formed part of the German Confederation, to which the King of Denmark belonged as Duke of Holstein. Both the Danish and the German national movements saw their opportunity in the revolutionary situation of 1848. The partisans of a modernised Danish monarchy wanted to include Schleswig, which did not belong to the German Confederation, in the new unitary Danish state which they were advocating. The German movement countered with the historically dubious argument that the Duchies had been promised they would remain "for ever undivided". This ruled out the compromise whereby Schleswig might have been incorporated in Denmark, while Holstein could have joined the new Germany. In any case the south of Schleswig was mainly inhabited by Germans, and ethnically the fairest frontier was that achieved by the plebiscite after the First World War which ceded North Schleswig to Denmark, while leaving everything to the South in German hands. For a fleeting moment, in March 1848, the Germans in the Duchies were prepared to accept a plebiscitary solution, but the beginning of armed hostilities silenced the voices of conciliation and reason. Both sides now adopted extreme positions; the Germans asked for the whole of both Duchies and the Danes demanded the restoration of the *status quo ante*, coupled, if possible, with a weakening of the rights of the Duchies.

The question was further complicated by the imminent extinction of the direct line of the House of Oldenburg which occupied the Danish throne. This raised the possibility of a separation of the Duchies from the Kingdom of Denmark, since the Danish Crown could devolve in the female line, whereas Schleswig and Holstein followed the German custom of the Salic Law. The Danes were in a dilemma. A strict observance of the Salic Law, to put the continued union of the Duchies with their Kingdom beyond doubt, was unthinkable in the circumstances, as it would have involved the succession of Christian Augustus, Duke of Augustenburg, who was in rebellion against Danish rule. They thus resorted to a near heir in the female line, Prince Christian of Glücksburg, the head of a junior branch of the house of Oldenburg. But there was no certainty that the Duchies would be prepared to accept this deviation from the Salic Law. They were, in fact, predominantly in favour of the eventual succession of the Duke of Augustenburg.

When the Duchies rose in March, they called on the German Confederation for help. The Prussians and some federal troops responded and, although they were originally told to confine themselves to Holstein, they soon crossed into Schleswig and even entered the Kingdom of Denmark proper. It was a moot point whether the Danes could, as a result of the German violation of indubitably Danish territory, demand protection from Britain in accordance with the terms of the guarantee of 1720.[1] Quite apart from that, Britain was vitally interested in preventing the passage from the North Sea to the Baltic falling into the hands of a potentially unfriendly great power. From the British point of view, it was better

---

[1] At first, Palmerston put forward the argument that a German annexation of Schleswig would bring the guarantee into play (see his despatch to Cowley, 10 May 1848, Public Record Office FO/96/22). But he did not adhere to this view.

that a normally friendly minor power like Denmark should control the "Dardanelles of the North" than that the influence of any major power, be it Russia or Germany, should be extended to this area. Commercial and naval arguments reinforced this reasoning. The Napoleonic Wars had shown how awkward a situation could arise if Danish naval power fell into enemy hands. The interests of peaceful trade also seemed to require the maintenance of the existing state of affairs. Palmerston was firm in opposing any extension of the German protectionist system to the Duchies. The economic aspect may well have been as important to the Foreign Secretary as the strategic one.[1]

Prince Albert favoured the German case. Holding a strong united Germany to be in the interests of Europe, he considered it vital that the entire project of German unity should not be allowed to fail over its first important venture. This does not imply, however, that he was happy about Germany tackling the thorny Schleswig-Holstein question before it had straightened out its internal problems.[2] He was impressed by the legal arguments put forward by the Germans. He felt that the Estates of the Duchies should be consulted before any change were made in their relations with Denmark.

The Foreign Secretary strove for the only possible policy which Britain could follow. He wanted the conflict to end as soon as possible without Russia obtaining a foothold in the area. Tsar Nicholas I, who considered himself responsible for the fate of the elder—Danish—line of his dynasty, might well be driven to military intervention to resist German penetration, though he preferred resorting to diplomatic and naval pressure.

Prince Albert took too one-sided a view to be able to show any understanding for the difficulties in which Palmerston found himself and which he did his best to master, particularly after Britain had undertaken to mediate in the dispute. The Prince felt it necessary to appeal to the Prime Minister, Lord John Russell:

> The Schleswig-Holstein question causes me much anxiety as I am afraid that we may be dragged by the Danish and Russian, perhaps even by French insinuation and diplomatic efforts, into an open opposition to Germany. I assure you that I try to divest myself of every particle of

---

[1] See Palmerston's draft to Cowley No. 62 of 24 February 1849 in which the Foreign Secretary reports a conversation with Bunsen. He writes that he remained silent about most of the German proposals over Schleswig, but reacted strongly against a plan to include Schleswig "in the line of customs of the German Confederation", which Bunsen dropped at once (Public Record Office FO/30/120).

[2] See Prince Albert's letter to Bunsen about Hungary, 21 August 1849, p. 125.

German feeling in considering this question and am looking solely to the interests of this country which may be most seriously endangered by a provocation on our part of the national passions of a people feeling for the first time since 1813 their nationality to be their highest good. . . . Our opposition must appear to them either as hostility to their regeneration and consolidation on account of interested motives, or as a proof of our despising in them a nationality which we recognise and protect in other nations like the Italian, the Swiss, the Polish and the Greek etc. perhaps as both.[1]

The Prince also complained about the attacks on the German cause in Parliament and in the press.[2] The chief culprit in the latter was *The Times*. Parliamentary criticism came in particular from Benjamin Disraeli, who made a strongly pro-Danish speech on 19 April.

The Prince received little encouragement from the Prime Minister, who concluded his reply by remarking pointedly:

I cannot prevent The Times taking its own view, still less Mr. d'Israeli. But I trust that the Germans will have too much sense to imagine that The Times and Mr. d'Israeli comprehend the whole of England.[3]

The Schleswig-Holstein question did not lead to an open conflict between the Court and the Foreign Secretary at this juncture, as the Prince did not have a case against Palmerston. It was different when the ground shifted to the South of Europe. Here the Foreign Secretary was laying himself wide open to royal criticism for "intermeddling", and in fact doing so with very unfortunate consequences. Palmerston's lecture to the Spanish Queen on her choice of ministers had been, in Peel's words, "calculated to give offence to a proud nation like Spain". Advice given in an insulting manner was worse than no advice at all. Even if some of the trouble could be attributed to the indiscretions of the Minister to Spain, Sir Henry Bulwer, the Foreign Secretary only had himself to blame if his bravado made matters worse. The expulsion of Sir Henry Bulwer by the Spanish authorities in May 1848 signalled his defeat, made worse by touching his own Sovereign very deeply, for Queen Victoria considered the treatment of "her Minister"[4] a direct insult to herself, for which she held the Foreign Secretary to blame. She was right to reprimand the Foreign Secretary, who had turned a deaf ear to her previous warnings about Bulwer. But Palmerston was to show the following month that even stronger measures on the part of the Sovereign were necessary to keep him within his constitutional

[1] Prince Albert to Russell, 1 May 1848 (Royal Archives I.4.7).   [2] Ibid.
[3] Russell to Prince Albert, 2 May 1848 (Royal Archives I.4.8).
[4] The Queen to Palmerston, 23 May 1848 (*Letters*).

limits. For the Foreign Secretary was about to repeat in Portugal what had already led to a severe diplomatic defeat in Spain.

It is hard to see why Palmerston should have stirred up trouble for himself over Portugal, realising fully from previous experience how sensitive his Court was about the treatment of their relations at Lisbon. In spite of that, he submitted a draft to the British Minister to Portugal, Sir Hamilton Seymour, in the middle of June 1848, which was difficult to justify on any score, particularly after what had happened in the neighbouring kingdom:

> As it is evident that the Queen and the Government of Portugal will listen to no advice except such that agrees with their own wishes, I have to instruct you to abstain in future from giving any longer any advice to them on political matters, taking care to explain both to the Queen and the Government your reasons for doing so. You will, however, at the same time positively declare to the Portuguese Government that if by the course of policy they are pursuing they should run into any difficulty, they must clearly understand that they will not have to expect any assistance from England.[1]

This reprimand could not do any good. If the British Foreign Secretary was right in not having any confidence in the Portuguese government, then that government was not likely to have the sense to heed his warning of the withdrawal of British support.

Queen Victoria would have failed in her duty if she had not tried to stop the despatch of so inexcusable a draft. The Queen was particularly annoyed at Lord Palmerston having turned an instruction to Seymour to keep out of party intrigues at Lisbon, which she had requested, into something offensive to the Portuguese government. She immediately referred the matter to the Prime Minister, expressing herself in terms which were fully justified:

> . . . The Queen thinks this almost a mockery of Lord John, the Cabinet, the Country and herself which can really not go on so.[2]

As the draft had arisen from a request of the Queen transmitted by the Prime Minister, Palmerston's action was an expression of contempt for the views of both. Queen Victoria also implied that the Prime Minister and the Cabinet had failed to keep the Foreign Secretary in order, thus placing an unfair burden of responsibility on the Queen's and the Prince's shoulders. The Cabinet was too big a body, met too infrequently, and had too many other pre-

---

[1] See *Letters*, footnote to 16 June 1848.
[2] The Queen to Russell, 16 June 1848 (Royal Archives C.8.22).

occupations to be able to carry out any day-to-day supervision of the activities of the Foreign Secretary. But Lord John could not plead similar excuses. In view of the importance of foreign affairs, the head of government has always kept a special eye on his colleague at the Foreign Office. In the case of Lord John Russell's government, a strict control of Lord Palmerston by the Prime Minister had been a condition of Lord Grey's entering the government. As the crisis of December 1845 had shown, Lord Grey's support was as essential for the formation of a Whig government as Lord Palmerston's. Lord Grey had thus been in a position to stipulate conditions. He soon realised, however, that Lord John was not carrying out his part of the bargain. Lord Grey was unable to insist on his doing so, for Lord John was not tough enough to take care of Palmerston. The Colonial Secretary feared that a serious disagreement about the control of foreign policy might lead to a break-up of the government. The Cabinet was thus unable to check the Foreign Secretary without the full assistance of the Prime Minister. It could reassure its conscience by pointing to its frequent agreement with the Foreign Secretary's policy even if it was not entirely satisfied about his methods.

Lord John was now beginning to find himself almost continuously in that position of umpire between Windsor and Broadlands in which he later claimed to have felt so uncomfortable.[1] But the very expression Lord John used about his position reveals his inability to live up to the responsibility of his task. It was not the Prime Minister's place to arbitrate between his Sovereign and a member of his government, but to captain his team, to enforce his authority on his difficult subordinate where he was found wanting and to deal with the Queen as the spokesman of a united cabinet. The notion of the umpire shows a curious conception of cabinet responsibility in the Prime Minister.

In spite of all his good qualities, his intelligence, his culture, his long experience of government and of the House of Commons, Lord John was ill fitted to be a leader of men. His treatment of Palmerston alternated between mildness and severity, and he succeeded only for short periods in keeping the Foreign Secretary in order. He usually failed to satisfy the Court that he was determined to grasp the Palmerston nettle. Shifting his ground constantly and uneasily, he succeeded in remaining in office until February 1852, but in the

---

[1] Russell to Clarendon, 23 December 1851 (See Sir H. Maxwell, "Life and Letters of the Fourth Earl of Clarendon", I, 337–8).

process almost completely destroyed his reputation for character and consistency.[1]

The handling of the despatch to Portugal illustrates Lord John's evasive attitude. The Prime Minister was desperately trying to square the circle, to comply with Palmerston's refusal to instruct Seymour on the necessity of neutrality without falling foul of the Court. At last he seemed to have found a solution: to do nothing. After corresponding with Palmerston, Lord John wrote to the Queen, taking everybody's side without being on anybody's:

> As it is evident that such a dispatch would not do any good, and Lord Palmerston will object to any positive injunction to Sir Hamilton Seymour to refrain from meddling, Lord John Russell is of opinion that it will be best to trust to the discretion and good temper of Sir Hamilton Seymour, and say nothing more to him on the subject, till he writes further.[2]

When the Queen was not prepared to accept this disregard of instructions with which Lord John had actually identified himself, the Prime Minister found it wise to come down on the Queen's side against the Foreign Secretary. He wrote to Lord Palmerston:

> I think after every consideration given to the subject, that it is necessary to draw up an instruction to Sir H. Seymour to take no part in the struggle of parties and to refrain from any interference, with respect to which he has not specific directions from the Government.[3]

He thought the tone adopted to the Portuguese government should be one of commendation rather than of reproach. He quoted extensively from recent despatches of Sir Hamilton Seymour to show that the Government then in power—that of the Duke of Saldhana —had in fact handled the situation well by remaining firm without being brutal. He rejected Palmerston's untenable view that British ministers abroad might be in confidential communication with parties endeavouring to overthrow existing governments:

> Our ministers abroad have credentials to the Sovereign and are by their permission entitled to certain privileges and immunities. It is . . . not consistent with [such a position] . . . that we should authorise or permit any participation in the efforts of parties who are seeking to overthrow a Ministry having the confidence of the Crown. Such conduct would be unfriendly and unfair to the foreign Sovereign, impolitic and perilous as regards ourselves. I hope therefore you will frame such a note as I have here intimated.[4]

---

[1] The case for Lord John is admirably put by G. P. Gooch in the "Later Correspondence of Lord John Russell" edited by him.

[2] Russell to the Queen, 17 June 1848 (Royal Archives A.79.4).

[3] Russell to Palmerston, 18 June 1848, copy submitted to the Queen (Royal Archives A.79.8).

[4] Ibid.

Queen Victoria was so delighted with Lord John's reply to Lord Palmerston, that she immediately let the Prime Minister know her feelings on the subject of the Foreign Secretary:

> Lord Palmerston has behaved about this draft really like a naughty child; because he was to do what he did not like, he insisted upon doing it in a manner which he knew must be displeasing to Lord John, and (the Queen cannot help suspecting) particularly to herself, and this without the slightest pretext for it.[1]

The Queen had thus already reached the conclusion that Lord Palmerston was deliberately flouting her proper constitutional authority.

Two days later—four days after the Queen's first complaint—Lord Palmerston declared his readiness to write a despatch in the sense of Lord John's letter to him.[2] This should have been the end of the matter but the correspondence between Buckingham Palace and Downing Street continued for more than another fortnight. Palmerston had not yet exhausted his tricks. He drafted a despatch, it is true, but it was such that Lord John could not accept it,[3] as the Foreign Secretary probably realised from the first. The draft was resubmitted to the Prime Minister six days later, the day before the Portuguese mail was due to go off. When Lord John rejected it and substituted one of his own, Lord Palmerston in turn objected and said he wished to consult a former despatch, "to avoid blaming Sir Hamilton Seymour". Lord John submitted. He informed the Queen:

> Lord John agrees with Lord Palmerston that it will not be right to blame Sir Hamilton Seymour, who only wishes to follow his instructions.[4]

Thus the Portuguese mail was missed a second time. It required another reminder from the Queen to ensure the despatch of the draft:

> The Queen wishes to remind Lord John Russell that it is today (and for the third time) the last day before the Portuguese Mail goes out,—and Lord Palmerston's draft has not yet made its appearance.[5]

The final draft dropped the offensive references to the Portuguese monarchy.

The internal correspondence of the Foreign Office shows that despatches were frequently sent off to ministers abroad without Crown authorisation and that this was done with Palmerston's full

---

[1] The Queen to Russell, 18 June 1848 (Royal Archives C.8.24); as so often with the Queen's letters during this period, the draft (A.79.9) is in Prince Albert's handwriting.
[2] Russell to the Queen, 20 June 1848 (Royal Archives A.79.10).
[3] Memorandum by Prince Albert, 26 June 1848 (Royal Archives A.79.11).
[4] Russell to the Queen, 27 June 1848 (Royal Archives A.79.14).
[5] The Queen to Russell, 6 July 1848 (Royal Archives A.79.16).

authority and not normally by accident. Officials would obtain the Foreign Secretary's permission to let drafts go which had not yet been seen by the Queen. During May and June, Palmerston authorised action of this kind with regard to despatches to Italy and Portugal.[1]

(ii)

Lord Palmerston's provocation of the British Court over Portugal is all the more surprising in view of the major diplomatic effort he was at that very time making to arrive at a solution of the Italian question. In this he was likely to be impeded by the opposition of the Queen and the Prince. In March, Lombardy and Venetia had revolted against their Austrian masters, and the King of Sardinia, Charles Albert, had come to their aid by invading Lombardy.[2] The Habsburg Monarchy, which was undergoing a desperate crisis following the March rising in Vienna, found itself unable to cope with this new threat and the Austrian troops under Marshal Radetzky fell back on the famous Quadrilateral in the Mantua region, leaving Milan to the insurgents. The town of Venice rose and established a republic. Sicily had already risen against the rule of the King of Naples. The smaller Princes, including the Pope, either had to submit to the demands of the revolutionary national movement, or flee.

Palmerston was delighted by the assertion of popular rights against the oppression of foreign and Italian despotism. He considered that the Austrians, hated by the Italians, had no moral right to be in Lombardy and Venetia. One may even credit him with some sincerity in his view that the Italian dominions weakened rather than strengthened the Habsburg Monarchy, whose general maintenance he considered desirable. Palmerston took for granted that Austria would not be able to muster the necessary military strength for the recovery of its territories in Northern Italy. In any case, he did not regard possession resting on military dictatorship as an agreeable state of affairs and believed that the Habsburg Monarchy would only gain discredit from the methods of oppression to which it would be driven.

While welcoming the progress of Italian unification and of liberal institutions, the Foreign Secretary was at the same time fully alive

---

[1] Public Record Office, FO/96/22.
[2] For the Italian question, see A. J. P. Taylor, "The Italian problem in European Diplomacy, 1847–9".

to the possible international complications. There was a danger that the men who had been put in power at Paris by the revolution there might intervene in Northern Italy by force of arms. The establishment of Republics, abhorrent both to Palmerston and to the British Court on ideological grounds, might even give France all the advantages of peaceful penetration, without the necessity of a military effort.

The vital practical question over which the Court disagreed with Palmerston's appreciation of the Italian situation concerned the attitude to be adopted by the British government towards France. To begin with, while Palmerston was prepared to deal with revolutionary governments on a basis of fact, Queen Victoria and Prince Albert regarded the men who had displaced Louis Philippe as usurpers still on probation. Neither side was quite consistent. Palmerston was prepared to pocket his objection to republican institutions in the case of France. It was, on the other hand, difficult for the Queen and the Prince to maintain a legitimist devotion to an ex-King who had himself usurped the throne.

Palmerston's main endeavour was to prevent war. He rightly judged that the risk of French intervention in Italy should be avoided at all costs. Whether or not one mistrusted the French government, and particularly if one did, it was best to tie it down by inviting it to co-operate with Britain and thus to prevent it from following a policy of its own. The Court, on the other hand, wanted the Foreign Secretary to concentrate on the mediation for which Austria had asked Britain. It advocated an effort to bring the conflict to a speedy close by helping to conclude a settlement between the belligerents before the French had been given an opportunity to intervene. Prince Albert wrote to Lord John Russell:

> We ought . . . to try and remove the different questions of dispute which might give France an opening. Amongst these the Italian is the one which is most fraught with danger, as it is evident, that whichever side is victorious in Italy, France will make it a pretext for war: If Austria, the French must come to the rescue of the Italians as "une nationalité opprimeé", if the Italians, France must have "une compensation". It is evident that negotiation and a treaty between the belligerents alone can stop the evil and that *we* alone can mediate with any effect.[1]

Prince Albert disliked the prospect of Austria being dislodged from Northern Italy, but he considered the prompt solution of the Italian question so important that he resigned himself to advocating

---

[1] Prince Albert to Russell, 17 May 1848 (Royal Archives C.16.56).

Austrian abandonment of the whole of Lombardy. He took what proved to be a far more realistic view of the military prospects of the Italians than Lord Palmerston and the majority of the Cabinet:

> Why should not the peace be re-established upon the footing that both parties keep what they now possess? The Italians have been beat at Verona and Austrian reinforcements will soon reach Radetzky. I think it *more* than doubtful that the Italians will ever dislodge the Austrians from their present strong position, without the aid of France, which would bring new misery upon Italy. The Austrians, even if they should retake Milan, can never hope to keep it with the whole of Italy against them and the French taking up its cause . . .[1]

He advocated the River Adige and the line of Verona and Mantua as the best boundary between Austria's Italian possessions and the rest of Italy. He suggested that Venice might become a Free Town on the model of the German Hanseatic cities and that Austrian Venetia, under an autonomous governor, should form part of an Italian League.[2]

Before Radetzky sallied forth from the Quadrilateral and drove the Sardinians out of Lombardy, these terms might have been obtained from Austria with English backing. Sardinia could then have achieved, without the necessity of a "tip" to France (which Prince Albert thus foresaw as early as 1848), as much as it received in 1859. But both the Italians and the pro-Italian party in the British Cabinet underrated the might of Austria. Lord John Russell and Lord Minto did not think that any proposal leaving Mantua and Verona to Austria was feasible. Lord John considered that any attempt to persuade the Italians to accept such terms would destroy British influence in Italy.[3] One of the greatest difficulties of the British Foreign Office at this time was to make the Italians take a realistic view of their own position. Lord John thought it necessary that the Austrians should abandon practically the whole of Venetia.

Prince Albert rejected French participation in an Italian settlement. He wrote to Lord John Russell that he objected to

> the mixing up of France with the present question in Italy or elsewhere. France has not assumed any settled shape and is sure to bring only developments of destruction into any matter that has to be settled.[4]

In Palmerston's view, this was the very reason for making sure of her co-operation.

[1] Prince Albert to Russell, 17 May 1848 (Royal Archives C.16.56).
[2] Ibid.
[3] Russell and Minto to Prince Albert, 17 May 1848 (Royal Archives C.16.55).
[4] Prince Albert to Russell, 17 May 1848 (Royal Archives C.16.54).

It is possible that the Foreign Secretary overestimated the likelihood of French intervention. When it came to the point, the French government refused all help to the Italians. It did not want to have a strong Italian kingdom on its south-eastern flank, and would have preferred a string of weak republics. But it was realised in Paris that military intervention to set up a series of republics and confine Sardinia to its previous boundaries would not be feasible. Both Lamartine and Bastide, his successor at the Foreign Ministry under the Cavaignac régime, were sensible enough to abstain from any drastic steps. But the degree to which these governments could be relied on to continue their resistance to the pressure of an inflamed public opinion was a different matter. Palmerston was right in not taking any chances.

The Queen and the Prince fought Palmerston's co-operation with France at every stage and only grudgingly and half-heartedly conceded that the Foreign Secretary had good reasons for the policy he was pursuing. They assumed that Lord Palmerston was using French diplomatic support to dictate the worst possible terms to Austria, to expel the Habsburgs completely from Italy and to found a Kingdom of Upper Italy which they dreaded. But the excessive strengthening of Sardinia was certainly not part of French policy at the time. It is true that the Foreign Secretary did not share the concern of the British Court for the maintenance of the Austrian position in Venetia and for the rights of the petty princes. But Palmerston was not as violently pro-Italian as Minto or Russell.

At the end of July, almost exactly at the time when Radetzky's advance changed the whole diplomatic situation, the Queen and the Prince made a determined attempt to force the Foreign Secretary to give up his policy of co-operation with France. The Queen wrote to Palmerston:

> Considering that it must be out of the question for a French Republic to *take a part* in any other arrangement except that of driving the Austrians out of Italy, the Queen thinks it quite uncalled for and would consider it very unfortunate if we were to treat with the French this question[1] and thus be the first to introduce French intervention or to enter into an entente cordiale with the *French Republic* against Austria.[2]

Palmerston replied that diplomatic co-operation with France was

---

[1] The grammar points to Prince Albert's drafting.
[2] The Queen to Palmerston, 22 July 1848 (Royal Archives J.4.15).

necessary to prevent a general war.[1] In spite of that, the Queen returned to the charge two days later:

> . . . a negotiation with France in order to agree with her upon a common line of policy to be followed with regard to the Italian question can lead to no good; it will make us the ally of a government which is not even legally constituted and which can accordingly not guarantee the fulfilment of any engagement it may enter into and it will call upon the very power to judge the Italian dispute which it is the interest of Europe to keep out of it.[2]

The Queen objected particularly to French schemes for a Venetian Republic.[3]

When the Queen and the Prince had come to the conclusion that direct representations to the Foreign Secretary were of no avail, they approached the Prime Minister on the following day:

> The Queen must tell Lord John what she has repeatedly told Lord Palmerston, but without apparent effect, that the establishment of an *entente Cordiale with the French Republic* for the purpose of driving the Austrians out of *their dominions* in Italy would be a *disgrace* to this country . . . How will England appear before the world *at the moment* when she is struggling to maintain her supremacy in Ireland and boasts to stand by treaties with regard to her European relations, having declined all this time to interfere in Italy or to address one word of caution to the Sardinian government on account of its most unjust and unscrupulous attack on Austria and having refused to mediate, when called upon to do so by Austria, because the terms were not good enough for Sardinia—if she should now ally herself with the Arch enemy of Austria to interfere *against her* . . .[4]

The letter is a strong indication of the heat the Italian question had engendered in the relations between the Court and Lord Palmerston. After what had happened over Portugal only a few weeks previously, the Queen and the Prince made the Foreign Secretary personally responsible for every act of foreign policy of which they disapproved, even if he was carrying out the policy of the Cabinet. At this stage the Prime Minister told the Queen he agreed with the Foreign Secretary[5] and there is no reason to doubt that a majority of the Cabinet did so too. Thus, the Queen was in this instance powerless to change the foreign policy and retreated:

> Though the Queen thinks that the French Republicans cannot safely be trusted in this matter, yet she must acknowledge the advantage of our

---

[1] Palmerston to the Queen, 22 July 1848 (Royal Archives J.4.16).
[2] The Queen to Palmerston, 24 July 1848 (Royal Archives J.4.17).
[3] Ibid.
[4] The Queen to Russell, 25 July 1848 (Royal Archives J.4.21).
[5] Russell to the Queen, 26 July 1848 (Royal Archives J.4.23).

trying to bind them to good conduct; only, this must be done in a way not to appear as a league with them against a friendly power, struggling to preserve to herself a territory granted to her by a treaty to which we were a party.[1]

On the same day, however, the Queen also wrote to Lord John accusing Palmerston of sabotaging the peace negotiations to obtain better terms for the Sardinians. The Queen claimed, and Lord John denied, that the Sardinians would have accepted the Adige line if they had not heard from London that Palmerston had advised them they could have better terms:

> The Queen is afraid that Lord Palmerston has a scheme for establishing a Kingdom of Upper Italy reaching from one sea to the other and that it is for that scheme that all considerations of ancient alliance with Austria, of the peace of Europe, the regard for treaties, etc., etc., are to be sacrificed . . . The new Kingdom will form *no* barrier against France, whilst it will dreadfully weaken Germany . . .[2]

Prince Albert's interest in the fate of Germany was now beginning to have a direct impact on relations between the Crown and the Foreign Secretary. The Prince considered that "Austria required the Venetian territory for her own and Germany's security".[3] He looked on the Austrians in Italy as fellow-Germans who had to be supported against other nationalities, however critical he might be of Austria's role in Germany. He was heartened by Radetzky's victory at Custozza on 25 July and the consequent expulsion of the Sardinians from Lombardy. He wrote to King Leopold:

> I am glad to see from your letter to Victoria that you are also delighted about the brilliant successes of old Radetzky. I am extraordinarily pleased about it: for the sake of the good old man himself, for that of the brave Austrian army, for the honour of German arms . . . and above all because of the just Nemesis which has . . . come over the ignominious Carlo Alberto and which has converted him from the Spada d'Italia to the Traditore in a week. Pilgerstein[4] still wants to establish his Kingdom of Upper Italy and can hardly hide his anger. Dietrichstein [the Austrian Chargé d'Affaires] thinks he has aged very much and that his eyes are very red and bathed in tears: "But not from sentiment," he adds quickly . . .[5]

He proceeded to give the Austrians advice as to what they should do,

[1] The Queen to Russell, 27 July 1848 (Royal Archives J.4.26).
[2] The Queen to Russell, 27 July 1848 (Royal Archives J.4.28).
[3] Memorandum by Prince Albert, 15 August 1848, submitted to the British Government (Royal Archives J.4.102).
[4] Footnote by Prince Albert that Pilgerstein stands for Palmerston.
[5] Prince Albert to King Leopold, 15 August 1848 (Royal Archives J.4.100), mainly tr.

making sure that it would reach them by sending copies of the letter to his cousin Alexander von Mensdorff at Vienna and to Prince Leiningen at Frankfurt.[1]

> If I were an Austrian Minister I would do the following: I would use the 15 days' armistice and the fury of the Milanese against the King of Sardinia to come to an understanding with the Milanese themselves, take up positions on the River Mincio [on the Mantua line] and come to an understanding with them about a Sovereign for Lombardy ... to obtain popular consent to my arrangement by universal suffrage which should be as easy to achieve under the guns of Austria as it was under those of Piedmont. I would not have any dealings with the mediating powers and the Spada d'Italia. Before the Armistice has expired, the new Kingdom of Lombardy *of my creation* and under my protection but according to the will of the people would have been founded, and all that Carlo Alberto and his auxiliary powers could do would be to sit still and to be annoyed or to start an inexcusable war *against* the independence of Lombardy and Tuscany.[2]

Prince Albert's crossing of the foreign policy of the British government in a major question requires some explanation, though it cannot be excused entirely. The Prince suspected the Foreign Secretary of duplicity[3] and he was certainly right in believing that Lord Palmerston was not being candid with the Crown and with the rest of the Cabinet. It was unfortunate that the Prince was beginning to lose faith in the possibility of redress through the normal constitutional channels. He found it hard to accept that the Crown would have to tolerate a foreign policy which it considered wrong, when its means of persuasion were exhausted.

The Queen endorsed the Prince's conclusions and, once having adopted them, put them forward with all her usual fervour. Her dislike of the Foreign Secretary seems to have become even stronger than the Prince's. She wrote to Lord John Russell at this time:

> The Queen must say, she is afraid that she will have no peace of mind and there will be no end of troubles as long as Lord Palmerston is at the head of the Foreign Office.[4]

In September, the Queen asked Lord John to replace Lord Palmerston at the Foreign Office, a request she was to repeat frequently during the next three years. On this occasion she suggested that the Foreign Secretary should change places with the

---

[1] Footnote by Prince Albert, ibid.
[2] Ibid.
[3] Private memorandum by Prince Albert, undated (Royal Archives J.4, summary of contents).
[4] The Queen to Russell, 11 August 1848 (Royal Archives J.4.84).

Lord Lieutenant of Ireland, Lord Clarendon. The Queen told the Prime Minister that she

> had proofs that he [Lord Palmerston] was not always straightforward in his conduct and kept back things which he did not like should be known . . .[1]

Lord John did not hold out much hope of a change, in view of the risk of offending Lord Palmerston. He had little reason to expose himself, since he was in agreement with the Foreign Secretary's policy. The Crown had the satisfaction, shortly afterwards, of over-coming Palmerston's opposition to the holding of a European Congress on the Italian question by securing the consent of the Prime Minister. The Queen and the Prince failed, however, to obtain the representation of Germany, that is of the German Central Power and of Prussia, which Palmerston felt would strengthen the Austrian side too much. All this was quickly becoming a question of academic interest as the Austrians were consolidating their position throughout their Italian possessions.

The Prince took care to emphasise Palmerston's—and perhaps even more Lord John's and Lord Minto's—miscalculation about the military prospects of the Italians:

> Had we accepted the Austrian offer for the relinquishment of Lombardy before the last bloody campaign, peace might have been settled in June. But these offers were peremptorily rejected . . . After the Austrians had reconquered Lombardy by a bloody campaign and at immense sacrifices, we *offered* our mediation (this time in conjunction with the French Republic) but upon the very basis which Austria had offered when in the greatest distress . . .[2]

The Prince had no doubt that Palmerston was to blame, for his methods were almost as bad as the policy which the Cabinet had approved:

> We have been . . . confining our diplomatic correspondence to that species of angry, irritating bullying, which has long characterised our relations with Spain, Portugal and Greece.[3]

The Austrian government was becoming increasingly annoyed at this time about the way Lord Palmerston was lecturing it on the policy it should follow.[4] Prince Schwarzenberg, who became the

[1] Memorandum by the Queen, 19 September 1848 (Royal Archives J.5.84).
[2] Prince Albert to Russell, 15 October 1848 (Royal Archives C.16.64).
[3] Ibid.
[4] Thus Palmerston's private letter to Ponsonby at Vienna of 7 November 1848 for communication to the Austrian Government, a mixture of persuasiveness and bullying (Public Record Office FO/96/22).

chief Austrian minister in November and soon infused new life into the tottering régime, was not the man to accept this kind of treatment. To show his disapproval of the British Foreign Secretary he chose a method likely to increase the tension between Lord Palmerston and his Court. In December, he refused to allow an Archduke to be despatched to London to announce the accession of the new Emperor Francis Joseph I on the abdication of the mentally feeble Ferdinand I, although this courtesy was extended to other courts of similar rank. To Queen Victoria and Prince Albert, this demonstration of an important foreign government's loathing for the British Foreign Secretary was further proof, if any were needed, of the failure of Palmerston's policy. Palmerston himself considered this slight of a despotic government as a compliment and a tribute to his appeal to public opinion on behalf of oppressed minorities and political parties.

Queen Victoria and Prince Albert asked King Leopold to convey their sympathy with the Austrian cause and their dislike of Lord Palmerston's Italian policy to the Austrian Court. The King of the Belgians informed his niece and nephew of the gratitude of the Austrian Cabinet for this attitude and promised to pass on some Austrian documents to the British Court.[1] Prince Albert was pleased about the success of King Leopold's activities as an intermediary. He wrote back to Brussels:

> I consider Austria's rancune against Pilgerstein quite natural and am glad that one expects better and more loyal feelings from Victoria and me ... than from this heartless, obstinate and revengeful man. We have perhaps been of more use to the Austrians than they can suspect and have incessantly waged war for them with Pilgerstein, in which he got many an ugly poke, as it says in the White Cat.[2] But we should regard any *acknowledged* separation between him and us as *exceedingly undesirable* politically and constitutionally. We therefore hope that no démarche of a kind which would involve such a separation will be made and that the private declaration through you will be regarded as sufficient ... One must not be cheeky [pfiffig] with him [Palmerston], for that puts weapons in his hands (vide Louis Philippe, Guizot, Metternich); but one has to be rough [grob] with him, for his whole system is bullying and nothing else.[3]

In his relations with the British Court, the Foreign Secretary's greatest liability was his excessive self-confidence, which led him periodically right up to the edge of the abyss and eventually pre-

---

[1] King Leopold to Prince Albert, 16 December 1848 (Royal Archives I.10.53).
[2] From the Fairy Tales of the Comtesse d'Aulnoy.
[3] Prince Albert to King Leopold, 20 December 1848 (Royal Archives I.10.66), mainly tr.

cipitated him into it. Palmerston was never on his guard for very long and as soon as he had overcome one crisis, it did not take much time for another to spring up. In January 1849 *The Times* accused the British Government of supplying arms to the Sicilian rebels in flagrant violation of Britain's policy of neutrality in this area. Though the original contention was an exaggeration, it was found on enquiry that the Foreign Secretary had on his own authority allowed a shipment of arms to be transferred from a government arsenal to oblige a contractor who needed the weapons to supply the Sicilian rebels. When pressed by the Prime Minister, Lord Palmerston eventually had to agree that he had acted hastily. As a result of the incident, the Prime Minister found himself closeted with the Queen and the Prince for nearly two hours at Windsor Castle on 24 January 1849. In recording the interview in just over one thousand words, the Prince excused himself for only giving an extract.[1]

It was clear from Lord John's report to the Queen and the Prince that the Foreign Secretary at first tried to brazen it out with the Court. He attempted to justify his action by quoting the Queen's and the Prince's endeavour to find a sovereign for Sicily, on its proposed separation from the Kingdom of Naples. Prince Albert pointed out that this contingency only arose once the Sicilians had established their independence; should this come about, a Sicilian Kingdom was preferable to a Republic there. In view of this argument on the part of the Foreign Secretary, the Prince thought that Palmerston had engaged in a lengthy intrigue against him over the question of the Sicilian succession:

> Now that Lord Palmerston referred to this . . . it struck me that there must have been some design in Lord Palmerston's asking our opinion on this subject in June last, for I had been very much surprised at Lord Carlisle,[2] in September last at Osborne, asking me pointedly . . .: "did not Your Royal Highness very much wish to see the Duke of Genoa[3] made King of Sicily?" as much as to say "you have no right to cast stones at Lord Palmerston".

He also thought it was suspicious that "Lord Palmerston was careful not to place anything in writing before us" when the Queen and the Prince had pointed out the danger of Sicily becoming a Republic, with which Lord Palmerston said he agreed.

[1] The following is taken from Prince Albert's memorandum of the interview 24 January 1849 (Royal Archives J.7.26).
[2] Then Chief Commissioner of Woods.
[3] A younger son of King Charles Albert of Sardinia.

Lord John Russell conceded that the British Government had to be prepared to make an apology to the Sicilian authorities.

> The Queen expressed herself to Lord John very strongly upon the want of ingenuousness in Lord Palmerston's conduct, the danger to which the Country was at every moment exposed by it and the humiliation for her to have to sanction an apology for an act, for which Lord Palmerston alone was responsible and ought to pay the penalty . . . The Queen mentioned her embarrassment at not being able to see Lord Palmerston any longer in her society towards whom she felt it repugnant to her character to show a degree of respect and politeness which was at variance with her real feelings towards him. Lord John admitted but regretted this, as Lord Palmerston's absence from Court had begun to be much noticed.

The Prince asked for a change at the Foreign Office at a "stated time" in the future, but the Prime Minister refused to commit himself as to what would happen when this crisis, in which the Government had to maintain solidarity, had been overcome. According to the Prince's record, he half admitted that Palmerston had mismanaged some affairs:

> Lord John said that at any rate he would take care that should we go again to Scotland in the Autumn, Lord Palmerston should not be left alone at home; he considered it was then that most mischief had been done.[1]

Presumably Lord John was referring to the impasse reached with Austria over Italy.

The episode of the Sicilian arms was practically the end of the impact of the Italian question on the relations between the Crown and Lord Palmerston for a decade. There was little England could do once the King of Naples had recovered control over Sicily. The final fling of King Charles Albert of Sardinia in the spring of 1849 was over too quickly for the diplomatists to move into action. Soon the Italian question was overshadowed by events in Germany.

(iii)

During 1848, while the Frankfurt National Assembly was debating the shape of the Germany to come, the only tangible problem which Germany offered to the British diplomat was the Schleswig-Holstein conflict. Prince Albert was largely unsuccessful in interesting the British Government in the intricacies of the German problem which Palmerston always insisted he could not understand. Thus the Prince's influence was exercised in his personal capacity

[1] Thus far Prince Albert's memorandum of 24 January 1849.

as a German prince, naturally strengthened by his standing as the husband of the Queen of England. But from the early part of 1849, German developments were beginning to move from the realm of speculation and theory into that of practical action. The British Government could no longer evade that formulation of views which King Leopold had considered necessary the previous year.

Gagern's solution of a German and an Austrian Empire linked in a loose association could not but be agreeable to the British Government, as it avoided the creation of an excessively powerful state in the heart of Europe. The natural consequence of the exclusion of Austria was the hegemony of Prussia in Germany. The British Government now had to decide, in a fluid situation, what it thought of this Prussian supremacy. It could certainly do something to influence the course of events and it might be a dangerous omission not to do so. For in the absence of a speedy solution, there was a risk either of the radical forces, bent on overthrowing the old order, getting the upper hand, or of a triumph of reaction, with disastrous long-term consequences.

Prince Albert and Lord Palmerston found themselves in somewhat unusual positions over the German question in 1849. The more the Frankfurt National Assembly moved to the left, the more Palmerston, the hero of the radicals in England and of the upholders of constitutional government all over Europe, became opposed to German unity achieved under the sponsorship of the *Paulskirche*. The Foreign Secretary did not want to see a radical extension of the franchise in Germany any more than in England. Prince Albert agreed with Lord Palmerston's objections to hasty constitutional reforms. But he differed from the Foreign Secretary in the inference he drew as to the desirability of action. Palmerston seemed to be ready, in pure passivity, to see the tide of reaction sweep over Germany again. Prince Albert, on the other hand, pleaded that a rare opportunity should not be missed decisively to influence developments in the centre of Europe in the interest of the whole continent and of Britain. In the context of Germany, their views on the Habsburg Monarchy were the reverse of those they held as far as Italy was concerned. Palmerston, the enemy of Austria in Italy, seemed to have no objection to the Habsburg Monarchy recovering its influence in Germany. Prince Albert, who continued to stand up for Austrian interests in Italy in 1849, considered it essential that Austria should keep out of German affairs. Palmerston was reluctant to see Austria excluded from Germany because he realised that this involved the supremacy of Prussia. He disliked the Prussian military tradition of Frederick II of which he saw fresh evidence in the Schleswig-Holstein conflict. In addition, he distrusted the "advanced" tendencies of the new Prussian constitution, with its universal suffrage. Thus he objected both to the traditions and to the democratic achievements of the Prussian state. He thought, indeed, that Prussia was flying the German national flag merely to cover up its designs of aggrandisement, that Schleswig-Holstein was a continuation of something like the old style conquest of Silesia by other means. It was certainly still an open question, whether Prussia would be able to find a synthesis between its Frederician past and a more liberal future.

Prince Albert was not an uncritical admirer of Prussia. But he felt that the only hope of a fruitful development in Germany lay in Prussian leadership. His emphasis on this grew stronger as Austrian policy under Prince Schwarzenberg revealed its hostility to any progress on the German question. Unfortunately, however, it was by then too late to ignore Austrian views on Germany and to impose its exclusion from Germany on the Habsburg Monarchy. Valuable months had been lost during which the Danube Empire had been so taken up with risings that it would have been compelled to acquiesce in any scheme proposed for Germany. By the end of 1848, the Monarchy was beginning to make a remarkable recovery, largely due to the ability and determination of its new leading minister.

From the moment that the project of a Prussian-led Germany, which would have to be established in the teeth of Austrian opposition, became the object of negotiation between the German governments, Britain could no longer stand entirely aloof. The British Foreign Office could not treat the plans of important German states with the same indifference with which it had regarded the schemes of the Frankfurt politicians.

The German Confederation, set up in Vienna in 1815 by the victorious powers—including Britain—had preserved for each of the individual thirty-eight states the right of diplomatic representation. Ministers of foreign powers, such as Russia and Britain, were thus to be found at all the more important German courts and even at some of the minor ones. Normally British ministers did not, unlike their Russian colleagues, interfere in the internal affairs of the German states to which they were accredited. Most of the British diplomats strongly favoured the maintenance of the sovereignty of these countries, if only for the obvious reason that their status and importance depended on it. Some of them were prepared to take a different view, such as Lord Cowley, who was accredited to the Central Power at Frankfurt.

As 1848 turned into 1849, Lord Cowley became convinced that the speedy election of the King of Prussia as Emperor of a Germany which excluded Austria was the only way out of a dangerous impasse. The Acting Reich Foreign Minister, Max von Gagern (a brother of the Minister-President), told Cowley that he was worried about the King of Württemberg's attitude to Prussia and asked him to intervene to secure the King's support for Frederick William IV. Gagern realised how useful the agreement of the other important sovereigns would be. He requested Cowley to write to the King of Württemberg to ask him "to put himself forward in favour of the election of the King of Prussia". The Ambassador felt, however, that he ought to secure the agreement of his Foreign Secretary before he took any active steps. He also obtained from Gagern an assurance that the constitution passed by the Frankfurt National Assembly would not be forced down the throats of the German sovereigns, but that there would be some consultation with them. Cowley made a strong appeal to Palmerston to let him go ahead:

> I conceive that I cannot be acting wrong in doing anything that may promote a good understanding between the Sovereigns and the Central Power. If I find upon going into the question with Gagern, which he offers to do fairly, that he can guarantee what he proposes—of his own sincerity I have no doubt—I think that I may do good in taking the step suggested by him.[1]

The Foreign Secretary refused Lord Cowley's request with Palmerstonian elegance. He wrote to the Queen:

> Any advice which Lord Cowley might give to the King of Württemberg on the subject in Question would probably only carry weight with him, in as far as it was considered by the King of Württemberg as being the advice of the British Government; and it appears to Viscount Palmerston that it would not be expedient for Your Majesty's Government to express opinions or to give advice upon a matter so complicated and affecting so variously a great number of different interests as the Reconstruction of Germany; the more especially as it is a matter with which Great Britain has no direct concern . . .[2]

If Palmerston had wished to intervene, the latter negation would not have deterred him any more than elsewhere in Europe. The

[1] Private letter from Cowley to Palmerston, 31 December 1848 (Royal Archives I.11.7), copy submitted to the Queen.
[2] Palmerston to the Queen, 5 January 1849 (Royal Archives I.11.6).

Queen and the Prince were displeased by the Foreign Secretary's attitude, but they could not challenge it. Still, an admission of British neutrality was valuable to the Court as it also cut the other way and barred attempts by Lord Cowley's colleagues in Germany to prevent unification. Soon, Prince Albert was to insist that if the British Government was not doing anything for German unity, neither should it do anything against it.

After Frederick William had rejected the imperial crown proffered by the Frankfurt National Assembly, he called a meeting of representatives of the governments of the old German Confederation at Berlin in May 1849. He proposed a modified form of the Gagern scheme providing for a German and an Austrian state linked in union. Austria was hostile, the South German states adopted a waiting attitude, but practically the whole of Northern Germany became part of the Prussian Union, whose Parliament later met at Erfurt. The Kings of Hanover and Saxony joined with the King of Prussia in the Alliance of the Three Kings which provided for the setting up of some federal governmental machinery under Prussian leadership and was designed to serve as the nucleus for a new Germany. It was vital to get support from Southern Germany, for Hanover and Saxony were reluctant to merge their particularist interests in the larger community. They had insisted on an escape clause in the event of the Southern States—and particularly Bavaria —refusing to join. Modifications were proposed in the Frankfurt constitution to make it more palatable to the German Sovereigns. The Basic Rights of the Frankfurt Parliament were watered down and the direct and equal suffrage was replaced by a system of indirect election by three classes.

Prince Albert was enthusiastic. He thought the Prussian plan offered the only way out of the anarchy which was threatening Germany. He feared that the French—particularly under their new Prince-President—might take advantage of the internal strife in Germany to intervene. The Prince failed to see that the main reason why many of the monarchs, such as the King of Saxony and the Grand-Duke of Baden, were co-operating with Prussia was because popular risings on their territory were threatening their very existence and because their only hope was to appeal for Prussian help. Once the emergency was over—largely due to Prussian assistance—the individual monarchs were far less keen to make sacrifices for the common cause. Whether Prince Albert liked it or not, revolutionary pressure was the great driving force behind

German unity. The Hungarian insurgents—who were keeping Austrian and Russian forces tied down—were actually its helpmates. With his respect for existing authority, the Prince could not be expected to see this connection between his German hopes and the rebellion of the Hungarians against their lawful masters. He did not share Palmerston's enthusiasm for the Hungarian independence movement and was horrified at a suggestion of Chevalier Bunsen that Hungary should be "the lever for bringing about German unity".[1] It need hardly be added that the Prussian Minister to the Court of St. James's was not putting forward this plan in his official capacity. The Prince replied to Bunsen:

> An alliance of Germany with England and France for *armed* mediation, *for the Hungarian cause*, would be a step which would excite many misgivings and could hardly be the basis of enabling England and France to support Prussian leadership in the German federal state . . . In my view Prussia should occupy itself with *one* subject at a time and should pursue it with all its might on the basis of its justice, importance and necessity: namely the effecting of the Alliance with the Constitution as it has been arranged by the three Kings . . . Once a state of law exists in Germany and a government which is put in a relationship of mutual effect with public opinion, *then* the time will have come to think of a European policy for Germany. Before this is the case, every appearance on the European field will only introduce new elements of disturbance into the internal process of regeneration. I say . . . vide Schleswig.[2]

The Prince took the opportunity of a letter of congratulation to the King of Saxony on his return to Dresden after the crushing of the Saxon rebellion, with Prussian help, to put in a word for continued co-operation with Prussia. He said that Prussia was the only purely German power which could bring about unification.[3] He was prompted to write this letter by the knowledge of the lukewarmness of Saxon and Hanoverian support for the Alliance of the Three Kings. Receiving reports from British and German sources, he was better informed on the situation in Germany than anybody else in Europe. He had for a time had the impression from reading despatches that some of the British diplomats in Germany were lending only too ready an ear to the grumbles of particularism and were even prepared to encourage local opposition to German unity. The Prince's letter to the King of Saxony was an attempt to counteract the prevailing impression that Britain encouraged particularist

---

[1] Prince Albert to Bunsen, 21 August 1849 (Royal Archives I.16.34), tr.
[2] Ibid.
[3] Prince Albert to the King of Saxony, 14 July 1849 (Royal Archives I.15.110).

opposition. He quoted with approval the radical *Examiner* which castigated British "Pumpernickel diplomats at the small German courts who fear the extinction of their twaddlesome nothingness".[1] This praise for Thackeray's description of the German state of Pumpernickel in "Vanity Fair", which had been published shortly before, throws a curious light on the Prince's sense of humour. The model for "Pumpernickel" was the Grand Duchy of Weimar, which Thackeray visited in 1830.[2] It may be wondered to what extent the Prince recognised that Pumpernickel diplomacy presupposed Pumpernickel states or that Coburg fell into this category.

In June 1849, Prince Albert had ample cause for accusing two British ministers in Germany of gross partiality and of violation of the very precept of non-intervention which Lord Palmerston had previously used to frustrate his suggestions. Queen Victoria and her husband objected to the British Ministers at Hanover and Dresden setting themselves up without authority as the champions of their dynastic rights in Germany. The Minister at Hanover, Bligh, reported that he had drawn the attention of the Hanoverian government to the effect which its abandonment of sovereign rights under the Prussian scheme might have on the rights of the British Royal Family, should it inherit the Hanoverian Crown.[3] This representation was doubly galling to Queen Victoria and Prince Albert. They could only regard it as an attempt to put obstacles in the way of Prussian plans. They had little tenderness for Ernest Augustus, the Queen's uncle on the Hanoverian throne, who was personally and politically obnoxious to them and about whose fate they could feel little concern. There was no sign of the extinction of the Cumberland branch in Hanover and of the claim to the Kingdom passing to the next male line of the British Royal Family, that of the Duke of Cambridge.

The British Minister to Saxony, Forbes, went even further in openly combating the Prussian scheme. He was asked by the Saxon Minister, Beust—who became a member of the Austrian government after the Saxon defeat of 1866—what he thought of the new German constitution framed at Berlin. Forbes replied:

> I . . . expressed my surprise at their [Saxony] consenting to make over to Prussia their rights of diplomatic representation . . . I said I could hardly

---

[1] Prince Albert to his brother, 23 March 1850; (H. Bolitho, "The Prince Consort and his brother").

[2] See "The Letters of W. M. Thackeray", edited by G. N. Ray.

[3] Despatch to the Foreign Office, 7 June 1849 (Public Record Office FO/34/56).

imagine that the Great Powers would allow Prussia to dictate to them and to order them to recall their Ministers from the other German Kingdoms or to submit to their being sent away; that in the instance of Great Britain, the Royal Family was closely allied to one branch of the House of Saxony [Coburg] . . .[1]

It is not surprising that Beust thereupon opened his heart to Forbes and told him that he was still hoping to escape from the Prussian alliance which he obviously heartily disliked. He said:

> La Prusse nous a mis le couteau sur la gorge. . . . I forgot to tell you that our final acceptance depends on that of Bavaria; we have made this a positive stipulation, which you may write to Lord Palmerston. I cannot speak of it here for it would be tantamount to saying to Bavaria: "refuse".[2]

It did not require great intelligence on the part of Forbes to draw the obvious conclusion:

> I cannot, by this observation, help thinking that His Excellency would be glad if a note of this fact reached the Bavarian Government . . . M. de Beust said their *greatest* embarrassment proceeded from the Hanoverian Government, who had not only finally accepted, but had been beforehand with every proposition of Prussia.[3]

Prince Albert immediately complained about Bligh and Forbes to the Foreign Secretary. Lord Palmerston's reply was uncompromising. He fully supported the action of the two Ministers. He stated that he had asked the British Ministers in Germany to refrain from championing any particular plan to bring about German unity. He denied, however, that this attitude of non-intervention precluded the Ministers from giving opinions when asked:

> Mr. Forbes . . . was asked by Baron Beust what he thought of the new constitution proposed by the Prussian Government . . .; being thus asked, he could not without affectation have declined to give an opinion.[4]

This is not a convincing argument. But the Foreign Secretary almost at once discarded any pretence of impartiality:

> In his [Forbes's] place I should certainly have expressed much stronger opinions, for it appears to me that the principle of universal suffrage upon which that constitution is founded, is scarcely compatible with the permanent existence of monarchical institutions . . . The fact is that universal suffrage is essentially a republican institution; and there cannot be much doubt that the men who originally proposed it in Germany meant it as an engine for the overthrow of Royalties, while the

---

[1] Forbes's despatch to the Foreign Office, 2 June 1849 (Royal Archives I.15.1).
[2] Ibid.   [3] Ibid.
[4] Palmerston to Prince Albert, 19 June 1849 (Royal Archives I.15.50).

weakminded men who adopted it have deluded themselves with the notion that its acceptance was the price by which monarchy was to be secured.[1]

Thus Palmerston—who was incidentally wrong in thinking that universal suffrage had been retained in the Prussian scheme—had completely outflanked Prince Albert on the "Right" by being even more strongly against "democracy" than the Queen's husband. It is a matter of speculation how welcome these Palmerstonian arguments would have been to Queen Victoria, with her natural conservatism, if she had not been so strongly influenced by the Prince. Later developments in Germany give an ironical ring to this British criticism of Germany for advancing too quickly on the road to democracy.

As so often happened with Palmerston, his blustering was only a cover for retreat. As a result of Prince Albert's representations, he had a closer look at the Prussian scheme, which he now welcomed in fresh instructions to the British ministers:

> The difference between this [Prussian] scheme and the Plan proposed at Frankfurt is obvious and great . . . By the Prussian Plan it would seem that separate nationalities would to a certain degree be preserved, whilst Prussia, retaining her position as an European Power, would be the head of a German Confederation combining in its organisation many of the advantages of unity, without destroying the moral springs of action which derive their strength and elasticity from feelings of local nationality.[2]

Nothing could have been more satisfactory to Prince Albert than this statement. As a result, when Saxony wanted to enlist British support for stiffening the attitude of the Hanoverian government against Prussia, Lord Palmerston refused to intervene.[3] Prince Albert on his part warned Bunsen about the Hanoverian and Saxon intrigues:

> . . . it is high time . . . to call the German parliament, for Hanover and Saxony are playing you false, Austria will be free to act within the shortest time, France clearly expresses her joy about that and about the importance "que l'Autriche reprenne sa position en Allemagne que la Prusse va usurper". . . . The leading article in The Times . . . is almost literally what Lord Aberdeen[4] still said yesterday. Every wish that Germany should be

---

[1] Palmerston to Prince Albert, 19 June 1849 (Royal Archives I.15.50).

[2] Draft to the Earl of Westmorland, the British Minister to Prussia, 13 July 1849 (Royal Archives I.15.109).

[3] Forbes's despatch No. 40 of 15 August 1849 (Royal Archives I.16.25). Palmerston to Forbes No. 8 of 28 August 1849 (Royal Archives I.16.61).

[4] This seems to have been one of the rare occasions at this time on which Lord Aberdeen found himself in agreement with Lord Palmerston.

strong and united, but union, federative state, nationality, parliament etc., etc. are nonsense. But how should it become strong and united?[1]

Prince Albert's ideas on German unity were encountering increasing resistance in his own family. The King of the Belgians was drifting more and more into the Austrian and anti-Prussian camp. Prince Albert defended Prussia to his uncle against charges that it was only interested in its own aggrandisement. He accused Austria of having influenced the German kings against Prussia by bribing them with the promise of the mediatisation of the smaller sovereigns. He also complained about the British diplomats in Germany:

> Our Ministers are all furiously *anti-Prussian* and very active in this sense, because they would lose their places if the Constitution of the Three Kings were accepted, and they put their hope in the method offered by Austria. A similar instinct of self-preservation also makes all the other diplomats . . . report strongly against the unity of Germany.[2]

If the Prussian scheme failed to make sufficient progress in 1849, it was mainly because of Frederick William's attitude. As usual the King wavered. In September, he concluded the "Interim" with Austria which provided for an intermediate period of six months during which Austria and Prussia were jointly to take over the German federal power. The office of Vicar of the Empire was to be abolished and in due course the Archduke John laid down his charge in December. The Prussian understanding with Austria made it safe for Hanover and Saxony to abandon the Alliance of the Three Kings in all but name. Prince Albert remained convinced, however, that Prussia would be able to reach its goal if it persevered. He had the satisfaction of Lord Palmerston administering a stern rebuke to Forbes, who had told the Saxon Minister Beust, "that Saxony could not remain as she was, and must either be swallowed up or regain part of what she once possessed". This was a clear incitement to Saxony to recover territories lost to Prussia in 1815, through finding herself on the losing side at the end of the Napoleonic Wars.[3] In a letter to his brother, Prince Albert spoke of "our ass Forbes".[4] The Prince was so worried about the course Saxony was adopting that he wrote direct to Beust reminding him of his obligations to his greater fatherland.[5]

[1] Prince Albert to Bunsen, 5 September 1849 (Royal Archives I.16.58), mainly tr.
[2] Prince Albert to King Leopold, 9 October 1849 (Royal Archives I.17.14), tr.
[3] Forbes to Palmerston, 15 March 1850 (Royal Archives I.19.34), Palmerston to Forbes, 20 March 1850 (Royal Archives I.19.44).
[4] Prince Albert to his brother, 23 March 1850 (*Bolitho*).
[5] Prince Albert to Beust, 20 February 1850 (Royal Archives I.18.43).

Chapter Eight

THE CLASH WITH PALMERSTON—II

(i)

THE German question was to contribute indirectly to a serious difference of opinion between the Court and the Foreign Secretary over Greece. Whereas Queen Victoria and Prince Albert were sympathetic to Otto, the Bavarian Prince on the Greek throne, Palmerston had only contempt for him because of his misrule. The claim of a Portuguese Jew born at Gibraltar, Don Pacifico, whose house in Athens had been sacked by the mob, gave the Foreign Secretary an opportunity to intervene in Greece on behalf of a British subject who had been wronged. Palmerston had some justification for becoming impatient, as the Greek government remained entirely inactive about the—admittedly excessive—claim, in spite of frequent diplomatic representations. But when he started acting, the Foreign Secretary overshot the mark. The British fleet was sent to the Piraeus and the Greek government informed that the claim must be settled within 48 hours. When this proved of no avail, the British naval commander seized some Greek ships. The highhanded action caused protests in Paris and St. Petersburg, and the British Cabinet became alarmed about the latitude allowed to its Foreign Secretary.

The Don Pacifico controversy was the most dramatic episode in the conflict between Lord Palmerston and the Court. Palmerston regarded King Otto as the "spoilt child of absolutism".[1] The Queen and her husband favoured the King because he was a German prince. The Foreign Secretary objected to small states sheltering behind all sorts of excuses, such as poverty, so as to avoid giving redress. The Court looked on Palmerston's cavalier treatment of small countries as sheer bullying. Lord Palmerston rather enjoyed a storm of disapproval from other capitals, which gave him an opportunity to exercise his diplomatic skill and parade as a British hero. The Queen and the Prince regarded the hostility of the other powers to Britain as a sign of the failure of the country's foreign policy, and as a reflection on the British Crown. To the Foreign

[1] Palmerston to his brother, Sir William Temple, 15 February 1850 (E. Ashley, "The Life of Viscount Palmerston", I, 191).

Secretary, the injustice of Don Pacifico's claim was an unimportant detail, whereas to the Queen and her husband it was a vital matter. As usual, when the Foreign Secretary felt that his policy was encountering opposition he moved stealthily, resorting to all sorts of ruses to carry out his programme before he was stopped. He thus offended against the stricter control by the Prime Minister and the Crown which he had undertaken to accept in June 1849,[1] encouraging the inference that the supervision was still not strict enough. Substance and procedure became so inextricably intermingled that it was difficult to disentangle them. The intensity of the clash is not surprising, as it came as the culmination of strong differences of opinion over Spain, Portugal, Italy and Germany. It was, indeed, a particularly explosive combination of some of the most dangerous ingredients of previous controversies. Palmerston had the Court at a disadvantage, however justified the objection of the Crown might be to the arbitrariness of his policy. For it was only too easy for him to set himself up as the champion of liberalism against despotism, as he had done over Spain, Portugal and Italy. In addition, he was able to appeal to the patriotic pride of every Britisher as the defender of his rights against the unfairness of the foreigner.

Now that the dust of the controversy has settled, it seems hard to defend Palmerston's handling of the affair. Don Pacifico's claim was vastly exaggerated. The pressure the Foreign Secretary employed to enforce the demand was out of all proportion to the original wrong done. Prince Albert unburdened himself to his uncle about it:

> *Our* policy I can only mourn about; it is as bad as *the one* who conducts it, but he is more stupid than I have considered him so far. The political combination which keeps him in power and which makes it ossible, for him to create so much mischief has never existed in history *like that*, for nine-tenths of England cry with The Times: "Why must this man be allowed to indulge his immoderate appetite for being hated?" and yet he does what he wants and commits one blunder after another [schießt einen Bock nach dem anderen], such as this one in Greece.[2]

Prince Albert put the strength of Palmerston's position too narrowly in believing that the Foreign Secretary was kept in power in spite of public opinion. The reverse was the case. Lord Palmerston was able to ignore the justified criticism of Crown and Cabinet because

---

[1] Drafts were to be submitted first to the Prime Minister, before they went to the Queen. Palmerston at once agreed to the new procedure. (See *Letters*, Russell to Prince Albert, 19 June 1849, ff.)

[2] Prince Albert to King Leopold, 10 February 1850 (Royal Archives I.18.36), mainly tr.

he could always appeal beyond them to public opinion. He was even able to do so with regard to Greece, although his case was a bad one. He knew more about the popular handling of a situation than any other statesman of his time. Lord John was an apprentice by comparison, in spite of his occasional successes. The Crown was always at a disadvantage in an appeal to public opinion, for it had to remain aloof. Understandably Prince Albert became thoroughly alarmed when the Prime Minister proposed in March 1850 to meet the objections of the Court to Lord Palmerston's handling of foreign affairs by yielding the leadership of the House of Commons to him, going to the Lords, and taking the Foreign Office himself. The Prince realised, perhaps more than the Prime Minister, the vital importance the leadership of the House of Commons had acquired. He wrote to Lord John:

> ... making Lord Palmerston leader of the House of Commons ... would make him Prime Minister "de facto" at once, and "de jure" necessarily afterwards. The leader of the House of Commons (in these days) has the real power in the Country and can dictate absolutely to his colleagues. So Lord Palmerston would more than ever influence the foreign policy, himself free from the responsibility of the Office, and whilst before the Prime Minister found it almost impossible to control him, he would begin to control the latter and on any difference of opinion between them keep the party with him, casting the Prime Minister in the House of Lords adrift.
>
> The Queen could never reconcile it with her duty towards the Country to allow Lord Palmerston to become its ruler. . . .[1]

The reasoning was cogent. If it was found necessary to move Palmerston from the Foreign Office because he had got out of control, the cure of giving him the leadership of the House of Commons was worse than the disease. From this time onward, the Queen and the Prince were haunted by the possibility of the leadership of the House of Commons falling into the hands of a politician who might wish to play a part as a great "democratic" leader, unfettered by any responsibility to the Crown.

The Prince recapitulated the relationship between the Crown and the Foreign Secretary, which had been outlined earlier in a memorandum by Stockmar[2] in one of his now rather rare interventions on the British political scene. He elaborated on Stockmar's first principle:

> As a Minister, the Sovereign has a right to demand from him [Lord Palmerston], that she be made thoroughly acquainted with the whole

---

[1] Prince Albert to Russell, 2 April 1850 (Royal Archives C.17.55).
[2] Memorandum by Stockmar, 12 March 1850 (*Letters*).

object and tendency of the policy to which her consent is required, and, having given that consent, that the policy is not arbitrarily altered from the original line, that important steps are not concealed from her, and her name used without her sanction.[1]

This was unexceptionable and the Prince was quite right in stating that Palmerston had deliberately offended against these principles. The Prince considered it wise to drop the second part of Stockmar's memorandum threatening an offending minister with the exercise of the Queen's "undoubted constitutional right" of dismissal. While this might perhaps be good constitutional theory, it was very bad government practice. The Sovereign would have been brought into the political arena. It is hard to see how any Prime Minister could have accepted a direct dismissal by the Crown of a member of his own cabinet. Prince Albert found himself in this new role of moderating his mentor as Stockmar was tending increasingly to encourage the Queen in autocratic tendencies which she was wise enough not to follow. Although the Baron was a rugged individualist, who valued the independence of his judgment, he had acquired during decades of service at Court a tendency frequently to give advice agreeable to the recipient. The Queen seems to have turned to Stockmar occasionally in preference to her husband when the Prince did not sufficiently fall in with her views. At this stage, the Prince's advice was so much sounder than Stockmar's that the Queen in the end followed her husband rather than the trusted family councillor.

In his letter to the Prime Minister, the Prince showed himself far more aware of the strength of Palmerston's popular position than previously:

> . . . his boldness pleases and his dexterity amuses the public; if his case be ever so bad a one he can represent it and dress it up to his advantage, and the public cries out: "Look how he got out of this scrape again, after all he is a very clever fellow!" His bullying tone to the weaker foreign powers is grateful [appeals] to the taste of our manufacturers and small traders, who look upon other countries only as upon markets . . . The Radicals like this also and, as much, his intrigues with foreign revolutionists and his unscrupulous hostility to the thrones and monarchs of different states; they are only afraid that they might one day have to pay with a war for their indulgence. If there is danger of that, they join in the general outcry against Lord Palmerston; the danger gone by, they uphold him again.[2]

---

[1] Prince Albert to Russell, 2 April 1850 (Royal Archives C.17.55).
[2] Ibid.

The Prince recognised Palmerston's ability but felt it was marred by the absence of principle:

> Lord Palmerston is an able politician with large views and an energetic mind, an indefatigable man of business and a good speaker; but a man of expediency, of easy temper, no very high standard of honour and not a grain of moral feeling. He is consequently quite unscrupulous as to any line of policy he is to follow, or any means he is to use, as long as they lead to his ends. Whilst he is a most easy colleague and minister with regard to other departments, never making any difficulty, he is self-willed and impatient of any control of his own: his obstinacy arises from personal conceit, which makes him almost pity those who differ from him in opinion.[1]

It can be inferred from this last remark, that the Prince must have been hurt by the Foreign Secretary's attitude to him. He could never quite overcome a certain diffidence in himself, and Palmerston's almost unshakable self-confidence must have irritated him.

The Prince was right in thinking that Palmerston was ready to resort to almost any expedient in carrying through his policy. But he was wrong in expecting the Foreign Secretary to be so wedded to office that he was prepared to accept meekly his removal to another department:

> His love of office generally, which he has held now for nearly 40 years, will in my opinion prevent his quitting the Government again upon losing the Foreign Office, and make him inclined to enter into such arrangements as are proposed to him in a friendly and conciliatory manner and with a view to save as much as possible the point of honour.[2]

Palmerston was not as "unprincipled" as that. The Prince made the mistake of underrating him and of putting the worst interpretation on his motives. Lord John knew the Foreign Secretary much better and was not so sure that he would submit.

As had so often happened before, Lord John vacillated. While he did not like Palmerston's use of force to settle the Greek claims, he did not stop him from pursuing a policy about which he had grave doubts,[3] shared by other members of the Government. The new procedure, started in June 1849, of channelling Foreign Office drafts to the Court through him had largely been a failure. The Prime Minister never faced up to important points of principle and policy, largely confining himself to niggardly haggling over details and to the occasional demonstration of the weak man that he was

---

[1] Prince Albert to Russell, 2 April 1850 (Royal Archives C.17.55).   [2] Ibid.
[3] Lord John informed the Foreign Secretary of his disapproval as early as 12 January 1850 (Walpole, Russell, II, 56).

still in charge. To cover up his failure, he tried to draw a meaningless distinction between the general aims of Palmerston's policy with which he agreed and the methods of the Foreign Secretary of which he often disapproved.[1] But where did the aims end and the methods begin? Into which category did the dramatic gestures fall which so endeared the Foreign Secretary to the British public? Surely it was an illusion to suppose that a "Palmerstonian" policy could be carried out without a Palmerston. It was never done or even attempted afterwards.

To get the best possible terms for Don Pacifico, the Foreign Secretary was dilatory about informing his Minister in Athens, Wyse, about a compromise reached in London thanks to the good offices of France. This allowed the British Minister to enforce exorbitant demands in Athens under the muzzles of the guns of the British fleet when the conflict had already been settled by negotiation. The French authorities were so disgusted with this insult to their activities as mediators that they withdrew their Ambassador from London in protest. The Russian government threatened to follow suit. Now the British Cabinet became seriously perturbed and insisted on a compromise, embodying the London settlement wherever possible.

Palmerston was in a weak position. He had encountered serious international difficulties for what seemed to be a paltry cause. In the course of the handling of the Greek affair, he had not been candid with the Crown, the Prime Minister, the Cabinet or the French. He had furthered his policy by suppressing or delaying agreed instructions. He had not given either Crown or Cabinet a clear idea in advance of the policy he was about to follow. The Crown was thus justified in demanding either his resignation or, if that was not possible, the enforcement of a stricter control.

The Queen, with the Prince's full agreement, thought the time had come for a definite decision that Lord Palmerston was to give up the Foreign Office.[2] Lord John might have fallen in with this desire, had not Lord Stanley put down a motion in the House of Lords challenging the Government's handling of the Greek affair. The Prime Minister therefore pleaded that no action should be taken until the end of the session, in order to give the Government an opportunity to defend itself.[3] But he wrote to Lord Palmerston

---

[1] Thus Russell to Prince Albert, 10 July 1850 (Royal Archives A.79.33).
[2] See Prince Albert to Russell, 18 May 1850, ff. (*Letters*).
[3] Memorandum by Prince Albert, 20 May 1850 (*Letters*).

that he was proposing to make a change at the Foreign Office at the end of the parliamentary session.[1] It has been assumed that Palmerston at this stage accepted his displacement. There is no evidence of that. He countered Lord John's letter by a method he had often found useful, by silence. The medieval tag that silence implies consent certainly had no application to Palmerston. By not reacting, he considered himself even less bound than by expressing agreement with a view he disliked.

Palmerston was saved by the delay. It gave him the opportunity for the greatest parliamentary triumph in his political career. The Foreign Secretary concluded a speech of five hours on the Greek question at the end of June with the famous challenge to the House:

> Whether, as the Roman in the days of old held himself free from indignity when he could say *Civis Romanus sum*, so also a British subject, in whatever land he may be, shall feel confident that the watchful eye and the strong arm of England will protect him against injustice and wrong?

This passage turned the scale and allowed Palmerston to emerge from the trials and tribulations of the Greek affair as the very incarnation of John Bull. His position was even further strengthened by the death of Sir Robert Peel a few days later, which left him the unrivalled master of the British political scene.

Prince Albert could not fail to realise the increased difficulty of moving Palmerston after his parliamentary triumph, but he considered that the arguments which made it essential to carry out the change were still valid:

> . . . the public reasons which made his quitting the Foreign Office of importance are all still in force . . . the change of position can only lie in the increased difficulty to move Lord Palmerston with his own consent . . . The ostentatious demonstrations of adherence to him made by the Radicals and in which they press all timid and wavering people to join (presentation of the Picture, Dinner at the Reform Club, got-up cheers when he enters the House of Commons etc.) are evidently made to intimidate those who might wish to move him from his post. There is a remarkable coincidence between their manœuvres at the end of every session. Whilst the [sic] foreign affairs are kept out of parliament during the session and Lord Palmerston is abandoned to the abuse of his opponents, just before the close of the session they give him the opportunity of delivering a clap-trap speech upon which they ground great rejoicings. This was the case last year about the Hungarian Refugees[2] and the year

---

[1] Russell to Palmerston, 22 May 1850 (Walpole, Russell, II, 60).

[2] Palmerston gave naval support to Turkey which enabled her to resist Austrian and Russian demands for the extradition of the Hungarian revolutionaries, of whom the most notable was Kossuth; see p. 150 ff.

before about Italy, evidently intended to bind over his colleagues to keep the peace during the recess.

Prudence will require not to provoke this phalanx . . . The move can only be made during the recess after the close of a particular diplomatic transaction and after his having been supported through the parliamentary struggle ensuing from it. This is the case now . . .[1]

Prince Albert suggested that Lord Palmerston should be moved to the Colonial Office, but without the compensation of the leadership of the House of Commons. He added that the Queen's objections to Lord Palmerston's leadership of the House of Commons were enhanced by Peel's death.[2]

Lord John replied the following day, accepting the necessity of Lord Palmerston's removal from the Foreign Office, but at the same time reiterating his distinction between the ends and means of Palmerston's policy:

. . . It must . . . . be borne in mind that . . . I concur in the position which England has held since 1848. Many of those who dislike and distrust Lord Palmerston would have had England take up a position totally different, viz. of intimate and cordial alliance with Austria and Russia, and of coldness and sullen peace with France . . . There remain the faults of carrying a good policy into effect by means too violent and abrupt, and a demeanour which causes undefined alarm.

Weighing all the difficulties I think that Lord Lansdowne never will be persuaded to take the Foreign Office, and that the appointment of Lord Clarendon,[3] the best on many accounts that could be made, would be particularly offensive to Lord Palmerston. I come to the conclusion that my going to the House of Lords, with the Foreign Office, would be the best course, leaving Sir George Grey[4] to lead in the House of Commons and asking Lord Grey to yield the Colonial Office to Lord Palmerston . . .[5]

The day after this letter was written, Lord John went to see the Queen and her husband.[6] He was beginning to waver once more and

showed symptoms of doubt whether after all Lord Palmerston might not have the lead in the House of Commons.

This frightened the Prince who feared that Lord Palmerston might emerge from the situation with increased power as a democratic leader independent of the Crown. He therefore saw Lord John alone at the end of the audience to acquaint him with

the full extent of the Queen's objections to Lord Palmerston which were

---

[1] Memorandum by Prince Albert sent to Russell, 8 July 1850 (Royal Archives A.79.32).
[2] Ibid.   [3] The Lord Lieutenant of Ireland.   [4] The Home Secretary.
[5] Russell to Prince Albert, 10 July 1850 (Royal Archives A.79.33).
[6] The following is taken from Prince Albert's memorandum of 11 July 1850 (Royal Archives A.79.34).

connected with her knowledge of Lord Palmerston's worthless private character.

Before giving the reasons for his opinion, the Prince in his usual rather complicated style put forward a somewhat involved constitutional argument which deserves close study:

> I had often heard it stated as the nature of the English constitution and the Royal Prerogatives, that the Sovereign could not interfere with the Government or the management of Parliament which are left to the sole control of the responsible Ministers, but that he was absolutely free in the choice of his Minister. Now I differed completely from that doctrine, I held the Sovereign to have an immense moral responsibility upon his shoulders with regard to his government and the duty to watch and control it, and *no* choice almost in the selection of his Ministers, if he understood his duties. The circumstances which led to a change of Ministry almost always pointed out also the men to succeed, public opinion and parliamentary position designated the candidates and there hardly was an instance in History, where, the Sovereign following the bent of his own inclination, had chosen another man than the one who had been brought forward by the circumstances, it had not produced the greatest difficulties to the Sovereign and danger to the Country. A sagacious Sovereign therefore would look forward and take his share in the preparatory arrangements of Party organisation even, when he could, in order to have those presented to his choice in times of emergency, who he had before recognised as eligible. Lord John knew, I continued, that the leader of the Majority in the House of Commons will always have the strongest claim.

To the extent that the Prince was merely trying to show that the leader of the House of Commons had a good prospect of becoming Prime Minister one day and that Palmerston's appointment to the leadership would strengthen his case for the eventual succession to the premiership, the argument is unexceptionable. It was perhaps rather an extravagant claim that the Crown could take its part "in the preparatory arrangements of party organisation", but not too much should be read into this clumsy and heavy-handed formula. If it simply meant, as it probably did, that the Crown should be aware of the eventual consequences of its agreement to Lord Palmerston becoming leader of the House of Commons, it was a dictate of foresight and common sense.

In his eagerness to reach the conclusion that Palmerston should be kept out of the leadership of the House of Commons, the Prince oversimplified the problems in the initial stages of argument. The next few years were to show that the Crown did not always have an obvious candidate for the premiership on the resignation of a government. As to the Crown's "interference" with affairs of government, it was not a matter of allowing or excluding it, but of the extent to which it should take place.

The most difficult issue in this conversation between Prince Albert and Lord John is posed by the charges of immorality:

> . . . how could the Queen consent to take a man as her chief adviser and confidential counsellor in all matters of state, religion, Society, Court, etc. who as her Secretary of State and while a guest under her roof at Windsor Castle had committed a brutal attack upon one of her Ladies? had at night by stealth introduced himself into her apartment, barricaded afterwards the door and would have consummated his fiendish scheme by violence had not the miraculous efforts of his victim and assistance attracted by her screams saved her?
>
> Lord John said, that was very bad and made it absolutely necessary to take care to protect the Queen from Lord Palmerston's being thrust upon her at any time as Prime Minister. He would keep the secret of which he felt the full importance, he unfortunately knew another Lady in Society upon whom he had tried the same thing.[1]

The incident to which the Prince referred was alleged to have taken place in the early days of the Queen's reign, before Lord Palmerston's marriage. The Prince does not appear in an altogether pleasant light in raking up this old story. On the other hand, he must have been sincere in believing that Palmerston's former way of life made him unsuitable as the leading adviser of the Crown and that his standards of public policy were conditioned by his private morality. The Prince took an important part in the natural Victorian —or rather Albertian—reaction against the loose morals of the Regency Court, which was as excessive as the original aberration.

Lord John cuts a miserable figure. Why did he fan the flames of discord by providing fresh evidence? One is almost driven to the conclusion that in spite of all his protestations, he enjoyed keeping the balance between Windsor and Broadlands.

Once more the Prime Minister evaded any definite undertaking to make a change. On the day of the audience he wrote to the Prince:

> Upon the whole I think it best not to make any communication to Lord Palmerston till the session has drawn nearer to its close. The Queen will then be more at liberty to direct the arrangements which Her Majesty may desire.
>
> I have not altered my opinion that the retirement of Lord Palmerston from the Ministry would make it impossible for me to hold my present position, unless some disagreement in the conduct of affairs should render such a step on his part unavoidable.[2]

---

[1] Thus far Prince Albert's memorandum of 11 July 1850.
[2] Russell to Prince Albert, 11 July 1850 (Royal Archives A.79.35).

Having earlier encouraged the Court, the Prime Minister now discouraged it. This may have appealed to his sense of fairness or fitted in with tactical requirements, but it did not make for efficient government. Not having succeeded in securing a change at the Foreign Office, the Crown now fell back on its second string. It attempted to tighten its control over the Foreign Secretary. Lord Palmerston was asked by the Prime Minister, at the request of the Queen, to agree to observe certain principles governing the relationship of the Foreign Secretary with the Crown, laid down in a memorandum.[1] Surprisingly Palmerston swallowed the bitter pill, for the memorandum not only put the supervision of the Foreign Office by the Crown beyond any doubt, but also backed any infringement of the rules with the liability to dismissal by the Crown. This ultimate sanction was the result of advice tendered by Stockmar, and the Prince may well have realised that it overshot its mark.

The memorandum did not prevent future transgression of the rules by Palmerston, for the weapon of dismissal could hardly be wielded without the concurrence of the Prime Minister, who was not prepared to do without Palmerston for the time being. The dismissal of Palmerston by the Crown would have resulted too easily in the resignation of the government. But the memorandum weakened Palmerston's position and it ensured that his fall, when it came, would be a heavy one. From now on, the more he struggled against control, the more he would become enmeshed in it. At first he was cowed; he asked for an interview with the Prince and promised to behave.[2] He got good marks from Prince Albert in a report to the Prime Minister:

> . . . Lord Palmerston is exceedingly attentive and active, writing and explaining to the Queen all that is going on. So far he shows that he has taken good resolution . . .[3]

But this did not last long. Only a few weeks passed before he had a complete relapse.

The Austrian general Haynau, who had acquired an odious reputation owing to his brutalities against Hungarians, was unwise enough to visit Britain in the summer of 1850 without even shaving off his notorious long moustachios. He was recognised by the draymen of Barclay's London brewery and beaten up. When Palmerston as Foreign Secretary had to tender an apology to the Austrian

---

[1] Queen Victoria to Russell, 12 August 1850 (*Letters*). See also Martin, II, 304 ff.
[2] See Martin, II, 307 ff.
[3] Prince Albert to Russell, 8 September 1850 (Royal Archives C.17.79).

Ambassador for this inhospitable act, he inserted on his own authority a paragraph criticising General Haynau's tactlessness in coming to Britain at all after his conduct in Hungary. The Queen at once objected to the inclusion of the paragraph and drew attention to the Foreign Secretary's reversion to his former behaviour. She turned to the Prime Minister:

> It seems (true to his old practice) that either the draft was already gone when Lord Palmerston sent it to Lord John Russell, or that Lord Palmerston sent it as it was nevertheless to Baron Koller [the Austrian Ambassador]. He has been all this time keeping back the draft which—to have the desired effect—ought to have been a spontaneous expression of regret at what had happened, about which (whatever the opinion concerning General Haynau may be) there can be but one feeling—except among the most violent democrats. This stickling for the retention of an objectionable paragraph reflecting on General Haynau, and not sending the draft till three weeks after the occurrence took place can only have a very bad effect and must irritate and annoy the feelings of the Austrian government, already very sensitive at all our communications with them.[1]

It is creditable to Palmerston that he felt strongly about the brutality of a military dictatorship. At the same time, it seems hard to justify an attack on the very government to which the apology is addressed. The Prime Minister could not but agree with the Queen's criticism and this was one of the rare occasions on which he backed her to the hilt. He replied to the Queen:

> ... Lord John Russell would advise Your Majesty to insist on the omission of the last paragraph which is derogatory to the honour of the Nation, as if no one could be safe in this country who is obnoxious to the public feeling. Should the letter have been sent to Baron Koller, Lord Palmerston should recall it in order to substitute a corrected draft.[2]

When the Queen instructed the Foreign Secretary accordingly,[3] he hesitated about complying, but both the Queen and the Prime Minister remained firm. The Queen complained to Lord John that Lord Palmerston

> ... has proven himself here, as on all occasions, without any proper feeling and solely governed by a spirit of vindictiveness against those who crossed his purpose.[4]

---

[1] The Queen to Russell, 29 September 1850 (Royal Archives A.79.55).
[2] Russell to the Queen, 1 October 1850 (Royal Archives A.79.56).
[3] The Queen to Palmerston, 4 October 1850 (Royal Archives A.79.57).
[4] The Queen to Russell, 11 October 1850 (Royal Archives A.79.59). See also Palmerston's letter to the Queen, 8 October 1850 (*Letters*).

But if the Heads of State and Government[1] remained adamant, so did the Foreign Secretary. He wrote to Lord John:

> I do not think that I could have consented to put my name to the note to Baron Koller without something to the effect of the concluding paragraph of my draft, even if the note was still unsent and capable of being altered, and even if I could have agreed so to alter it before it was sent, it is surely needless to detail the reasons which would make it impossible for me to withdraw a Note which has been already received at Vienna and to substitute another in its stead.
>
> Under these circumstances, if the note which has been sent is to be withdrawn, and an altered note is to be substituted in its room, this must be done by another Secretary of State for Foreign Affairs, and I must in that case place my office at your disposal. . . .[2]

It is surprising that Lord Palmerston thought he could achieve anything by a threat of resignation at this stage, when both the Queen and the Prime Minister had committed themselves too far to retreat, even if they had wished. Lord John wisely asked the Foreign Secretary to reconsider his decision to resign, while insisting on the correction of the despatch.[3] Lord Minto, with whom the Prime Minister had been staying, supported him and also asked Lord Palmerston to give way. As a result, Palmerston withdrew his threat of resignation as spontaneously as he had made it:

> I do not myself see how my last paragraph to Koller can be considered derogatory to the honour of England and it is evident that you cannot protect an obnoxious foreigner from insult except by having him always accompanied by policeman . . . However as that is your opinion of the interpretation that might be put upon the passage in question, I have withdrawn it and have sent Koller a copy of the note without that passage to be substituted for the former copy, giving him this reason for the change . . .[4]

When the dust of battle was beginning to settle, Lord John advised the Court to be just as firm in the future:

> The same course may be adopted with advantage if a despatch is ever again sent which has been objected to, and to which the Queen's sanction had not been given.[5]

(ii)

In the meantime, the Court had been disagreeing with the Foreign Secretary in a major diplomatic issue, the Schleswig-Holstein

---

[1] Lord John wrote again to Lord Palmerston on 11 October 1850, expressing his full agreement with the Queen's objections (Royal Archives A.79.63).
[2] Palmerston to Russell, 13 October 1850 (Royal Archives A.79.65).
[3] Russell to Palmerston, 16 October 1850 (Royal Archives A.79.66).
[4] Palmerston to Russell, 17 October 1850 (Royal Archives A.79.67).
[5] Russell to Prince Albert, 18 October 1850 (Royal Archives A.79.69).

question. It has been shown how Palmerston's apparent partisan-ship for Denmark had been one of the first points of friction between the Court and the Foreign Secretary in the spring of 1848. The early successes of German arms in the Duchies and in Jutland had given an exaggerated impression of the strength of the German position. The backbone of the German army in the North consisted of Prussian troops which—in spite of the independence displayed by local commanders—in the last resort followed orders from Berlin. Frederick William IV had agreed to a "German" policy for the Duchies as reluctantly as he did generally. The further the March risings receded into memory, to become a terrible nightmare for him, the more the King felt encouraged to free himself from the shackles of the advisers imposed on him by the revolution. He had never liked to obey the summons of a popular national movement in the Duchies which was, to him, in rebellion against its lawful masters. But in the early days of the revolution he had no option. He then feared the Berlin populace more than his irate brother-in-law, Tsar Nicholas I, who called his conduct "infamous".[1] Frederick William was never prepared to brave Russian wrath for very long. As soon as he conveniently could, he tried to liquidate the Schleswig-Holstein affair. In August 1848, he concluded the Armistice of Malmö with the Danes which provided for the withdrawal of both Danish and Prussian troops from the Duchies and for their tem-porary administration by a joint Prusso-Danish commission. This betrayal of Germany's most sacred cause by the Prussian Govern-ment provoked a storm of disapproval at Frankfurt. Prince Leinin-gen, as Minister-President, had accepted the armistice, but when he realised the strength of opposition to it, he resigned. Eventually the National Assembly had to acquiesce in the Armistice. The dis-proportion between its unlimited pretensions and its nebulous power revealed by the Malmö crisis proved an important factor in the gradual disintegration of the Assembly and the resultant disorder at Frankfurt in October 1848.

The Armistice of Malmö did not settle the problem of the Duchies, which continued to occupy European diplomacy. In the summer of 1850, a serious effort was made by Palmerston, as mediator, to settle the question and thus to remove a cause of friction which was always liable to lead to a major outbreak of hostilities. The Duchies

---

[1] Bloomfield (St. Petersburg) to Palmerston No. 144 of 12 May 1848 (Royal Archives I.4.37).

were still in revolt against Denmark, and Palmerston was determined to regularise the position before Prussia returned to a policy
of intervention which might call forth the counteraction of other
powers, particularly of Russia. The Foreign Secretary was determined
to prevent a Russian protectorship of Denmark against Germany,
although the Queen complained to Lord John:

> The Queen is personally convinced that Lord Palmerston at this moment is
> secretly planning an armed Russian intervention in Schleswig, which may
> produce a renewal of revolutions in Germany, and possibly a general war.[1]

But to keep in step with Russia, Britain had to be largely pro-
Danish, for the Tsar was not prepared to sacrifice Danish interests.
Thus, the solution which Palmerston sponsored was unfavourable
to the German point of view. The *status quo* before March 1848 was
to be restored with the help of the German Confederation, which
was being revived under Austrian auspices. A "Federal Execution"
of the German Confederation was to re-establish the King of Denmark in effective possession as Duke of Holstein in the teeth of the
opposition of his rebellious subjects. Thus the German national
movement in the Duchies was to be broken with German help.
Palmerston nearly succeeded in achieving a settlement along these
lines in the summer of 1850. In July his terms were embodied in a
preliminary arrangement at Berlin. But when the permanent treaty,
the London Protocol, was ready for signature the following month,
Prussia's signature was missing. Frederick William had again changed
his mind.

Prince Albert had made a close study of the problem of the
Duchies, and Queen Victoria, who was not conversant with all
the details, accepted his conclusions. The royal couple objected to
Palmerston's solution because it did not take account of the feelings
of the inhabitants of the Duchies and because no attempt was made
to consult their representatives, the Estates. They were on strong
ground in contrasting Palmerston's indifference to national rights
in Schleswig-Holstein with his care for them in Italy. But they were
unable to grasp that the Foreign Secretary had valid and objective
reasons for his policy. Prince Albert assumed the worst motives.
Two years later, when he might have been expected to feel somewhat more dispassionate, he noted in a private memorandum:

> My personal belief is that the [London] Protocol [of 1850] was a bargain
> between Lord Palmerston and Baron Brunnow [the Russian Ambas-

---

[1] The Queen to Russell, 28 July 1850 (*Letters*).

sador] who engaged in return for it to withdraw the hostility of Russia and Austria against Lord Palmerston personally, which was most harassing to him during his trial [sic] in Parliament on the Greek affair.[1]

At the time Prince Albert went even further:

> I was long aware that the rights of the poor people of Schleswig and Holstein were to be the price for which Lord Palmerston would repurchase the good will of France and particularly Russia and he has paid with them at once also Mr. Reeve and The Times, who are thought to have received a large bribe in Danish stock.[2]

Curiously enough, the same memorandum also contained a report of Palmerston's complaints about a plot of *The Times* and Mr. Reeve against him. The newspaper certainly had an Olympian versatility.

Lord Palmerston was following a policy in accordance with the interests of Britain as they were then understood and the opposition of the Court did not move him from his course. He went so far as to accuse the Queen of wanting him to be Minister for the German Confederation, when she asked for it to be represented in the settlement.[3] In vain the Queen attempted to enlist the co-operation of the Cabinet. It was useless for Prince Albert to write to the Prime Minister:

> The Queen has never got an answer upon her letter to you asking that her correspondence with Lord Palmerston on the Holstein Protocol should be brought before the Cabinet. I understand that Lord Palmerston is going on with his Protocol as if no such correspondence had ever taken place.[4]

That summed up the position.

It has been seen that Prussia, which had been a party to the Treaty of Berlin in July, refused to join the London Protocol in August. This change of front was due to another of the periodic, if only short-lived, bursts of Prussian enthusiasm for its German mission. For a time the King was under the influence of his Foreign Minister, Josef Maria von Radowitz, a conservative Catholic with German ideals. Radowitz wanted Prussia to become the leading exponent of constitutional monarchy in Germany by taking up the cause of those who were being deprived of their legal rights by the Elector of Hesse. This prince, whose despotic record before the revolution has been noted, had attempted to collect taxes which had

---

[1] Memorandum by Prince Albert, 14 July 1852 (Royal Archives A.81.32).
[2] Memorandum by Prince Albert, 8 August 1850 (Royal Archives A.79.42).
[3] Palmerston to Russell, 23 June 1850 (*Letters*).
[4] Prince Albert to Russell, 2 July 1850 (Royal Archives C.17.74).

not been voted by the Hessian Diet, as required by the constitution. Some officials and army officers had been courageous enough to resign their jobs, as they were unwilling to be parties to unconstitutional acts. Many citizens risked imprisonment with their refusal to pay the taxes. The Elector called on the Austrian sponsored German Confederation—which Prussia still boycotted—to come to his aid. This was a magnificent opportunity for Prussia. But as the King and the Prime Minister, Count Brandenburg, only gave lukewarm backing to von Radowitz, the fervour generated by the Hessian cause was soon allowed to evaporate. The King did not like to fight on a constitutional issue against his fellow sovereigns. He thought it was better for him to make a stand on the contractual right of his troops to pass through the Electorate on the way to the Prussian Rhineland, over the question of the *Etappenstrassen*. The problem became one of the relations of military commanders: would the Prussian commander stationed on the lines of communications in Hesse prevent his Bavarian fellow general from moving troops into the Electorate? The Bavarian general had been commissioned to carry out the "federal execution" of the Austrian-led German Confederation in support of the Elector. This way of presenting the controversy was certainly effective in ensuring that there would not be any popular enthusiasm for Prussia's German cause. As Palmerston remarked contemptuously the Hessian problem had been "narrowed down to a question to be settled by the road books".[1]

Prince Albert was very dissatisfied with the handling of Prussian policy:

> . . . for Prussia to have irresistible strength she must make herself an honest, sincere and enthusiastic champion of constitutional freedom in Germany. If she only wants to be a Prussia longing for the Holy Alliance, without any confidence in the constitutional system, and does not want to defend anything in Hesse except Etappenstrassen, then it remains in spite of its immense fortifications merely what it was, the humble servant of Austria and Russia, only with the difference that it is now despised by them.[2]

But as long as there was a hope that Prussia would adopt its new role in Germany, the Prince supported it. He and Stockmar pleaded with the British Government to encourage Prussia in its German plans. This was asking rather too much of Lord Palmerston, after all the difficulties he had for years encountered from Prussia in the

[1] Palmerston to Russell, 26 November 1850 (Royal Archives I.23.46).
[2] Prince Albert to his brother, 1 December 1850 (Royal Archives I.23.54), tr.

Schleswig-Holstein question. As far as the Duchies were concerned, Austria was at this stage an ally, and not the opponent of the Foreign Secretary, as she was elsewhere. It is a curious irony that the Prince in this question found himself ranged against Austria, with Palmerston as the ally of the Habsburg Monarchy.

Prussia surrendered to Austria and Russia at Olmütz, in November 1850. It gave way completely over Hesse. The Elector was to be aided without giving any guarantees to his subjects. Palmerston could only be pleased about Austria's victory over Prussia, which now had to give up any independent policy in Schleswig-Holstein and to agree to the Federal Execution in Holstein which Denmark had requested. Palmerston had, after all, been more correct in his cynical appraisal of Prussian policy than Prince Albert with all his enthusiasm. The Prince was disgusted with Prussia. He wrote to Stockmar:

> The King [of Prussia] is in his Seventh Heaven in delight about the marvellous solution and says, Schwarzenberg had given more than he had demanded! ! He believes that war would only have profited democracy, which intends to bring about *his* fall, though he would of necessity have won, for all Hungary, Italy, even Vienna wanted to rise, the Saxons would have gone over to them! Now he is, as it were by the goodness of fate, freed from this danger! ! ! ! Please let Bunsen know of these lines and advise him to put on sackcloth and to cover his head with ashes for serving *such a master*.[1]

Thus Prince Albert recognised for a moment, when it was too late, the link between the aspirations of the German and of other national movements. Olmütz effectively put paid to any hopes for German unity under Prussian leadership for the time being. Radowitz resigned and gave Prince Albert a tale of woe when he came to Britain on a fruitless mission to investigate the possibility of an alliance between Britain and Prussia. The reactionary Otto von Manteuffel became Prussian Minister-President. Prince Albert's friend, the heir to the Prussian throne, withdrew from active participation in affairs of state as he disapproved of the "see-saw system" (*Schaukelsystem*) for conducting foreign policy.[2] It took many years before Prince Albert could again work for German unity.

The Prussian surrender was the beginning of the end for German hopes in the Duchies. The Federal Execution took its course. Holstein was subjected and handed back to the King of Denmark,

---

[1] Prince Albert to Stockmar, 8 December 1850 (Royal Archives I.23.83), tr.
[2] The Prince of Prussia to Bunsen, 23 December 1850. Copy sent to Prince Albert (Royal Archives I.23.121).

the "King-Duke". A conservative government, with Lord Malmesbury as Foreign Secretary, was in 1852 to put the finishing touches
to the settlement with the London Protocol regulating the Danish
succession which had been foreshadowed in 1850. The pro-German
Augustenburg line was excluded. On the extinction of the direct
male line the junior pro-Danish branch of Glücksburg was to succeed to Denmark and the Duchies. Queen Victoria and her husband
opposed this arrangement. Prince Albert wrote to the Prince of
Prussia in the middle of August 1850, just after the signature of the
first London Protocol:

> It will not be so easy to get rid of the succession question by European
> protocols: and if the Augustenburgs remain determined not to give up
> their good right [to the Duchies], the politicians [die Politik] will in the
> end have to make up their minds to give up their good wishes,[1]

Prince Albert in January 1851 went so far as to write to his cousin
Alexander von Mensdorff, who had been sent to Holstein as Austrian Commissioner with the Federal Troops of Execution, that what
the Powers were trying to do was "illegal" (*rechtswidrig*).[2] But he
still considered that the treaties which had been concluded were
binding, as long as the Danes carried out their commitments. This
is clear from advice he gave to the Duke of Augustenburg in
February 1852. The Duke appealed to the Queen and the Prince to
intervene with the King of Denmark for the return of his property
which had been confiscated. Prince Albert advised the Duke to
accept a Danish offer of compensation. He added:

> As far as Your Highness's possible [eventuelle] claims to the succession
> in any part of the territories of His Majesty the King of Denmark may be
> concerned, I may be permitted to voice my opinion that Your Highness
> will leave this point to the judgment [Ausspruch] of Austria and Prussia,[3]
> as the Federal Assembly has empowered these two governments to settle
> that question . . .[4]

Prince Albert considered the claim of the Augustenburg line to
the succession in the Duchies strong and perhaps unanswerable in
abstract law. But he felt that in the circumstances, with the Great
Powers committed to the Glücksburg succession in the whole of
the Danish monarchy, including the Duchies, it was better to face

[1] Prince Albert to the Prince of Prussia, 20 August 1850 (Royal Archives I.21.42),
tr.
[2] Prince Albert to Mensdorff, 20 January 1851 (Royal Archives I.24.43), tr.
[3] Both these powers accepted the exclusion of the Augustenburg branch.
[4] Prince Albert to the Duke of Augustenburg, 24 February 1852 (Royal
Archives I.27.63), tr.

facts. This is important in view of the part Queen Victoria played in the question of the Duchies after her husband's death, when the "Protocol-Prince" succeeded to the Danish throne in 1863.

In one of his sweeping, if rather meaningless generalisations, Lord Palmerston had stated in November 1850 that in a war between the two major powers in the German Confederation, the sympathies of the British nation would be with Prussia, "Protestant and liberal", rather than with Austria.[1] The emphasis on a common Protestant heritage is not a matter of coincidence, for the Foreign Secretary was at this period concerned with the diplomatic answer to the "Papal aggression" committed by the creation of Roman Catholic territorial sees in England. Lord John retaliated with his "Ecclesiastical Titles Bill" which helped to bring down the government. Lord Palmerston's position was so strong that he was sought after not only by the Whigs but also by the Protectionists who attempted to form a new administration. Only the Peelites spoke the Court's language about Palmerston. Prince Albert recorded a conversation with two of the leading Peelites:

> One subject seemed uppermost in the minds of Lord Aberdeen and Sir James [Graham] viz: The impossibility to have Lord Palmerston in the Cabinet and the House of Commons. Sir James said he would prefer seeing him as leader of the Protectionists opposite to him to having him on the Treasury Bench next to him, after his having seen him play falsely to his former colleagues, intriguing with the Radical and Irish fraction of their supporters, detaching that party from them and using it and *his influence over it* as a means of coercing his colleagues. This was behaviour which he [Sir James] could not expose himself to and would strongly resent. On my saying that Lord John had thought of the possibility of giving him the lead in the House of Lords, Lord Aberdeen looked very black and assured me that the House would never submit to that. They thought the Lord Lieutenancy with a Peerage was the right thing to offer him. Lord Aberdeen declared that he personally had no objection to sit with him in the Cabinet, but well remembered that, when he had been in office with him under the Duke of Wellington, the constant disputes with him (who was then only Secretary at War) on the foreign policy were anything but pleasant.[2]

One may wonder to what extent the happenings during Wellington's ministry in 1828 were relevant to the situation of 1851. It is regrettable that politicians of all parties saw fit to widen the gulf between the Court and Lord Palmerston even further.

[1] Palmerston to Russell, 26 November 1850 (Royal Archives I.23.46).
[2] Memorandum by Prince Albert, 24 February 1851 (Royal Archives C.46.31).

The Queen's mind on the subject of Lord Palmerston seemed to have been made up. She told Lord Lansdowne:

> One man the Queen could not allow to be reinstated . . . and indeed had a promise from Lord John that he should not be thrust upon her again and that was Lord Palmerston to [sic] the Foreign Office.

The Duke of Wellington had agreed with the Queen that Palmerston's return would be a terrible misfortune.[1] But all this was in vain. When Lord John's government returned to power at the beginning of March after all other solutions had failed, Lord Palmerston came back with it. There was a tense atmosphere when Lord John told the Queen and the Prince of his determination to restore the *status quo ante* at the Foreign Office:

> The Queen was made very low by this announcement and could not be appeased by the expectation which Lord John held out that their whole tenure of office would be very short.[2]

Prince Albert had engaged in wishful thinking when he drew up a scheme for a coalition government "for his own amusement" which listed Lord Palmerston as Lord Lieutenant outside the cabinet.[3]

(iii)

The autumn of 1851 saw fresh manifestations of the tension between the Court and the Foreign Secretary, which was ever present under the surface. The cause was connected with the finale of the liberal national movement of 1848. In 1849, Lord Palmerston had saved the lives and liberty of many Hungarian refugees, including their leader Kossuth, by preventing the Turks from obeying Austrian demands to extradite them. Kossuth came to Britain in October 1851. The Court insisted that Palmerston should be restrained from receiving him, so as to avoid insulting Austria.[4] Lord John had the unenviable task of arguing out the matter with the Foreign Secretary in the Cabinet. He reported to the Queen:

> . . . The Cabinet met today when Lord John Russell stated his views respecting Kossuth, and said he wished to hear the opinion of the members of the Cabinet separately, but would not ask for any collective resolution.
> Lord Palmerston replied and enforced [sic] his opinion.
> Lord Lansdowne said he thought that after Kossuth's speeches it would

---

[1] Memorandum by Prince Albert on the conversations with Lord Lansdowne and the Duke of Wellington, 1 March 1851 (Royal Archives C.46.105).
[2] Memorandum by Prince Albert, 3 March 1851 (Royal Archives C.46.117).
[3] Memorandum by Prince Albert, 1 or 2 March 1851 (Royal Archives C.46.106).
[4] Queen Victoria to Russell, 24 October 1851, ff. (*Letters.*)

be a great pity there should be any misconstruction [sic] as to the views of the Government. That he thought the reception of Kossuth might give rise to such misconstruction, and he therefore hoped Lord Palmerston would not receive him. At the same time he thought he had a right to receive him, and would defend that right if Lord Palmerston thought proper to act upon it.

The other members of the Cabinet all, in various manner, and in different degrees expressed their wish that Lord Palmerston should not receive M. Kossuth.

Lord Palmerston yielding to the general sense said he thought he could avoid any interview with Kossuth. But he wishes the matter to be left in his hands, and not to be publicly talked of. The Cabinet willingly assented, and thus the matter rests.

Lord John Russell trusts the matter will be quietly disposed of, and will be no more heard of.[1]

It would not have been in accordance with Palmerston's usual behaviour, if this had been the end of the matter. Soon afterwards, a deputation from the London boroughs of Finsbury and Islington called on the Foreign Secretary with a petition praising Kossuth and denouncing the Emperors of Austria and Russia; Lord Palmerston did not dissociate himself from its terms. The Queen took a serious view of Palmerston's conduct and asked for it to be referred to the Cabinet,[2] which happened on 4 December. The Prime Minister's report must have been cold comfort to the Queen and the Prince:

Lord John Russell . . . has this day brought before the Cabinet the substance of Your Majesty's communications . . . The Cabinet were deeply impressed with the necessity of guarding the honour of the Crown and maintaining the dignity of Your Majesty's position towards foreign countries. Nor could they fail to discern a want of caution in Lord Palmerston's proceedings in respect to the Finsbury deputation . . . The Cabinet however declined to come to any formal resolution. Mr. Labouchère [President of the Board of Trade] and Lord Grey might probably have been willing to do so; but Lord Lansdowne, and all the rest of the Cabinet were decidedly opposed to such a step.

It is to be hoped that the expression of opinion elicited will have its effect on Lord Palmerston to whom Lord John Russell has written a private letter, urging the necessity of a guarded conduct, in the present very critical condition of Europe.[3]

Lord John's hope was in vain. The day before, news of Louis Napoleon's *coup d'état* on 2 December reached this country. The Foreign Secretary, at once and without authorisation, expressed his

[1] Russell to the Queen, 3 November 1851 (Royal Archives A.79.86). See also Walpole, Russell, II, 134 ff.
[2] The Queen to Russell, 21 November 1851 (*Letters*).
[3] Russell to the Queen, 4 December 1851 (Royal Archives A.79.110).

approval to the French Ambassador. Meantime at the request of the Queen, the British Ambassador in Paris, the Marquis of Normanby, was asked to remain a passive observer of the course of events. When he called on the French Foreign Minister after receiving a despatch instructing him accordingly, he was told that Lord Palmerston had already expressed approval of the *coup d'état* to the French Ambassador in London. On Lord Normanby asking his Foreign Secretary about this apparent inconsistency in British policy, Lord Palmerston justified his approval of the coup in an official despatch. He adopted his usual flamboyant attitude, although he had already been made aware by a letter from the Prime Minister that the Queen was questioning his conduct and asking for an explanation. After two days had elapsed without a reply from the Foreign Secretary, the Prime Minister had to write again more urgently pointing out the discourtesy to the Sovereign. Lord Palmerston only had a partial answer to the charges, that he had given his opinion to the French Ambassador in his private capacity. He also pointed out that the Prime Minister himself and other members of the Cabinet had expressed similar views to the Ambassador. But even if this is accepted, there still remains the despatch to Lord Normanby which was a flagrant contravention of official policy. In any case, all this was the last straw. On 19 December Lord John dismissed the Foreign Secretary. Lord Palmerston contemptuously rejected Lord John's offer of the Lord Lieutenancy.[1]

The Queen and her husband were delighted. The Prince wrote to the Prime Minister on the following day:

> She [the Queen] feels naturally much relieved as it had been much on her mind, whether it was not her duty to put an end *herself* to the dangerous proceedings of Lord Palmerston, which might however have brought the Crown too prominently into discussion, in which it had no means of making a public defence.[2]

The Prince made a forecast about the situation of the government which proved only partially correct:

> I hope your Cabinet will see no reason why it should not go on; I consider it strengthened, not weakened by Lord Palmerston's secession, nor do I think that public opinion will support his sympathising with the coup d'état.[3]

---

[1] The ample literature on Lord Palmerston's dismissal includes "The Letters of Queen Victoria"; Martin, II, 411 ff.; Walpole, Russell, II, 138 ff.; Gooch, Russell, II, 83 ff.; E. Ashley, Viscount Palmerston, I, 284 ff.; Bell, Palmerston, II, 46 ff.
[2] Prince Albert to Russell, 20 December 1851 (Royal Archives C.19.35).
[3] Ibid.

The Prime Minister had certainly borne in mind that he for once had Palmerston at a disadvantage over his support for Louis Napoleon in the suppression of constitutional liberties. The feared enemy of the continental tyrants, the upholder of liberal movements in Europe, had congratulated the dictator who had trampled on a constitution and arrested his political enemies. For Palmerston found himself exposed to the full glare of publicity in a decidedly unfortunate posture. He did not have a good press. Early in February 1852, he received a further blow to his prestige when the Prime Minister read out the Queen's memorandum about the relations of the Foreign Secretary and the Crown[1] during the debate on his dismissal. This revealed the apparently imperturbable and self-confident Foreign Secretary as being on probation, accepting a stinging rebuke which even a lesser man would have found hard to swallow. Lord Palmerston's delay in replying to the Queen's objections in December also created an unfortunate impression.

Thus Prince Albert was right in thinking Lord Palmerston would not come off too well with public opinion. He misjudged the effect of his loss on the strength of the Cabinet. Lord John proposed Lord Granville to the Queen as Palmerston's successor, which met with royal approval. A young hereditary Whig, an amiable if perhaps somewhat too smooth personality, Granville had won Prince Albert's confidence by his work for the Great Exhibition. When Lord John called a meeting of the Cabinet to discuss the situation created by Palmerston's dismissal, he secured a nearly unanimous approval of his action. But his colleagues were not so happy about Granville as a successor. They naturally wanted another Foreign Secretary of calibre. The Home Secretary, Sir George Grey, asked for the appointment of Lord Clarendon, with which the other members of the Cabinet agreed. Lord John was so delighted to carry the Cabinet with him over the dismissal that he handled the succession question badly. He agreed to Clarendon being approached. He should not have allowed the Cabinet to come to any conclusion on this. Ministers are appointed by the Crown on the recommendation of the Prime Minister, and the Queen was quite right to protest "against the Cabinet taking upon itself the appointment of its own members".[2]

The history of Lord Clarendon's relations with the Court is a curious one. He alternated between being a favourite and almost *persona non grata*. As late as the summer of 1850, the Queen and

---

[1] The memorandum of 12 August 1850 (see above p. 140).
[2] See memorandum by Prince Albert, 23 December 1851 (*Letters*).

the Prince had suggested recalling him from Ireland, where he was Lord Lieutenant, to succeed Palmerston, but Lord John then objected to him as a candidate for the Foreign Office. Now that the question became acute, the position was reversed. When Lord John informed the Queen and the Prince that he had veered round to Clarendon after all,[1]

> the Queen . . . declared that, much as she esteemed and liked Lord Clarendon personally, he would not possess her confidence as Foreign Secretary, for which his imprudence in communications, his connection with News Papers, his antecedents as an intriguing diplomatist in Spain,[2] his undisguised hatred of the French, were serious obstacles.

Prince Albert continued the report of the audience:

> I assisted the Queen by giving it as my opinion, that we would have Lord Palmerston over again in Lord Clarendon, as, with the difference of a milder temper and more gentlemanly feeling, he possessed the same love for intrigue and the same lax morality which formed the chief danger in the character of a Foreign Secretary; everything depended (I said) on inspiring confidence in the honesty and straightforwardness of the British Government; Lord Clarendon would fail in inspiring this confidence.

The Prince put a cynical interpretation on a letter from Lord Clarendon expressing his reluctance to succeed Lord Palmerston, coupled with a willingness, if necessary, to sacrifice himself for his country:

> I rejoined that this letter appeared to me to mean nothing else, than: "Offer me the place as I am ready to accept it (and with the advantage of its having been imposed on me)." If therefore a communication with Lord Clarendon was necessary, the only mode of doing this would be for Lord John to take the letter of Lord Clarendon as a refusal of the Foreign Office and to inform him that knowing the offer would have been disagreeable to him it had not been made.
>
> After a long discussion, Lord John agreed to do this and to say that he had received the Queen's permission to make the offer to Lord Granville, but this would be contrary to the wish expressed by the Cabinet. I remarked that if the Cabinet had known the Queen's determination not to accept Lord Clarendon, they might probably have come to a different decision.

Lord John saw the prospects of the cabinet's survival deteriorating as a result of the refusal of the Crown to have another strong man at the Foreign Office. In his exasperation with the attitude of the

---

[1] The following is taken from Prince Albert's memorandum on the discussion with Lord John of 23 December 1851 (Royal Archives A.80.1).
[2] Lord Clarendon represented Britain in Madrid from 1833 to 1839.

Court, he referred to Lord Stanley's offer of the Foreign Office to Lord Canning, the later Governor-General of India, during the cabinet crisis at the beginning of the year:

> Lord John said he would mention that at that time it had been said by somebody, Lord Canning had been named only to please the Court, who liked to have a young man, whom they could manage. I [Prince Albert] interrupted Lord John by saying that such talk should not deter us from insisting upon it, that a new Secretary for Foreign Affairs, let him be young or old, ought to be honest; for that was the main point.[1]

The Court's rejection of Clarendon was certainly open to misinterpretation. It is rather ironical in view of his sweeping condemnation of Lord Palmerston's policy in a letter to Lord John Russell the following month. Clarendon challenged the essence of Palmerston's policy, that British interests and constitutional government could be furthered by adopting an offensive attitude to foreign states. He instanced the success of the reaction as proof of Palmerston's failure to advance the cause of constitutional government in Europe.[2]

The royal couple's objection to Clarendon at this time did not concern his ideas on foreign policy so much as his person. They regarded him as too much inclined to follow expediency to attain political power. They had mistrusted his sudden change of front about Lord Palmerston the previous year. After having advocated the Foreign Secretary's removal for some time, Clarendon told Lord John at the beginning of August 1850 that he no longer considered the moment appropriate. This was not surprising after the Don Pacifico debate, but Prince Albert concluded differently:

> My belief was that Lord Clarendon had expressed his new opinion on account of the postponement of the Lord Lieutenancy Bill which will prevent his leaving Ireland for the next year and therefore make it impossible at present to succeed *himself* to Lord Palmerston, and this belief was strengthened by the fact of his having still lately spoken in unmeasured terms of Lord Palmerston to Lord Normanby and upon the latter cautioning him to be prudent, as Lord Palmerston was already very jealous of him, said: "I know that, but I don't care, for Palmerston's jealousies are the jealousies of a Footman." [3]

The Queen and her husband seem to have come to the conclusion that Clarendon had "let them down" against Palmerston for purely selfish reasons.

Granville's appointment led to suspicions that the Queen and

---

[1] Thus far Prince Albert's memorandum of 23 December 1851.
[2] Clarendon to Russell, 22 January 1852 (Gooch, Russell, II, 97 ff.).
[3] Memorandum of Prince Albert, 5 August 1850 (Royal Archives A.79.41).

particularly the Prince wanted to take over complete control of foreign affairs. It gave apparent plausibility to vague—and sometimes more direct—allegations of the Palmerston circle that their hero had been the victim of a dark Court intrigue. It lengthened the odds against the government's survival. Lord John's fall was not, in fact, long delayed. He was brought down by Palmerston's "tit for tat" at the end of February. The Queen's and the Prince's wish to retain Lord John without Lord Palmerston had thus proved unworkable, at any rate without Lord Clarendon at the Foreign Office. The royal couple had overestimated the weight of the rest of Lord John's Government and underestimated Lord Palmerston's prestige. The dismissed Foreign Secretary emerged from his ordeal strengthened, the most sought-after politician in the country. The Protectionists wanted him as much as the Whigs. The Queen and the Prince had failed to foresee that their wish to get rid of Lord Palmerston might force them to swallow as bitter a pill as the behaviour of the autocratic Foreign Secretary, in having to accept a Protectionist government under Lord Stanley, now Earl of Derby. They considered the maintenance of Peel's achievements a sacred trust, particularly after Sir Robert's death. They had to accept as their Prime Minister the very man who had been the bitterest opponent of their hero. In fact, in addition to a Protectionist government, they nearly got Lord Palmerston as leader of the House of Commons.

The victory over Palmerston was a Pyrrhic one. That it was so derived to some extent from the lack of moderation the Court showed in its hour of triumph. The distinction between a healthy and an excessive supervision on the part of the Head of State is always a nice one, and Queen Victoria and Prince Albert may have just overstepped it after Palmerston's fall. Since Granville's first tenure of the Foreign Office was so short, it is impossible to decide whether the charge of undue interference by the Crown was justified. The course of events swept past any intentions the Prince might have had of running the Foreign Office. These ideas seem as unlikely as they were impracticable. Soon the Queen and her husband were more than busy with the sheer task of ensuring that the country had a government.

Just as there were really no victors or defeated in the country's most dramatic extra-parliamentary political struggle in the century, neither side was completely in the right. The Crown was justified in complaining about Palmerston's violations of the essential rules of constitutional government. It could claim to be the trustee of the other parties affected by the practice of the Foreign Secretary, such as the Prime Minister and other members of the government who for various reasons remained mute. The Crown had cause to be dissatisfied with the lack of moral courage shown by ministers who agreed with its criticism of the handling of the Foreign Office, or seemed to agree with it. Partly as a result of the requirements of Court etiquette, the Queen and the Prince received a distorted picture of the political situation in as far as it affected Palmerston's position. Still, this could have been largely avoided, if politicians had shown more uprightness in dealing with the Court. If they wished to criticise Lord Palmerston, they should have addressed themselves to him in the first instance, instead of complaining to the Queen and the Prince behind his back, thus aggravating the tension.

The mediators failed signally, each in their own way. Lord John never tried properly, for reasons which can only be guessed; he may well have been content to find himself in apparent control as the arbiter between his powerful colleague and the Sovereign. Lord Lansdowne was thoroughly honest and straightforward, trusted by all concerned, but he was getting on in years and never—at this period—progressed beyond the Wellingtonian common sense of the elder statesman. Lord Granville was too smooth and soothing, and too young and inexperienced, to make much impact. Lord Clarendon was the self-opinionated, rather too keen professional mediator, whose protestations of disinterestedness did not ring quite true.

Questions of constitutional procedure played so vital a part in the whole controversy, apparently quite out of proportion to their importance, because Lord Palmerston felt unsure of being able to carry out his policy openly. He came to the conclusion that if he stated his intentions at the outset, he would be overborne by the opposition in the Cabinet. If he had really been able to carry the Cabinet with him, the Crown would have been powerless to stop his policy.

The Crown had to concern itself with the details of Palmerston's diplomacy, because these were a vital part of it. The dramatic gesture, conceived on the spur of the moment and as quickly put into effect, was part and parcel of the Palmerstonian system. Perhaps the Foreign Secretary was really willing, in August 1850, to make an effort to reform himself. But he was incapable of it at the time. He had become the slave of his own propaganda, he had to go on living up to the image of the John Bull who always had his own way. The Prince was shrewd in assuming that Palmerston needed success,

constant success. His strength was the appeal of his foreign policy
to public opinion at home. If he could no longer lecture the tyrants
abroad on the unrivalled advantages of British constitutional government, the source of his power was removed. This was his Achilles
heel. If the Crown attacked it, it was not so much because the Prince
and the Queen realised that this was his vulnerable spot, but because
they could see the danger of foreign policy becoming a matter of
mass emotion. They also felt that the Crown was at a disadvantage
in this appeal to public opinion. They wanted the issues of foreign
policy to be judged dispassionately in the confidential atmosphere of
the council chamber, instead of being thrown open to national
debate. To the Court, foreign policy was an end in itself. It could thus
be put to simple tests, such as whether Britain had succeeded in
keeping on reasonable terms with the other powers, and whether the
prospects for peace had improved. Judged by these criteria, Palmerston's handling of affairs in Spain, Portugal and Greece had been a
failure. But Palmerston himself reached different conclusions, because he considered foreign policy partly a means to an end and
inseparable from domestic policy and ideology. He is one of the few
statesmen who have succeeded in running liberalism and nationalism in harness by making the propagation of British constitutionalism
the watchword of his foreign policy. This enabled him to gain
popularity at home by making every Britisher feel that whatever was
still wrong at home, Britain was a better country than the despotic
states of the continent. Thus the way in which Palmerston captured
the imagination of the British public contributed to keeping this
country comparatively quiet in these troublesome years.

To what extent had Palmerston's policy been successful, within
his own wide definition? Clarendon pointed out that whereas
Palmerston had sought to support constitutional government on the
continent, reaction had triumphed everywhere.[1] This was a telling
argument, but Palmerston considered the very long-term future. His
main aim was to keep the cause of constitutional government alive
and in the public eye. He thought that the despotic system of the
Eastern Powers would wither away as a result of its own contra-
dictions, to anticipate Marxist terminology. He and Britain could
afford to wait.

In the absence of the Prince, Palmerston might well have
persuaded the Queen to agree to a policy which fitted in so well
with many of her views. Fundamentally, Palmerston's instinctive

[1] Clarendon to Russell, 22 January 1852 (Gooch, Russell, II, 97 ff.).

approach, his coming to a decision in a flash, appealed to her temperament. If Prince Albert had not been there, Palmerston would have been able to put his case to the Queen direct, and she might have become as eager a partisan of his policy of standing up for British rights abroad as she later in widowhood became a devotee of Disraeli's imperialism. With the Prince as the Queen's main adviser on foreign affairs, this was not possible. The Foreign Secretary was no longer, as in the early days of the reign, dealing with a Queen who had little knowledge of foreign affairs and who had never been out of Britain, but with the wife of a German prince, whose knowledge of Europe matched his own. The Foreign Secretary's impressive and apparently unanswerable sweeping statements were to be questioned and then to be challenged. The Prince was cautious and painstaking, the Foreign Secretary a brilliant gambler. The former thought out everything, the latter—like the Queen and later Bismarck—had often decided on his course of action before the process of intellectual reasoning set in. To differences of temperament were added divergences of outlook. Palmerston had no time for the Prince's constant reiteration of moral and legal arguments. The Prince objected to the Foreign Secretary's high-handed methods which often paid no attention to undoubted rights. The Prince dismissed the pressure on small countries to adopt constitutional government as "bullying", but the same could be said of the treatment of opposition movements by the governments of these states. Palmerston sincerely felt for the persecuted, whereas the Prince was, on the whole, indifferent to their sufferings. Neither side was completely consistent. As a result of his belief in his fatherland, Prince Albert wanted to help those inhabitants of Schleswig-Holstein who had resisted the Danes because they felt—rightly or wrongly—that the Duchies should form part of a united Germany. But Palmerston would not sympathise in the Duchies with the kind of nationalist movement which he was quite prepared to accept in Northern Italy. The divergence of opinion between Prince and Foreign Secretary over Germany certainly loomed large in the tension between the Court and Lord Palmerston. The Austria struggling to maintain its hold over Lombardy and Venetia was to the Prince a German power. Its victories were those of German arms. In Portugal, the Foreign Secretary fell foul of a Coburg prince, in Greece of a Bavarian. In the Haynau and Kossuth incidents, a "German" power was involved in Austria. It is ironical that in the only question where the Prince was anti-Austrian, over Prussian leadership in Germany, the Foreign Secretary found it prudent to suppress his hostility to the Habsburg Monarchy. As a German of the upper classes, the Prince was also more anti-French than the ordinary Briton. He was thus too partisan to see Palmerston's solid reasons for co-operating with France—revolutionary or even Napoleonic—over Italy.

The Crown often had a case against Palmerston. At other times it made the execution of patient diplomatic negotiation more difficult. Tempers became frayed and allegations were made—on both sides—which are hard to sustain. The conflict was so intense because it was conditioned by the most critical events on the continent of Europe since 1815, as a result of which Britain for a time became more exposed than ever to the wind blowing from the continent. It transcended foreign affairs. Perhaps it was a necessary cataclysm in the circumstances. Britain could not be spared some disturbance and it was better that the contest was fought out mainly in Parliament and in the council chambers than in the streets.

Chapter Nine

DOMESTIC AFFAIRS

(i)

IN his intense preoccupation with foreign affairs following the revolution of 1848, the Prince did not neglect domestic developments. His part in the Great Exhibition of 1851 is best known. It forms the culmination of a long interest in industrial development and the welfare of the working classes. Similarly, the Prince's hand can be seen in the shaping of government policy during the complicated religious controversies of the day and the Cabinet crisis early in 1851 which arose in their train. The Irish question, on which he also expressed his views, forms a link between the two sets of problems.

Prince Albert shared the determination of Lord John's government to deal firmly with any disturbances and to resist Chartist mass pressure. He was forced to watch the decisive day in the capital, 10 April 1848, from the quietness of Osborne, but not without taking an active interest in all that was happening. While the news from London of 9 April was generally satisfactory, the Prince considered it necessary that the Chartist orators should be prosecuted. He thought that "their language is . . . going beyond all bounds". His prescription was:

> Work for the suffering and unemployed, maintenance of order by police arrangements, and prosecution of the agitators . . .[1]

The Prince was not satisfied with purely repressive measures unaccompanied by positive action. He believed in fighting not only the symptoms, but preferably the underlying causes. From his extensive social work he was aware of the economic causes of so much political discontent among the industrial working classes.

In another letter to the Prime Minister on the very day that the Chartist demonstration in London collapsed, he developed more fully his positive ideas for preventing a revolution:

> I have inquired a good deal into the state of employment about London, and I find to my great regret that the number of workmen of all trades out of employment is *very* large and that it has been increased by the reduction

---

[1] Prince Albert to Russell, 10 April 1848 (Royal Archives C.16.47).

of all the works under government owing to the clamour for economy in the House of Commons. Several hundred workmen have been discharged at Westminster Palace; at Buckingham Palace much fewer hands are employed than are really wanted . . . Surely this is not the moment for the tax payers to economise upon the working classes! and though I don't wish our Government to follow Louis Blanc in his system of "organisation du travail" I think the Government is bound to do what it can to help the working classes over the present moment of distress.[1]

On 11 April news of the failure of the Chartist demonstration in London reached Osborne. The Prince was delighted:

The Day of yesterday terminated gloriously for England! I must congratulate you . . . as the measures that had been taken by the Government have been admirable.[2]

In pursuing his interest in the welfare of the working classes, the Prince encountered the same difficulty from the Whigs as he had from Sir Robert Peel. Lord John and his Home Secretary, Sir George Grey, were just as frightened of any incident in which the Prince might be involved as Peel and Graham had been. Prince Albert was asked, in April 1848, to take the chair at a meeting of the "Labourers' Friends Society", but Lord John opposed this, as he feared that trouble might arise. When Lord Ashley would not take "no" for an answer, the Prince approached the Prime Minister again. After quoting from Lord Ashley's reasons why he should attend after all, the Prince wrote:

I confess that holding the advantages of the step against the possible risk, that they very much overbalance it, but I conceive that one has moreover a *Duty* to perform towards the great mass of the working classes (and particularly at this moment), which will not allow one's yielding to the fear for some possible inconvenience . . . All this considered, I am inclined to adhere to my first resolution of attending the meeting and hope that you will think me right in doing so.[3]

The Prime Minister did not like the Prince to take this firm line in opposition to his wishes. In particular, he objected to the Prince speaking about his duty of attending. The Prince replied:

You have misunderstood me with regard to what I meant in speaking of my *Duty*; all I meant to say was that I feel it to be a duty, in these days not from fear of some risk or inconvenience to neglect doing what one can in showing one's interest and sympathy for the lower orders.—What I wish is: with your aid to come to the best decision upon the subject of my

---

[1] Prince Albert to Russell, 10 April 1848 (Royal Archives C.56.12).
[2] Prince Albert to Russell, 11 April 1848 (Royal Archives C.16.49).
[3] Prince Albert to Russell, 27 April 1848 (Royal Archives C.16.51).

presiding at the meeting; to do this, the *degree* of risk attending it ought to be ascertained as nearly as possible, and I should wish Sir George Grey to see Lord Ashley and to talk the matter over with him and with the Police Commissioners.—The real danger I conceive would be that the Chartists might attend and that some ill-disposed member of them might make a violent speech or propose a violent resolution, which might create confusion and be unseemly in my presence. On the other hand this is very unlikely and the general feeling would not countenance such a step.[1]

When one recalls the many attempts on the life of Queen Victoria—often when accompanied by the Prince—his insistence on appearing in public at a critical time is all the more noteworthy.

Finally, Lord John's flank was turned:

The book which you sent me certainly exhibits great disposition on the part of some mischievous folks to attack the Royal Family, but this rather furnishes me with a reason more for attending the meeting and thereby showing to those who are thus to be misguided that the Royal Family are *not* merely living upon the earnings of the people (as the publications try to represent) without caring for the poor labourer, but that they are anxious about their welfare and ready to co-operate in any scheme for the amelioration of their condition. We may possess those feelings and still the mass of people may be ignorant of it, because they have never heard it expressed to them or seen any tangible proof of it . . .[2]

After this it is not surprising that the Prince had his way. The Prime Minister took it in a good part and actually attended the meeting[3] at which the Prince presided. The Prince was particularly keen to go since the opening of the first great Model Lodging House was being celebrated. This was a project in which he had interested himself for some time.

The story of Prince Albert's vital part in the Great Exhibition of 1851 has often been told.[4] It is characteristic of the Prince that he was determined, only slightly more than a year after the revolutionary outbreak of 1848, to look ahead and to formulate long-term plans. The Prince attached special importance to keeping the Crown in touch with industry and the working classes. The Great Exhibition, among many other achievements, did just that:

It inaugurated a new relationship between the Court, the manufacturing and moneyed classes and most important the new mechanic class.[5]

---

[1] Prince Albert to Russell, 29 April 1848 (Royal Archives C.16.52).
[2] Ibid.
[3] Prince Albert to Russell, 17 May 1848 (Royal Archives C.16.54).
[4] In view of the vast literature on the subject I will refrain from adding to its detail.
[5] R. H. Mottram, Town Life, in "Early Victorian England", edited by G. M. Young, I, 222 ff.

With its newly-won prestige and popularity, the monarchy could all the more effectively fulfil its role of the strongest bulwark of the existing order against revolution.

In another way the Prince wanted the exhibition to be a manifestation of British achievement in peaceful competition with other nations, in contrast to Palmerston's pandering to nationalistic pride. The Prince thought that an aggressive foreign policy was a poor foundation for national unity, as he was later to tell his Prussian son-in-law.[1] The solid attainment of industrial progress in which all classes could join was a more lasting basis. The Great Exhibition did more for the preservation of law and order than troops and policemen:

> The great event brought to London thousands who perhaps had never seen a train before, people speaking the strange tongues of Lancashire and Durham, and the official reports of their behaviour as they flocked through museums and gardens are full of unconcealed pride. Not a flower was picked, not a picture smashed. And ten years before, the Londoner who now welcomed them had stood silent in the street to watch the guns going north to Lancashire.[2]

The exhibition was a much more convincing demonstration of the adaptability of British political institutions than the Palmerstonian frigates which terrorised Athens. It was thus quite logical from their anti-constitutional point of view that the Court Camarilla at Berlin should try to prevent the Prince of Prussia from accepting the invitation to come over to Britain for the Exhibition. The Gerlachs maintained that Britain was not sufficiently settled for the Prince of Prussia to visit it. This was a curious way of thanking the country which had sheltered that very prince when his life was not safe at home. The Prince and Princess of Prussia did, however, come. A strange leaflet was distributed in London during May 1851. Composed in atrocious German, it reads in translation:

> GERMAN PATRIOTS! THE PRINCE OF PRUSSIA is here, other tyrants are expected daily from the Continent. Should we not show to these traitors of their Fatherland how despised and hated they are in England, too? Could we not welcome them as Barclay's noble brewerymen welcomed the bloodthirsty Haynau? . . . Come on. Teutonia's sons and take revenge! . . .

The leaflet bore the signature: Democratischer Verein, May 8 1851.[3]

---

[1] See p. 248.   [2] R. H. Mottram, p. 212 (op. cit.).
[3] The Home Secretary, Sir G. Grey to Prince Albert, 12 May 1851, enclosing copy of the leaflet (Royal Archives F.24.146-7).

The Prince did not take the alleged origin of the "Democratic Association" seriously. He commented:

> My opinion is that the placard comes from the Russian or Austrian Embassy, who wish to be able to say that their apprehensions were not untrue and want to punish the Prince of Prussia for his coming here against the wish of the reactionary governments.[1]

The Russian Ambassador, Brunnow, went so far as to prevent the Diplomatic Corps from presenting an address to the Queen on the opening of the Exhibition.

The Crystal Palace was a vindication of Free Trade. It sounded the death-knell of Protection. It was a monument of the Queen's and the Prince's devotion to the ideas of Sir Robert Peel, who had helped to prepare the exhibition but did not live to see its triumph.

The hope that the Great Exhibition would usher in a long period of peace in Europe was doomed to disappointment. Three years later many of the nations which exhibited in the Crystal Palace were at war. The Exhibition was more successful in its limited aim of stabilising the domestic situation in Britain than of leading a world crusade for peace. There was one recurrent internal British problem which the Great Exhibition did not touch, though its methods and ideas also had some application to it, that of Ireland.

Prince Albert did not feel any more moral qualms about the title of the English Crown to Ireland than the Queen or English opinion in general. Denying the justification of Irish national aspirations he failed to understand the intensity of Irish hatred for the English conqueror. It was unfortunate that by the time the Prince started taking a serious interest in the Irish question under the influence of the events of 1848, a reasonable solution had become even more difficult. By 1848 the stock ideas of the Prince, economic improvement, model housing and the like, were no longer sufficient to deal with Ireland. For shortly before, the radical Young Ireland movement of O'Brien and Mitchel had triumphed over the more moderate older generation of O'Connell. As Sir Llewellyn Woodward said, "They made it almost impossible for any British government to cure Irish discontent by kindness."[2] Prince Albert was aware of the seriousness and of the international ramifications of the Irish question, without realising all the implications of the victory of the Young Ireland movement over the ideas of O'Connell. Early in April 1848,

---

[1] Note by Prince Albert (Royal Archives F.24.146).
[2] Sir Llewellyn Woodward, "The Age of Reform", 335.

when there was news from Ireland of an impending rebellion and of an appeal for French help, he wrote to the Prime Minister:

> The affairs of Ireland give us a great deal of anxiety the more we think of them. I hope that, whatever you may find it possible to do for that Country will be done soon, in order that the unfortunate motto of 1848: "trop tard" may not apply to us likewise. The Lord Lieutenant ought not to postpone the issue of a proclamation setting forth the evil intentions of the agitators, the certain misery which their success must bring upon Ireland and the readiness on the part of the Government to listen to any complaint and to take any proposition for the amelioration of Ireland into their most serious consideration; that the way of petition is open to the Queen and to Parliament and that Parliament has at all times bestowed the greatest care and attention on the investigation of any plan of improvement . . .[1]

No appeal to sweet reasonableness could stop the insurrection of O'Brien, fired by the news of the continental revolutions, though disappointed by the refusal of the French revolutionary régime to help. The Irish believed in their national aspiration as much as the Germans of Holstein or the Italians of Lombardy.

The Prince also misjudged the situation in Ireland when he supported Lord John's plan in 1847 to abolish the Lord Lieutenancy in Dublin. Irish opinion regarded it as an attempt to destroy the last "phantom of independence". It is true that the English government had some sound technical reasons for reorganising the conduct of Irish affairs. With improving communications, the Lord Lieutenant at Dublin was gradually losing some of his independence from London and becoming increasingly the instrument for the execution of orders from the Cabinet transmitted by the Irish Secretary. It was proposed to recall Lord Clarendon, the Lord Lieutenant, from Dublin, and to ask him to organise a new department under a fully-fledged Secretary of State for Ireland. Prince Albert realised that the planned change would need careful handling:

> It is very desirable that the abolition of the Lord Lieutenancy of Ireland should in the mind of the Irish not be considered as a degradation, but as an elevation, not as a sinking to the level of a mere province, but as an admission to equality with England and Scotland. Nothing will tend more to accomplish this, than a visit of the Sovereign in Person after the departure of his representative and the providing of means for the occasional residence of the Sovereign in Ireland for the future. The measure would thereby lose all that could make it offensive to the feelings of the Irish and ought on the contrary to be rendered popular amongst them. The chief opposition which is to be expected to the abolition of the

---

[1] Prince Albert to Russell, 5 April 1848 (Royal Archives C.16.46).

Lieutenancy will come from Dublin, which town must naturally dread the loss of the Court, which now forms its centre of life and is the main support and customer of the Dublin trades people. Would it not be the best way of conciliating this interest, which may justly consider itself as injured, to substitute for the mock Court which leaves Dublin a part or branch of the real one and occasionally that Court itself?[1]

The Prince, in advocating occasional Court residence in Ireland, was foreshadowing, on a small scale, the modern Court occasionally visiting various parts of the Commonwealth just over a century later. Actually, the scheme for abolishing the Lord Lieutenancy had to be dropped owing to English and Irish opposition.

The Queen and the Prince visited Ireland in August 1849. They were received with enthusiasm. But the situation had reached a stage where no radical improvement in the atmosphere could be expected from a royal visit. The following year tension in Ireland was to be increased by a reminder of the difficulties under which the Catholic Church laboured in the United Kingdom.

(ii)

The revolutionary era of 1848 was a time of intense religious passion in England. The tension, which elsewhere led to the overthrow of governments, in England found one outlet in some of the bitterest religious strife which the country had seen for some time. The original issue was the reform of the Church of England. But thanks to the peculiar nature of the attack on the existing order, it ended as a contest between the Church of England and Rome. The Oxford Movement led by men like Newman, Keble and Pusey set out to purify the Church of England by re-emphasising its orthodoxy and catholicity, by raising the standard of services and by fighting heterodoxy and liberalism. The sweeping and merciless criticism found in the Oxford tracts edited by W. G. Ward was regarded by many in authority, including the Bishop of Oxford, Dr. Wilberforce, as a challenge to the episcopal bench. This created a dilemma for the Oxford reformers. They had always emphasised the importance of the visible Church and the duty of obedience to its rulers. As a result of their own doctrines, they were denied an appeal to their own biblical interpretation on which they might, like Luther and Wesley, have founded their independence of existing church authority. Caught in the maze of their own dogmas,

[1] Memorandum by Prince Albert, 26 September 1847, submitted to the Prime Minister (Royal Archives C.16.18).

some capitulated. Many, like Newman, left the apparently unsatisfactory half-way house and made their submission to Rome. The
Oxford reform movement thus became tainted with the suspicion
of "Popery".

The Prince, like the Queen and the Prime Minister, came into
conflict with the Oxford Movement. Brought up as a Lutheran, the
Prince was bound to resent the Tractarians' emphasis on the catholicism of the Church of England and their rejection of any protestant
tradition. The Prince saw the Church of England as part of the
great movement of the Reformation. Furthermore, he suspected the
Tractarians of wishing to go beyond a legitimate non-Roman
catholicism by paving the way for a reconciliation with Rome. The
Tractarians, on the other hand, objected to the Prince's sympathies
for Presbyterianism, which was one of the links binding him to
Scotland. It was even put about that the Prince was not a good
Christian, or at any rate not a good Churchman. To the German
Protestant—whether he was a Lutheran or a Calvinist—the divided
Church Visible could not play as important a part as the single State
Church did for the English non-Catholic; for political disunity had
its counterpart in the religious sphere.

The charges levelled against Prince Albert in England reflect the
religious tension of the day. The Prince was certainly a believing and
practising Christian. His moral perfectionism may, however, have
prevented him from fully accepting the Christian theory of redemp-
tion. He was not a worse churchman for being identified with the
"Broad Church" Movement which was the greatest object of Tractarian abhorrence.

The Broad Church Movement sought to counter not only the
Tractarians on the right, but also the Evangelicals—like Lord Ashley
—on the left. It was a via media which appealed to the Prince. With
his support Lord John, as a liberal churchman, made several appointments to the episcopal bench of men not connected with either
extreme. Among these were Dr. James Prince Lee and Dr. Hampden
who were elevated to the sees of Manchester and Hereford. Hampden was one of the pioneers of biblical criticism in England and
had emphasised the inferiority of a fallible church authority to
the infallibility of the Bible. This outlook was as agreeable to the
Protestantism of Prince Albert as it was irksome to the High Church
Party.

The new nominees were accused of unsound views by several
bishops belonging to the High Church Party. In Dr. Hampden's

case, the bishops pointed to his having been deprived, while Professor of Divinity at Oxford, of the right to assist in the appointment of select preachers owing to unorthodox views put forward in his lectures. The Prince approved wholeheartedly of Lord John's rejection of the bishops' criticism as an interference with the right of the State to make appointments. He congratulated the Prime Minister on his firmness:

> The Queen wishes me to acknowledge your letter of yesterday respecting Dr. Hampden. She quite approves of your letter to the Bishops which takes a strong constitutional ground and although the violent Party in the Church will visit you with their resentment, the Queen thinks your recommendation will prove to do good to the Church.[1]

The controversy over Dr. Hampden's appointment to the see of Hereford estranged the Prince from Dr. Wilberforce, the Bishop of Oxford, who had earlier been his chaplain. When Dr. Wilberforce took his seat on the episcopal bench in 1845, the Prince had outlined to him his views on the position of a Bishop in the House of Lords. He had exhorted him to give general support to the Queen's Government of the day. Dr. Wilberforce now took a prominent part against the government by questioning Dr. Hampden's appointment. With twelve of his colleagues, including Dr. Phillpotts, Bishop of Exeter, he signed a petition asking for the trial of Dr. Hampden by the Court of Arches. When he also approached the Prime Minister and the Prince's Private Secretary, George Anson, the Prince reacted strongly. He asked his Private Secretary to express his displeasure to his former Chaplain.[2] He condemned the Protesters' proposal that a tribunal of bishops should examine the soundness of their prospective colleague's theological views. The Prince rejected "a tribunal composed of accusers to decide upon a point of theological controversy according to their own peculiar opinions". He went on:

> ... the history of the Christian Church in all parts of the globe shows the objectionable nature of such judgments of divines upon others on points of doctrine. Why! The greatest crimes and abominations bringing disgrace upon the name of Christianity have been perpetrated in all times by such Councils of Divines, and all under the plea of maintaining purity of faith.[3]

There then followed a long enumeration of acts of persecution beginning with the Council of Nicaea and ending up with Calvin burning Servetus.

---

[1] Prince Albert to Russell, 5 December 1847 (Royal Archives C.16.29).
[2] Prince Albert to Anson, 18 December 1847 (Royal Archives C.55.23).
[3] Ibid.

If the spirit of the times would allow of it, the Bishop of Exeter might not be disinclined to have Hampden burnt. Had we an infallible Pope we might say: let him decide and we shall abide by his inspired judgment, but we have to do with a majority and a minority in a given Commission who are to decide according to their opinion upon the doctrine of the Established Church.[1]

There followed a dig at the Oxford Movement:

Is the Church agreed upon her own doctrines? Have we not seen Clergymen maintain that they might hold all the Roman Catholic doctrines and remain with sincerity in our Church, whilst she boasts of being *protestant*? Have we not seen her divided and perplexed upon the most trivial questions: whether the Clergyman is to preach in a white or a black gown etc. etc.?[2]

The Prince also instructed Anson to communicate a memorandum of his to the Bishop of Oxford. The Bishop was severely reprimanded for having protested against Dr. Hampden's appointment:

Did he [the Bishop of Oxford] think a Minister would expose himself and his Sovereign to the just charge of making appointments without due consideration? He calls the Protest a *private* one, but was it not immediately seen in all the newspapers and sent in, by those who had taken this private step?

The doctrine that it is the duty of the Bishops to head every insurrectionary movement in the Church is monstrous, and the admission that the consequence of the Bishops following the example of the Bishop of Norwich[3] would have been a large secession to Rome a fearful one.

It was then in order to accommodate within the Church persons who otherwise would have turned to Rome that the Bishops thought it necessary to run down one of their fellow clergymen and to wage war upon the Minister of the Crown and the Sovereign, bringing into jeopardy the law of supremacy and exposing the Church to a schism. . . .

The true motive for his action is however contained in the letter in the passage "what could I have done if after voting in Convocation [at Oxford University] with the great body of the Clergy against Dr. Hampden's soundness of old, I had now been suddenly satisfied". The Bishop will know best whether at that time *of old* when he took part in the movement it was a Tractarian move or not.[4]

The intervention of the Prince may well have contributed to the Bishop of Oxford's withdrawal from the protest.

The threat by the Dean of Hereford, Dr. Merewether, to prevent

[1] Prince Albert to Anson, 18 December 1847 (Royal Archives C.55.23).
[2] Ibid.
[3] Edward Stanley, a bishop of liberal views particularly disliked by the High Church.
[4] Memorandum by Prince Albert (communicated to the Bishop of Oxford by Anson), undated (Royal Archives C.55.42).

Dr. Hampden's election by the Chapter, incurred the Prince's wrath and he was delighted with the Prime Minister's terse answer to the Dean.[1] He considered the Dean's action "the climax of the bigoted warfare about Dr. Hampden".[2] He asked the Prime Minister to consider prosecuting Dr. Merewether:

... Dr. Hampden has been elected at Hereford, but the Dean's behaviour has been such that I think you can hardly let it pass unnoticed. The inconvenience and impolicy of raising a man like him to the honour of Martyrdom I fully admit, but on the other hand the example of resistance to the law remaining unpunished might induce others at the next opportunity to set the authority of the Crown at defiance.[3]

Early in January 1848 the Prince summed up the crisis:

The storm about Dr. Hampden is subsiding, but the impression left behind is a very deep one. The public generally is indignant at the spirit of persecution which the thirteen Bishops and the High Church Party have shown. I have been told by a Clergyman of the "Low Church" Party that the Tractarians had prepared the whole move for Dr. Lee, but when Hampden appeared who was so much better game for them, they changed their aim and assailed him. Their tactics are clever: three points can, if urged against a Divine, stop his road to the Mitre: 1. Want of learning; 2. unsoundness of doctrine; 3. immoral life. The Tractarians have reason to dread both Lee and Hampden as friends of inquiry and as liberal Churchmen ... In Lee's case, they got a man of the name of Gutteridge to accuse him of different vices, then the whole party and many Bishops cry out and say: this is most likely a *very* unjust accusation, but for the peace of the Church and the honour of the Mitre there must be an investigation in order that Dr. Lee may justify himself before the world before he can be consecrated ... Dr. Lee saw himself obliged (though it was most repugnant to his charitable and truly christian feelings) to prosecute his reviler for a libel in the Court of Queen's Bench. Everybody knows the unpleasant nature of such a trial and that, even if successful,[4] the prosecutor is damaged in public opinion. The same course exactly was taken in the case of Hampden ... The Bishop of Oxford is the one who has damaged himself most. Lord Aberdeen told me: I am only sorry for one, and that is the Bishop of Oxford.[5]

After all this religious strife the Prince considered Lord John's proposal in April 1850 for a commission to inquire into the discipline, state and revenues of the Universities[6] to be singularly ill-timed. The

---

[1] The letter only contained one sentence: "I have had the honour to receive your letter ... in which you intimate to me your intention of violating the law." (Walpole, Russell, I, 480).

[2] Prince Albert to Russell, 27 December 1847 (Royal Archives C.16.32).

[3] Prince Albert to Russell, 30 December 1847 (Royal Archives C.16.33).

[4] The charges were found to be baseless.

[5] Memorandum by Prince Albert, 7 January 1848 (Royal Archives C.55.67).

[6] See Morley, "Life of Gladstone", I, 496 ff.

Prince was affected personally as Chancellor of Cambridge University, an office in which he had initiated an extensive reorganisation of the whole curriculum. He thought the proposal would result in "the enmity of vested and strong interests and further ferment in the Church".[1] He contacted his opposite number at Oxford, the Duke of Wellington. Early in May he reported to the Prime Minister:

> I am afraid the opposition will be very decided. I tried to pacify the Duke yesterday, who is very willing to make the best of matters, but feels like myself the embarrassment of the situation, having urged reforms and carried them and finding the Universities now attacked notwithstanding.[2]

The Prince did his best to smooth the rough edges. He proposed that the Universities should be given a chance to collect the requisite information voluntarily themselves and so to avoid inquiry at the hands of a Royal Commission,[3] but the Prime Minister remained firm. The Prince then made a last appeal to Lord John:

> As a politician in Parliament you would certainly gain strength by taking a more antagonistic line against the opponents of Reform in the University, but as representing the Crown I hope you will maintain that attitude of "*paternal solicitude*" towards the Universities which becomes it.[4]

The Commission's report was published in 1852 and an erstwhile opponent, Gladstone, carried out its recommendations as a member of the Aberdeen government. The representative principle was strengthened and, to Pusey's horror, religious tests were partially abolished at Oxford and Cambridge. In spite of his opposition to the Tractarians, the Prince's attitude in this question of university reform shows that he did not want to carry the war into the enemy's camp. He disliked stirring up controversy where it could possibly be avoided.

Lord John did not heed the Prince's exhortation to moderation in religious affairs and soon precipitated a crisis which led to the resignation of his government. In September 1850 the Pope created twelve territorial sees for England and Wales and appointed Dr. Wiseman Archbishop of Westminster. The Pope had some reason for expecting that the English government would not oppose these steps. The creation of a Catholic Archbishopric had been mooted for some time and Lord Minto did not express any disapproval of it during his mission to Rome in the winter of 1847-8. However, the

[1] Prince Albert to Russell, 23 April 1850 (Royal Archives C.17.60).
[2] Prince Albert to Russell, 2 May 1850 (Royal Archives C.17.62).
[3] Prince Albert to Russell, 3 May 1850 (Royal Archives C.17.64).
[4] Prince Albert to Russell, 8 May 1850 (Royal Archives C.17.65).

situation was badly handled by Cardinal Wiseman. He issued a
pastoral letter whose tone was bound to be irksome to Anglican
ears. In any case the atmosphere was tense, owing to the long list
of Tractarian submissions to the Church of Rome. To an excited
public, the Pope's step could only appear as a further instalment of
a systematic attempt to reconvert England.

The Prime Minister decided to strike. He was on edge after the
constant bickerings between Windsor and Broadlands. His government was weakened by the death of Sir Robert Peel and dependent
on a precarious and heterogeneous majority. He thought he could
utilise the vigorous anti-Papal feeling in the country to strengthen
his government so that he could crush all opposition. An additional
advantage to him was that he could deal the Puseyites a blow at the
same time. In a violently partisan letter to the Bishop of Durham,
he not only condemned the Pope's action in the severest terms, but
also spoke of "the unworthy sons of the Church of England" who
indulged in the "mummeries of superstition".[1] This declaration of
war against what he termed the "Papal Aggression" widened the
breach which it should have been the Prime Minister's duty to try
to heal. Lord John's nice tactical calculation completely miscarried.
The new policy weakened his support, particularly among the Irish,
and it prevented the accession of the Peelites to his government for
which he had been striving.

The Prince's strong anti-Catholicism could not be doubted and he
felt just as bitter as Lord John about the Tractarians. But he had a
far clearer appreciation of the endless harm this unnecessary em-
bitterment of the whole issue was bound to bring with it. He thus
began to work hard for a settlement. He asked the government to
postpone its Ecclesiastical Titles Bill, which prohibited the establishment of Roman Catholic sees and stimulated the forfeiture to the
Crown of money willed to persons holding prohibited titles. He first
wanted an effort to be made to get the Holy See to revoke its
measures. In this he advised caution. He objected to contacts by
unofficial agents who might be indiscreet. He criticised the choice
of Lord Arundel, the heir of the Duke of Norfolk, who had been
proposed for a mission to Rome:

> Lord Arundel is very weak minded and entirely in the hands of the
> Jesuits, who are in fact our opponents, and in dealing with whom the
> utmost care and circumspection is required: any secret transaction with

---

[1] Russell to Dr. Maltby, Bishop of Durham, one of the Prime Minister's closest
advisers on church affairs, 4 November 1850 (Walpole, Russell, II, 120).

the Pope may be construed into a symptom of weakness on our part: and if by any indiscretion it should transpire that the Government was tampering with Rome, it would rouse great public indignation . . .[1]

He preferred that an official agent be sent:

If . . . the Pope really be anxious for a reconciliation, why should not an official agent go to Rome and declare on the part of the Government: that they consider the effect of the last Bull as most injurious to the position and well-being of the Roman Catholics themselves in the United Kingdom; that it will be very difficult for the Government to protect them from new measures of restriction which Parliament will be likely to demand: that the hostility of the Protestants has been roused to an extraordinary height and that nothing, in the opinion of the Government, will allay it, but the revocation of the late Bull; that they understand the revocation of such Bulls, having reference to discipline only, to have often taken place in other countries under similar circumstances, and that they put it to the Pope, whether he will not best consider his own interests in taking this step.[2]

The Prince thought that the Government could not lose anything by this action, and even if the mission failed, it would have the advantage of strengthening its parliamentary case. When Lord John reacted favourably to the suggestion, the Prince elaborated the tactics which were to be followed at the Vatican:

The great object . . . ought . . . to be: to produce the impression on the Pope that the Government is well meaning and kindly disposed towards the Catholics, but determined to uphold the dignity and independence of this Country in Church and State. *No negotiation* should therefore be entered into . . . The . . . object [was] to inspire the Vatican with dread of the determination of the Government and with confidence in its intentions . . .[3]

He advocated that steps should be taken to secure the support of some of the Catholic Powers:

Austria is unfortunately hostile to us and France not to be trusted in any way. It struck me, however, that a personal letter from the King of the Belgians to the Pope might be a desirable auxiliary. The King has great influence at Rome from the support he has always given to the Hierarchy in Belgium against the attacks of the liberal party, and his advice would have the more weight, as he can speak from his own knowledge and experience of the public feeling in England and the nature of British institutions . . .[4]

The Prince was disappointed when Lord John refused to delay the

[1] Prince Albert to Russell, 11 January 1851 (Royal Archives C.19.1).
[2] Ibid.
[3] Prince Albert to Russell, 12 January 1851 (Royal Archives C.19.2).
[4] Ibid.

tabling of the Ecclesiastical Titles Bill in order to give negotiations a chance.[1] Palmerston in fact poured cold water on the suggestion of approaching the Vatican.[2] There was, indeed, very little the British Government could offer the Pope. He was being asked to make a concession in return for possible rather shadowy future benefits. But the Cabinet did agree that feelers should be put out through the British Ambassador in Paris, Lord Normanby, to get the Pope to withdraw Cardinal Wiseman from England.[3]

The Ecclesiastical Titles Bill proposed by Lord John struck the Prince as "simple and to the purpose". The Prince wrote to the Prime Minister, however, that he

> could not help being struck . . . by the Clause excepting the Scotch Bishops from its operation who in fact stand entirely in the same position as the Roman Catholic Bishops, viz: assuming territorial titles not derived from the Crown and being rival to the Established Church of the Country.[4]

The Prime Minister immediately had the Clause removed. It was replaced by one about the introduction of bulls.[5]

The Ecclesiastical Titles Bill was launched on its parliamentary career by an impressive majority, but the government was beaten soon afterwards on the question of the county franchise, whereupon Lord John resigned, on 22 February 1851. The Papal Bill now proved the major stumbling block to the formation of a new government by making a Whig–Peelite coalition impossible. Lord Aberdeen, Sir James Graham and Mr. Gladstone, the most prominent followers of the late Sir Robert Peel, who were agreed about so little else, were at any rate united in their dislike of penal measures against Catholics which, they thought, would make Ireland ungovernable. On the other hand neither the Whigs nor the Peelites—nor indeed the Radicals or the Irish—were prepared to allow a Tory Government to reintroduce protection, even partially. Lord Stanley, the leader of the Protectionists, who was asked by the Queen to form a new government, therefore declined to do so until all other combinations had been attempted. The Whigs and Peelites were tried, and after their inability to agree Lord Stanley was summoned again, but failed to form a government. The Queen and the Prince worked hard to solve the crisis and gave Lord Stanley every chance, however much they disapproved of his protectionist ideas. Following a

[1] Prince Albert to Russell, 16 January 1851 (Royal Archives C.19.4).
[2] Palmerston to the Queen, 21 January 1851 (Royal Archives C.51.114).
[3] Russell to the Queen, 17 January 1851 (Royal Archives C.51.113).
[4] Prince Albert to Russell, 16 January 1851 (Royal Archives C.19.4).
[5] Russell to the Queen, 17 January 1851 (Royal Archives C.51.113).

conversation between Baron Stockmar and Lord Aberdeen on 27 February,[1] the Prince proposed to Lord John Russell that the Crown should pause in its efforts to find another government until the various party leaders had made their explanations in Parliament on the following day. The Prince asked Lord John whether he saw any constitutional objections to this procedure.[2] Lord John replied that he first wished to consult his former colleagues, but he thought that

> the course proposed is obviously liable to the objection that it leaves to the House of Commons an initiative which belongs to the Crown . . .[3]

He again wrote on the following day:

> . . . I am very glad to hear that the Queen has sent for the Duke of Wellington, and not sorry that he is at Strathfieldsaye. It will be an excellent reason for the Queen's not sending for anyone today. I own that without some such reason I was afraid that the prerogative of the Crown might pass to the House of Commons; a serious step in the road to democracy . . .[4]

The Prince now proposed that the Whigs and the Peelites should join forces immediately, "leaving the Papal measure an *open question*, allowing Lord John to bring it forward and Sir James Graham to oppose it".[5] Lord Lansdowne, who was one of the "elder statesmen" consulted by the Queen and her husband, demurred to this:

> . . . a government newly composed, speaking and voting against each other on the first question which engaged their attention, would present itself to the public under the most unfavourable aspect.[6]

At the same time, Lord Lansdowne made a suggestion for overcoming the crisis:

> . . . the best, if not the only mode of meeting the difficulty would be for the persons recently composing the Government to remain in for a time precisely as they are, but avowing distinctly that they only so remained in the confident expectation of one of the bars to its reconstruction being speedily removed, whilst no time should be lost in providing for that fortunate contingency, by such confidential communications taking place, and prospective arrangements being considered, as might then insure a settlement on a broader and firmer basis.[7]

---

[1] Memorandum by Baron Stockmar, 27 February 1851 (Royal Archives C.46.72).
[2] Prince Albert to Russell, 27 February 1851 (Royal Archives C.46.75).
[3] Russell to Prince Albert, 27 February 1851 (Royal Archives C.46.78).
[4] Russell to Prince Albert, 28 February 1851 (Royal Archives C.46.89).
[5] Memorandum by Prince Albert, 1 March 1851 (Martin, II, 350 ff.).
[6] Memorandum by Lord Lansdowne, submitted to the Queen, presumably of 1 March 1851 (Royal Archives C.46.111).
[7] Ibid.

The crisis was finally solved—to the extent that it was capable of solution—by the Duke of Wellington. When he saw the Queen and her husband, he asked

> whether "Her Majesty had any reason to be dissatisfied with Lord John Russell's Government" and on being assured by the Queen of the contrary, he said: "very well then, as they are in *possession* it will be the easiest thing to leave them there". We [the Queen and the Prince] then explained that it could hardly be said that the Whigs were in possession, that Lord John had distinctly stated . . . in the House of Commons that there was *no* government at the time.[1]

The Prince was not very satisfied with the Duke's mastery of the details of the situation:

> . . . The Duke . . . had tried to make himself acquainted with the Debate of yesterday since his return to town, but appeared hardly to have studied all the points which are to be taken into consideration. One point he was very strong upon viz. that the Papal Aggression Bill ought to be gone on with, it might be modified . . . but a Bill must be persevered in.[2]

The Duke's advice was followed. Lord John returned with his old government. The Cabinet dropped most of the clauses of the Ecclesiastical Titles Bill, which was passed in its mutilated form and almost immediately consigned to oblivion.

The Lord Lieutenant of Ireland, Lord Clarendon, was delighted about the omission of the clauses which would have hit Ireland most. He wrote to Lord John:

> I am very glad to learn the decision of the Cabinet. Clause 2 and 3[3] were not worth a religious Civil War, and to judge from the present state of exasperation, things would have taken a bad turn here long before the Bill could have been passed.
>
> The only formidable resistance to the measure has proceeded from Ireland. This need not, I think, have been the case, if matters had been better managed, and if by adopting, even at the eleventh hour, the Solicitor-General's[4] suggestions the long established practice of the Irish Roman Catholic Church had been less interfered with. The Papal Aggression might then have been resisted as far as Ireland was concerned, to any extent in England, for there is no real sympathy between English and Irish Catholics. The Irish Clergy have a particular hatred of Wiseman and the laity secretly delight in any check given to the Pope. Hughes [the Solicitor-General for Ireland] himself told me there *ought* to be

---

[1] Memorandum by Prince Albert, 1 March 1851 (Royal Archives C.46.105).
[2] Ibid.
[3] These clauses dealt with the introduction of bulls and with the confiscation of money willed to persons holding prohibited titles.
[4] Henry George Hughes, an Irish barrister, Solicitor-General for Ireland from 1850 to 1852.

8⁰

stringent Legislation in England, and in order to facilitate it, he wished for the least possible interference with Ireland.

When, however, it appeared that the Bill would be more severe in its operation here than in England, the excitement it raised would hardly have been stopped by excluding Ireland, for the Clergy would have made it a point of honour to persevere in *giving a lesson* to the Government.[1]

The Prime Minister passed on the letter to the Queen without enthusiasm:

> Lord Clarendon's letter will shew his view of the state of Ireland—others think that this view is much exaggerated, and in truth, except in [some] instances, the Bill would not have affected Ireland. But the Irish are so ready to take up the least cause of offence, and so fond of meetings and declamation that in the progress of the Bill, the discontent might have assumed a most unpleasant if not a formidable shape.[2]

The Prime Minister remembered too late that Ireland still belonged to the United Kingdom. His handling of "Papal Aggression" did not enhance his reputation and it was a much weakened government which returned to power. A number of questions in which the Prime Minister could not count on a united Cabinet or on a dependable parliamentary majority were becoming acute, particularly those of electoral reform and of defence.

(iii)

In February 1851 Lord John had on his own authority given a promise to the House of Commons that a measure of electoral reform would be introduced. The Prince was not happy about Lord John's scheme. The detailed proposal of the Prime Minister in August 1851 foresaw transfer of representation from the smallest boroughs to the more populous areas and the reduction of the rateable value required for the franchise. The Prime Minister also planned the formation of various trades and professions into guilds whose members should have certain limited voting rights in the borough in which they resided. The Cabinet was divided; Lord Lansdowne and Lord Palmerston were against the extension of the franchise and the reform proposals were an additional obstacle to any Peelites joining the government. In September, Sir James Graham declined an invitation from the Prime Minister to enter the Cabinet. Prince Albert thought that this was due not only to his objection to Palmerston's tenure of the Foreign Office, but also to a fear of being involved in greater concessions to the reform party than he was pre-

[1] Clarendon to Russell, 7 March 1851 (Royal Archives C.52.30).
[2] Lord John Russell to the Queen, 8 March 1851 (Royal Archives C.52.29).

pared to make.[1] Although the dreaded secret ballot was not part of Lord John's proposal, Sir James evidently felt that the government might be forced to accept it once they were fully launched on their reform schemes. Commenting on Sir James's letter to the Prime Minister declining office, the Prince wrote to Lord John:

> What he says about the Ballot he stated to me in the strongest terms already last spring . . . he thought that without determined firmness upon that point on the part of the Queen's Government, the institutions of the country would run most serious risk. He may have been further strengthened in his apprehension if what the "Daily News" propounds is the real feeling of the Reform Party. I find it declared in a leading article . . . that "the very first principle of this determination (not to be bought off) should be: *no extension of the Franchise without the Ballot.*" [2]

The press was, indeed, causing considerable harm:

> I was very much surprised and annoyed to see your plan debated between the "Daily News" and the "Globe". The "Daily News" raises already a general outcry against it and misrepresents it as a scheme for introducing *indirect* elections, borrowed from the absolutist governments of the Continent! You must absolutely gag your organ, the "Globe", if you mean to secure the success of your measure by bringing it *intact* before the House of Commons. The replies of the "Globe" seem to have made matters worse.[3]

Electoral reform was one of the few topics on which Lord John felt strongly. Palmerston's resignation weakened the opposition to it in the Cabinet and this consideration may well have contributed to his decision to remove him. Once more the Prince counselled moderation. He wrote to the Prime Minister in the middle of January 1852:

> A measure "for the extension of the suffrage", having been promised by the Government, will have to be introduced. But we are in that peculiarly fortunate situation that no particular measure has been promised, nor does there exist any excitement in the country as to its nature, nor any consequent pressure from without on the Government. Your hands are then quite free to prepare such a measure as will meet with the greatest amount of support, and the Crown has an interest, which is identical with the best interests of the Country, that *no more* changes should be proposed by the Government than there is a fair probability of being accepted by Parliament, in order not to produce that state of things which you describe . . . as dangerous to the Crown viz. "if the question of the suffrage and its attendant propositions of ballot and short parliaments were made the topic of a general election".[4]

---

[1] Prince Albert to Russell, 27 September 1851 (Royal Archives C.19.32).
[2] Ibid.
[3] Ibid.
[4] Prince Albert to Russell, 13 January 1852 (Royal Archives C.19.36).

The following month, Lord John was able to introduce a Reform Bill, which was a modified form of his original proposals. But on 20 February 1852, he was himself defeated on another question and resigned. Lord Palmerston, who had always taken a strong interest in national defence, found the government's scheme for reorganising the local militia insufficient. He carried an amendment to compel militiamen to serve in any part of the country. Sir James Graham, who was no friend of Palmerston's, was fair enough to write to Baron Stockmar that "on the merits of the question respecting the Militia, Palmerston has the best of it". He left the chamber without voting as he could not make up his mind "to disparage the Queen's Government at the instance of the new Opposition Leader".[1] With regard to this question, Prince Albert was much closer to Lord Palmerston than to Lord John. The Prince had for years stressed the importance of national preparedness and opposed reductions in the armed forces. Similarly, his letter about electoral reform in January would have pleased Palmerston. Thus soon after Lord John had at last acceded to the Court's wishes in dismissing Palmerston, the expelled Foreign Secretary was voicing its ideas—on defence and reform—far better than the Prime Minister. In spite of that, Lord John's defeat was naturally a great blow to the Court, which was left at the mercy of its two main aversions, Lord Palmerston and Lord Derby (as Lord Stanley had in the meantime become). A painful period of readjustment began for the political life of the country in general and for the Court in particular, bringing in its train results which nobody would have forecast on that day in February 1852 when Lord John was finally beaten.

[1] Graham to Stockmar 20 February 1852 (Royal Archives C.27.1).

PART THREE

Hope and Disappointment

1852–1861

Chapter Ten

PARTY CONFUSION

(i)

WHEN the Queen and the Prince were heartened by Palmerston's fall in December 1851, they did not anticipate that the late Foreign Secretary would be able to set off a chain of events which would bring into power a Protectionist Government. The Court disliked Palmerston, but possibly dreaded the prospect of Derby in office even more. In view of the obvious collapse of Whig unity, a Protectionist government was, however, inevitable, although it was bound to find itself a minority in the House of Commons and would thus be dependent on the toleration of the majority. As long as the anti-Protectionists did not form a united front, as long as the Peelites continued to nurse their idiosyncrasies and as long as Lord John and Palmerston would not speak to each other, there was nothing to be done but to let the Protectionists reign, even if they could not rule.

It was worrying for the Court to have a change of government at the very time when Europe was unsettled by Louis Napoleon's *coup d'état* and Britain's defences needed strengthening. The connection of events was not, however, a fortuitous one. The Bonapartist stroke had been the occasion of Palmerston's fall and it provided the background for the defeat of the government over the militia question. At first glance, the Court might seem to have only itself to blame, with its dislike of Palmerston. While the Court was pleased about Palmerston's removal from the Foreign Office, it had always been in favour of his transfer rather than his dismissal. If the Queen and the Prince had been consulted before Lord John acted, which they were not, they would have advised using the opportunity to shunt him to a quiet siding. It is true that Lord John offered Palmerston the Lord Lieutenancy of Ireland, but only as an afterthought and in circumstances which made it practically impossible for the ex-Foreign Secretary to accept. On the other hand, if the Court and some of the senior ministers—such as Lord Lansdowne—had been taken into the Prime Minister's confidence at an early stage, the incident might have yielded the desired result without leading to the fall of the government.

The majority of the votes which had brought down Lord John had been Protectionist and in accordance with constitutional usage the burden of forming the new government should fall in the first instance on Lord Derby. This was certainly Prince Albert's view, but the Queen for a time seems to have held out against it. For the first time since 1841 the Queen challenged her husband's view on an important political question. She called on Baron Stockmar for his opinion. The man who had been the Prince's political mentor during his early days in Britain was becoming increasingly the adviser of the Queen rather than of her husband. During his intermittent stays in the country, Stockmar occasionally became the rival of his old pupil.

On the day of the fateful division, 20 February 1852, Buckingham Palace followed attentively every move on the parliamentary chessboard. Even before the division had taken place, the Court had little hope that the Government would survive. In this position of uncertainty, the Queen approached Baron Stockmar:

> I send you *my* impressions and feelings on the present critical state of *our own* affairs and I hope you will consider them and give me *your* opinion. I can't *say how* strongly I feel the danger I speak of.[1]

The memorandum[2] reveals clearly the difficulties the Queen had in subordinating her own strong personal views to the dictates of strict impartiality towards all political parties exacted by constitutional government. It also shows how seriously she took her responsibilities:

> I cannot resist putting *down* a few hasty remarks on the present critical state of the government.
>
> In ordinary cases when a government is turned out by another party, that party is called upon to form another government, but I think that the state of the country and the state of Europe—threatening in every direction—must be *first* considered. This country is flourishing and prosperous, which is an immense blessing. If, however, a protectionist government comes in, or tries to do so, maintaining protection, I feel *convinced* the country will become *excited* so that there will be commotions; the manufacturing districts and the towns never *can* and *will* permit any return to protection and the *trial* I consider one *far* too dangerous to undertake or to wish trying—for we are in the midst of measures of the utmost importance for the safety of the country, and the ministerial crisis, without any of these important measures provided for, which place us in a weak and defenceless position and exposes us to the very dangers we are trying to avoid. France seeing us divided and weak, would readily *press all* the

---

[1] The Queen to Stockmar, 20 February 1852 (Royal Archives C.27.4).

[2] Memorandum by the Queen, 20 February 1852 (Royal Archives C.27.5). The text has been left in its original form, as deciphered from the Queen's not always very easily legible handwriting. As to the construction of sentences, the Queen might well have pleaded "Regina supra grammaticam", to adapt the legendary utterance of the Emperor Sigismund.

questions which we are trying to keep quiet and dormant, and cause some outbreaks which would kindle the flame of war in an instant. I am *deeply impressed* with this truth, *so much* so that I *hardly* think Lord Derby *wishes to succeed* and to saddle himself with these immense difficulties, not to say *dangers*. I repeat that I am *very* strongly impressed with these *great dangers* and that therefore I think the country should be *spared a trial* of them. *All* should be done to avert a calamity and I am very much impressed with the *duty* which I have to perform in saving the country from this. *My* opinion therefore is, that should the government be beat, I should *not* send for Lord Derby (nothing being *changed since* this time *last* year)[1] but for Lord Aberdeen or Sir J. Graham, and with them we might at last perhaps effect the junction which is so necessary. Much depends on the manner in which the government are beat, but *I do not* consider myself in the least *bound* to call upon Lord Derby *because* other parties think it will be advantageous to their personal character and position that he should try.

These are my impressions, and I can assure you *I think* the danger of a *trial* of a Protectionist government *cannot* be sufficiently overrated. Believe me *everything* should be done to avoid it.[2]

The Queen believed that she would be acting against the best interests of the country if she called on Lord Derby to form a government. She did not feel herself bound to ask the Protectionists to take power, even if they had brought down Lord John Russell. Though the division had not yet taken place, it was clear that the government would only fall if the Protectionists voted against it. In Prince Albert's view the Queen had no option but to turn to Lord Derby. The Queen was right in thinking that the Protectionist leader did not relish the task of heading a minority government. But in the Prince's opinion he should have thought of that before. Once the Protectionists had taken the lion's share in bringing down the government, the part of the Queen and opposition leader were predetermined. The Prince was thus in February 1852 struggling for the maintenance of the doctrines he had established in the summer of 1841. He disliked the Protectionists as much as the Queen, and was as devoted as she was to the memory of Sir Robert Peel and to the maintenance of his achievements. But he realised more clearly than his wife the impossibility of permanently attaching the Crown's support to one political party. It was ironical that in 1852 he had to struggle as much against the Queen's passionate attachment to Peel's ideas as he had to break down her hostility to Sir Robert himself in 1841.

Whereas in 1841 the Queen took her stand on a comparatively

[1] When the Protectionist leader was unable to form a government.
[2] Memorandum by the Queen, 20 February 1852 (Royal Archives C.27.5).

minor issue, that of the appointment of the Ladies of the Bedchamber, in February 1852 she based her attitude on major considerations of domestic and foreign policy. She judged that the formation of a Protectionist government would lead to unrest at home and to an increased danger of foreign invasion. In contemplating a deviation from constitutional usage, the Queen thus saw herself more as a provider of "good" government than as the guardian of self-government. This was a reversion to the doctrines of her grandfather, George III, to the ideal of the "King's friends" and of the permanent opposition. Not much importance need be attached to the argument that the Protectionists had forfeited their claim to power by their inability to form a government the previous year. It is worth noting that the Queen's attitude to Lord Derby had stiffened since the 1851 crisis. Like her husband, the Queen had then been unfavourably impressed by an apparent lack of candour on the part of the Protectionist leader.[1]

While Lord Derby did not particularly covet power, it would have been unwise to pass him over and so to aggravate needlessly the tension between the Protectionists and the Court, which had so decidedly taken the part of Sir Robert Peel. It could not be in the interest of the monarchy to revive the danger of an anti-Royalist Country party, as in 1839. The Queen does not seem to have had a sufficient belief in the healing power of the swing of the pendulum. The danger arising from a permanent Protectionist opposition was far greater than that from a Protectionist government existing on sufferance. The Queen's fears happily proved largely unfounded. Generally, the country took the eventual formation of a Protectionist government quietly. The threat of a Napoleonic invasion turned out to be a false alarm, but neither the Queen nor the Prince could complain about any unwillingness of their new ministers to take measures to defend the country.

In February 1852 the Prince no longer had the support of Baron Stockmar which had been so valuable to him in the summer of 1841. The Baron's reply[2] to the Queen's *cri de cœur* did not follow the line taken by the Prince. Stockmar wrote:

> The crisis is *portentous*. It is composed of many and great difficulties at *Home*, and an almost unexampled perplexed and dangerous state of the political affairs *abroad*. It is the juncture which forms great danger to

---

[1] See *Letters*, 22 February 1851, ff.

[2] Memorandum by Stockmar, 21 February 1852 (Royal Archives C.27.7).

England in the present hour, for an unsettled state of her government renders her *doubly weak* and *vulnerable*.

My *chief anxiety* is that the Queen as Sovereign should take the right and safe line. This line I take to be the line of her constitutional duty and that duty understood and exercised in the highest and most rational sense of the word. The constitutional doctrine is that the Queen never *is* and never can *act without constitutional adviser*.

There is *one* very important point for the Queen to keep firmly in mind. During the whole course of her reign, the Queen has gone with Liberal Ministers and *with her People*. In doing so, She could not always avoid coming into collision with the prejudices and imaginary interests of the Aristocracy. This may be in itself a disadvantage, but considering how sound, constitutional and right the general line of the Sovereign's policy has been and is, that disadvantage is only a *minor* and *unavoidable* evil.

If Lord Derby is to be sent for, *his greatest difficulty* appears to me to be to keep the Queen's position integer [sic], and to avoid to make the Sovereign appear *by his acts* that with Her Minister, She has also changed Her Character and means now to go with the Ultra-Party of the Aristocracy *against* the People.

In this present hour I take the Liberty of urging that the Queen in the construction of a new Cabinet *should move step by step*.[1]

This is a curious memorandum. It is difficult to reconcile its partiality to the Whigs with their condemnation by the Baron in January 1854 as "partly conscious, partly unconscious Republicans".[2] Admittedly, the Tories of the day were also dismissed there as "degenerate bastards of their predecessors".[3] Why did Stockmar develop this fervour for "liberalism" in February 1852? One is almost driven to the conclusion that he wrote what he knew the Queen wished to hear. Again this is in contrast to his usual behaviour, to his readiness to speak his mind openly.

Stockmar not only echoed the views put forward in the Queen's memorandum, he also supplied arguments with which she could support her attitude. All the doctrines of the pre-1841 era were resurrected. The policy of the government is treated as the personal affair of the Sovereign who is closely identified with it. The Queen's "character" is involved in the composition and acts of her government. The old dilemma of reconciling changes of government with her reputation for consistency is revived. A bogus distinction is introduced between governments of a "liberal complexion", supported by "the people", and governments which are not liberal and are not supported by the people. In putting forward the doctrine

[1] Ibid.
[2] Stockmar to Prince Albert, 5 January 1854 (Martin, II, 546), tr.
[3] Ibid.

of the Sovereign as the trustee of the people against the encroach-ments of the aristocracy, the Baron evoked traditions going back to George III and beyond to earlier times, although it was dubious whether this was a propitious moment for advancing them. The contrast between the aristocratic Tories and the plebeian Whigs bordered on the ridiculous.

The memorandum was not helpful from a practical point of view. When it came down to brass tacks, it advised caution, an obvious requirement. It also stated that the Queen is never without a proper constitutional adviser. This is incorrect, as Prince Albert was to emphasise again at the end of the year. To the present day the primary responsibility for the appointment of a new Prime Minister on the fall of a government lies with the Sovereign. The Sovereign may take advice, but he is not bound by it and the final decision is exclusively his. This is natural, as one of the most important functions of every head of state—republican or monarchic—is to act as a trustee for the whole community at times when no government is in existence.

In criticising Stockmar's views, his great merits in the service of the British Crown and of the House of Coburg should not be over-looked. It is not fair to judge the Baron exclusively by his attitude in this crisis. Although only in his middle sixties, he considered himself old, like so many other men of his age at the time. He also had hypochondriac tendencies. He may well have been broken spiritually by the failure of his hopes for the realisation of German unity after 1848.

The Queen did not in the end refuse to call on Lord Derby. The situation proved too strong for her. She offered Lord John a disso-lution, but the Cabinet decided against it and formally resigned on 21 February 1852. The Queen immediately called on Lord Derby,[1] who saw her and the Prince the following day. Lord Derby was prepared to try to form a government, but did not underestimate the difficulties caused by his weak parliamentary position and by his shortage of men with experience of office.[2] When the Queen blamed him for the defeat of Lord John's government, he tried to minimise his party's share in this:

> . . . it had not been his party, which had upset the Queen's government, for no notes had been sent out to his followers to vote, he himself had been absent at Badminton, but . . . he supposed the Ministers had rather

---

[1] The Queen to Derby, 21 February 1852 (*Letters*).
[2] Memorandum by Prince Albert, 22 February 1852 (*Letters*).

chosen the opportunity to resign for they felt they could no have gone on. They dreaded the motion on the Cape[1] and, should they even have survived that, they must have known that their Reform measure opposed by one part of the House was not popular with the other. They would very likely have carried the second reading, but would have found it very difficult to get it through the Committee . . .[2]

The Prince did not let Lord Derby get away with this special pleading:

> . . . it was quite true that the Government had resigned upon Lord Palmerston's motion on the Militia Bill, but . . . they had been attacked by Lord Derby and his party and would have been defeated by him some days later on the Cape question. The Queen had then a right to expect according to the constitutional maxims, that the party which drove out the government was prepared to replace it and . . . he must have foreseen this in leading his party to the fight. To the question whether I had stated the constitutional doctrine correctly, he assented.

It would have been best to leave it at that, but the Queen now tried Stockmar's constitutional ideas[3] on the Premier-designate:

> The Queen then said that she wished Lord Derby to recollect that since her accession she had identified herself with a liberal policy which was in conformity with the wishes of the People, that her three governments had been more or less liberal and that therefore she felt alarmed lest it should be considered that she had changed her opinions with the change of Ministers, and that she hoped therefore that what he would propose would not be in direct opposition to a liberal policy.

The argument was not left unanswered:

> Lord Derby, warming up, said he thought there existed different opinions upon what the real wishes of the people were, and that the measures he might have to propose would not be in opposition to them; he did not mean to go back to 1842, although he could not be expected to carry out the policy of Sir Robert Peel of 1846. Constitutionally the government were responsible for their measures and if these were objected to by the Country, they would be rejected in Parliament, upon which the government would retire. He added: "I hope Your Majesty will rest assured that your honour and character are safe in my hands", and that nothing would be done by him to expose it to any risk.

The Prince now decided to intervene:

> I reassured him [Lord Derby] that the Queen had merely wished him to

---

[1] The policy of the Colonial Secretary, Earl Grey, had encountered considerable criticism.

[2] The details of the conversation with the Earl of Derby are taken from a memorandum by Prince Albert of 22 February 1852 (Royal Archives C.27.14).

[3] See p. 186 ff.

bear in mind that besides her constitutional position there was a personal one that had to be taken care of . . .

Lord Derby's replies to the Queen could not be challenged. In any case he did not have the parliamentary majority necessary to revert to protection. Earlier in the interview he had assured the Queen that "he would try to get through the session without proposing any important measures leading to discussion, except what was quite necessary".[1]

The new Prime Minister told the Queen that he considered it advisable to offer Lord Palmerston a seat in the government. But he said at once that it could not be the Foreign Office "on account of what had lately passed, and . . . the 'well-known personal feelings of the Queen'."[2] He thought of the Chancellorship of the Exchequer, with the lead of the House of Commons:

> The Queen did not conceal how disagreeable this proposal must be to her, but would not, by refusing, throw additional difficulties in Lord Derby's way.[3]

The Prince remarked that Lord Derby probably would not remain Prime Minister very long once Lord Palmerston had been installed as leader of the House of Commons.[4]

Lord Derby said the Foreign Office was a difficulty:

> He could not propose Lord Aberdeen for the Foreign Office, as from what had passed last year,[5] he felt he could not induce him to accept. He could not propose Sir Stratford Canning whom he had offered it then with the Queen's permission, because he was aware that, besides his violent temper, several of the Courts of Europe, with whom it was most important for us to stand well at this conjuncture, entertained the strongest prejudices against him. His distance (Constantinople) would be an additional bar to his selection. The least objectionable person he could name was Lord Malmesbury (!) [sic], a man of fair abilities and a personal friend of his, for whose obedience he could vouch.
>
> On the Queen's expressing her doubts as to Lord Malmesbury's abilities, he said he would undertake to control the Office himself and hoped to be allowed to keep the Under Secretaryship open for his son[6] (on his way home from India). This the Queen sanctioned with some complimentary observations on the promising talents of Lord Stanley,

---

[1] Thus far Prince Albert's memorandum, 22 February 1852 (Royal Archives C.27.14).

[2] Memorandum by Prince Albert, 22 February 1852 (*Letters*).

[3] Memorandum by Prince Albert, 22 February 1852 (Royal Archives C.27.14).

[4] Memorandum by Prince Albert, 22 February 1852 (*Letters*).

[5] During the previous cabinet crisis.

[6] Lord Stanley (later the fifteenth Earl of Derby), who served as Foreign Secretary in Conservative administrations from 1866 to 1868 and from 1874 to 1878, but later took office under Gladstone.

at which Lord Derby seemed much pleased and said, he had hitherto done all well he had to do and was very ambitious.[1]

He mentioned that he had only seen Mr. Disraeli, whom he wished to offer a post:

> He was sorry he could not offer persons of whom the Queen could say more than "that she did *not object* to them".[2]

He was gloomy about the prospects:

> Should his government not be able to maintain itself, he would resign and be ready to support any government the Queen might appoint, which opposed the democratic movement which threatens our institutions . . .[3]

Lord Palmerston refused office, though the Prime Minister undertook to leave the protection issue in abeyance until a General Election had clarified the state of public opinion on the subject. Lord Derby reported to the Queen:

> . . . while he feels his own difficulties increased Lord Derby cannot but rejoice that Your Majesty had been spared a sacrifice of personal feeling, which nothing but an imperative sense of the public interests could have induced him to ask at Your Majesty's hands.[4]

The offer of the post was, however, a good tactical move and secured Palmerston's parliamentary support for a time. This left the Exchequer and the leadership of the House of Commons for Mr. Disraeli, although he had never held office before. Lord Malmesbury became Foreign Secretary and Spencer Walpole, who later wrote the official life of Lord John Russell, Home Secretary.

On behalf of the Queen the Prince pointed out to the Prime Minister the Sovereign's insistence that the persons composing the Court should not be on the verge of bankruptcy and that their moral character should bear investigation. In the Prince's opinion the Prime Minister was a kind of Keeper of the Queen's conscience who should help the Crown to keep up the necessary moral standards:

> Lord Derby seemed struck and said now he must reverse the position and make me his Confessor. He had certainly been very much pressed by a near relative, (Lord Wilton) to be made Master of the Horse; he felt that after this declaration he could hardly propose him, yet it would cause him great difficulties; he thought Lord Wilton had been much belied. I replied that a man bearing the nickname of "the wicked Earl" could hardly be put at the head of one of the departments of the Queen's Household.

---

[1] Memorandum by Prince Albert, 22 February 1852 (Royal Archives C.27.14).   [2] Ibid.   [3] Ibid.
[4] Derby to the Queen, 22 February 1852 (Royal Archives C.27.16).

We agreed that he should send a list of persons out of whom the Queen could select . . .[1]

Lord Derby did not find it too easy, however, to resist the solicitations of his racing companions. The Prince was horrified:

For the Household appointments Lord Derby had submitted a list of Peers and young gentlemen of which the greater part were the Dandies and Roués of London and the Turf. I prepared a counter list of some twenty respectable Peers of property . . . I had to tell him [Lord Derby] that he seemed hardly to understand the importance of these selections: I must remind him that of all the things which contributed to the French Revolution of February [1848] none did more harm than the murder of the Duchesse de Praslin by her husband who was attached to the King's Household. The King could not be supposed to have been answerable for that act and yet it was visited by the people personally upon him; now I was not meaning to imply that Lord Derby's racing friends were capable of such acts, but the lawsuit of Lady Gardner against her husband Lord Gardner (a Lord-in-Waiting in 1839) had done the Queen a good deal of harm in public estimation at the time; we could judge of what people were likely to do best from the reputation they had acquired at the time when they were recommended.

I saw that all this placed Lord Derby into considerable difficulties; however, he said he would take care and not apply Lord Melbourne's epithet [about this "damned morality"] to the objections.[2]

The veto on Lord Wilton put the Prime Minister in an awkward position. When informed by Lord Derby that he could not be considered for a Court appointment, Lord Wilton replied with a long and pathetic letter, mourning the blow which had fallen on him. He wrote that he "hoped passages in earlier life . . . had been buried in oblivion".[3] The Queen had little sympathy with Lord Wilton's disappointed hopes:

He [Prince Albert] told me . . . that Lord Derby had got over this difficulty with Lord Wilton, but not without wounding him terribly, for he foolishly called himself disgraced.[4]

In principle the requirements of the Prince about character and solvency were unexceptionable, but they were sometimes carried to extraordinary lengths. The Queen decided to maintain the ban on the reception of the wife of the new Lord Chancellor, Sir Edward Sugden (Lord St. Leonards)[5] at Court, which had been imposed

---

[1] The details of this conversation with Lord Derby are taken from a memorandum by the Prince of 23 February 1852 (Royal Archives C.27.25).
[2] Memorandum by Prince Albert, 26 February 1852 (Royal Archives C.27.46).
[3] Wilton to Derby, 26 February 1852 (Royal Archives C.27.51).
[4] Memorandum by the Queen, 26 February 1852 (Royal Archives C.27.50).
[5] This is Sir A. B. in Prince Albert's memorandum of 27 February 1852 (*Letters*).

because she had run away with her husband while he was still at school, and had lived with him for some years before they were married in 1808. The lady was now nearly, and her husband over seventy; he died at the ripe old age of ninety-three. The old gentleman was put in the embarrassing situation of finding himself asked to Court singly, although every other married man brought his wife. The Prime Minister's appeal for a withdrawal of the ban proved unavailing:

> . . . The Queen had been considering the case of Lady Sugden and has come to the conclusion that upon the whole it will not do for the Queen to make any difference on account of his election to the Peerage and therefore cannot receive her at Court. Lord Derby of course will understand that the Queen does not in any way thereby [wish] to interfere with what other people may wish to do in their own houses.[1]

In the end the faithful old husband requested that he should not be asked to Court as long as the prohibition on his wife continued.

(ii)

Lord Derby soon saw that it paid him to secure the co-operation of the Prince in the general running of affairs. In the Prince's judgment, every support had to be given to him now that he had taken over the government. He did his best to secure the new government a respite from Whig attacks. When Lord John came to take leave of the Queen and her husband, the Prince

> expressed the hope that this government, bad as it was, would be left unmolested till it had really shown its inability; their being driven from office rapidly would only increase the future difficulties of governing. This entirely concurred with Lord John's own opinion.[2]

But the personal sympathies of the Prince, as of the Queen, remained with the Whigs and the Peelites:

> He [Lord John] said Sir James Graham had been with him and told him nothing stood now in the way of their acting together. We rejoiced at this and impressed upon Lord John that it was now entirely in his hands in opposition to form and organise a party which when called upon to take office could form a government which possessed the strength to carry on the business of the country for five or six years. He replied he doubted sometimes whether he was quite the man to be at the head of such a coalition; it was almost impossible for a man to get through the work of Prime Minister and leader of the House of Commons, he thought a man

---

[1] The Queen to Derby, 28 February 1852 (Royal Archives C.27.64).
[2] Memorandum by Prince Albert, 26 February 1852 (Royal Archives C.27.46).

like Lord Clarendon more fit for such a position. If Lord Lansdowne were twelve years younger he would be just the man . . .[1]

It was certainly desirable for the smooth working of parliamentary government that the Peelites should make up their minds to join one or other of the major parties. Though speculation never ceased, it had become very difficult for them to rejoin the Tories. Their alliance with the Whigs, with whom they were agreed over Free Trade, was the obvious choice. The Derby government helped to crystallise the situation.

The Prince kept in touch with Lord John in a perfectly fair manner which was, indeed, advantageous to the government. Lord John considered it wise, in view of his undertaking to abstain from any factious opposition to the new government, to give the Prince a personal report about a meeting of Whig politicians held at his house in the middle of March 1852.[2] In his reply, the Prince assured him that he regarded his action as reasonable:

> I consider it of the highest importance to the well working of the constitutional machine, that the parliamentary opposition should be well organised and following the directions of a Leader after having agreed upon the political principles upon which it means to act. Its course becomes thereby intelligible and consistent and can be kept within proper bounds. The Government of the day can take it into its calculations in shaping its course, whilst nothing is more embarrassing than the irregular warfare and the desultory attacks to which your Government was liable from all sides of the House.[3]

Lord John's meeting was only a small beginning. Lord Palmerston refused to attend and continued to keep aloof from the official Whig party. The Peelites maintained their sphinx-like attitude, though more from confusion than intention. The general election in the summer of 1852, however disappointing both to the government and to the Opposition (except for the Irish), led to some clarification. In view of the loose party discipline at the time, all figures are approximations. The Derby Tories had the satisfaction of increasing their strength in the House of Commons from about 200 to 300 votes, but they fell at least thirty or forty short of proper control of the House. To consolidate their position, they were in need of allies. They could not very well consider the Irish Brigade of fifty members, which would have bridged the difference. The hope of the Peelites rejoining the party was never completely given up. Both Derby and his lieutenant Disraeli made repeated efforts to secure Palmerston's support, if possible with some of the Peelites. Palmerston's accession would have made the House of Commons more manageable even if it had not greatly strengthened the Government in numbers.

Perhaps the most important asset the Conservatives gained from the election was the ability to free themselves, with comparative dignity, from the millstone of their Protectionist past. Lord Derby had been willing to leave the protection issue in abeyance pending a general election and to bow to the verdict of the electorate. The Prince correctly predicted the effect of the election:

> Protection will be buried . . . for ever and we must be grateful for the prospect of seeing the commercial policy of this country settled on sound and fixed principles.[1]

The Whigs and the Peelites could gain satisfaction from this aspect of the election results, but apart from that they had little to gladden their hearts. The Peelites dropped from something in the neighbourhood of one hundred to under fifty.[2] The Whigs, even with Radical support, were now inferior in numbers to the solid Conservative block on the benches opposite.

Lord Derby and Disraeli tried hard to propitiate the Queen and the Prince, but only with limited success. The Prime Minister was flattering in his comments about suggestions by the Prince for the creation of a reserve force,[3] though they were not embodied in the amended Militia Bill which the new government passed through parliament. The Chancellor of the Exchequer was forced by the Cabinet to yield to the Prince's pressure for an expansion of the armed forces to such an extent that this may well have contributed to the failure of the Budget which was to bring down the government.[4]

The Prince never felt quite easy about the new men. In his attitude, differences of opinion and personal prejudices were so interwoven that it is hard to disentangle the one from the other. Whatever the government did about protection, it laid itself open to criticism by

---

[1] Prince Albert to Russell, 12 June 1852 (Royal Archives C.19.47).

[2] All estimates of Peelite strength should be treated with caution, as this group was not a proper party like the Whigs or the Protectionists. By December, only Aberdeen thought there were still 50 Peelites left in the Commons (memorandum by Queen Victoria, 25 December 1852, *Letters*). Derby speaks of 30 (memorandum by Prince Albert, 18 December 1852, *Letters*). Halévy, "History of the English People", IV, 180, gives them 35–40 in the election results.

[3] Memorandum by the Queen, 26 February 1852 (*Letters*); Martin, II, 433 ff.

[4] See W. F. Monypenny and G. E. Buckle, "The Life of Benjamin Disraeli", I, 1222 ff.

the Prince. If it had tried to re-introduce corn duties, under whatever name, the Prince would have accused it of harming the country. On the other hand, if it abandoned old ideas, it was charged with lack of principle. In Disraeli's case in particular, his gradual change of front over protection to the Prince confirmed the impression of demagogy and irresponsible ambition suggested by the career of the Chancellor of the Exchequer. For the Prince Disraeli and Palmerston were birds of the same feather, in "the laxity of the political conscious-ness which both these gentlemen have hitherto exhibited." [1] Lord Derby's situation was aggravated by the kind of company he kept. Both the Queen and the Prince were acutely aware of the ministers' lack of government experience. With the Queen the strongest objection to the Protectionists lay in their attitude to Peel in 1846. Her mind was made up: no further evidence against the Protection-ists was needed. The past spoke clearly.

As the budget was approaching, Derby and Disraeli felt that another effort should be made to strengthen the basis of the govern-ment. They still hoped to obtain the accession of Lord Palmerston and of the Peelites. They were encouraged to make approaches to Palmerston, when he tabled a face-saving amendment to a motion by the uncompromising Free Trader Villiers which was designed to bring down the government. Lord Derby thought that Palmerston was acting in concert with the Peelites. He immediately proceeded to Windsor in order to obtain the Queen's approval for an offer of a post to Lord Palmerston. Derby's precise attitude to Palmerston at this juncture is important, for the government's fate was sealed once it was certain that its basis could not be broadened.

Prince Albert recorded a conversation he had with the Prime Minister at Windsor on the evening of 24 November 1852:[2]

> Lord Derby . . . reported on the state of affairs which he considered very critical. There was a probability of the Government being defeated on Mr. Villiers's motion if it persevered in its own amendment. Late in the evening of the Debate, however, Lord Palmerston moved an amendment which if adopted by the Government would give them very likely a major-ity of not less than thirty, probably much more. This amendment was preconcerted by Lord Palmerston, Mr. Gladstone, Mr. Sidney Herbert [and] their Peelite following. It must not be concealed from us (Lord Derby said) that this is done with a view to office and to joining the Government. Lord Palmerston was anxious to join, and the Peelites, he understood, equally so; on the other hand it was impossible for the present

---

[1] Prince Albert to Derby, 26 November 1852 (Monypenny and Buckle, I, 1239).
[2] Memorandum by Prince Albert, 25 November 1852 (Royal Archives C.42.21).

government to go on without an accession of strength in the House of Commons and with all the talent united against it. He knew the introduction of Lord Palmerston would be very unpleasant to the Queen and myself, but that he felt in duty bound to declare that he would avoid it if he possibly could, but did not see how it was to be done: his own office was entirely at the Queen's disposal if that could assist in any way.

I said I had heard that Lord Palmerston was anxious to come into office again, he looked to becoming leader of the House of Commons and then to supplant Lord Derby very soon: I did not know whether he could trust Mr. Disraeli as leader, but that with Lord Palmerston I did not give his Government a long lease.

Lord Derby replied he had no reason to complain of Mr. Disraeli who was ready to do anything for him . . . Mr. Disraeli knew that he (Lord Derby) possessed the confidence of three hundred of his supporters, whilst Mr. Disraeli, if he separated himself from him, would very likely not carry five with him.

It was understood (he continued) that Lord Palmerston could neither come to the Foreign Office, nor become leader, and he would consent to Disraeli keeping the lead. What had been thought of for him had been the Home Office . . .[1]

This clearly disposes of the theory that it was the Crown which prevented the survival of the Derby government by vetoing the only possible terms which Palmerston was likely to accept, that is an offer of the lead in the House of Commons.[2] Lord Derby did not try to obtain the Queen's sanction for any arrangement of this kind. When he saw the Queen on the following morning, he merely repeated what the Prince had already noted.[3] The Prince closes his memorandum on Lord Derby's visit with this passage:

The Queen allowed him to enter into negotiations with the Peelites and Lord Palmerston on the distinct understanding that the latter could not receive the lead of the House of Commons.[4]

This was an acceptance by the Queen of the terms which the Prime Minister wished to offer, not a refusal of something for which he had asked. It will be recalled that the Crown had been prepared to accept Lord Palmerston as leader on the formation of the government.

The Prince's scepticism about the existence of an understanding between Lord Palmerston and the Peelites was only too well justified. When the Prime Minister sketched out the proposed reconstructed government with Gladstone at the Colonial Office, the Prince "asked whether Lord Derby was quite sure of all this and would not be left with Lord Palmerston alone?"[5] The Prime Minister soon saw

[1] Ibid.
[2] The argument put forward in Monypenny and Buckle, I, 1238.
[3] Memorandum by Prince Albert of 25 November 1852 (Royal Archives C.42.21).
[4] Ibid.   [5] Ibid.

that the Peelites were not acting in concert with Lord Palmerston
and he did not consider it worth while to raise the terms to the latter
in order to obtain him alone. It is doubtful whether Palmerston ever
seriously considered joining the Derby government. When the Prince
wrote on 26 November to Lord Derby about the "Queen's duty" to
prevent Palmerston from obtaining the leadership of the House of
Commons at which he was aiming "in order to possess himself of
absolute power",[1] the Prime Minister was not proposing to make
any offer of this kind. The Prince's sponsorship of Gladstone for the
leadership if Disraeli relinquished it[2] is only of interest in so far as it
reveals his personal predilections.

It has also been suggested that the Queen and the Prince rather
encouraged a limited offer to Lord Palmerston so as to ruin him
politically by an alliance with Lord Derby.[3] This argument relies
on the information the Queen and her husband are supposed to have
gleaned from a conversation Stockmar had with Cobden:

> Dined with Cobden. On my [Stockmar] saying "Your proceedings in
> the House yesterday [when the government survived owing to its accep-
> tance of Palmerston's amendment to the Villiers motion] have made
> Palmerston master of the situation," (said on purpose to sting him) he
> replied: "I deny that, Palmerston is not a whit stronger than he was and
> has in the whole House not more than three personal followers. If he
> joins Derby now, he is sure to be ruined somewhat earlier than he will
> be without it. The Manchester Party know him well and will take care
> that he does not longer humbug the public in the garb of a Liberal . . .
> I will do what I can to prevent Palmerston from getting into a position
> that he can pretend to lead the Commons . . .[4]

Stockmar's memorandum is dated 27 November, and this date is
confirmed by the reference to events in the House of Commons on
the previous day. By then, the negotiations with Palmerston, which
were always rather shadowy, had been discontinued. The opinion
of the Prince was taken on 24 November and that of the Queen on
the following morning. On his return to London in the afternoon
Lord Derby found that it was not worth while "exercising the
Queen's discretion" with regard to Lord Palmerston.[5]

At the same time it is clear that the Queen and the Prince were
in principle against the leadership of the Commons going to Lord
Palmerston, as they rightly considered it the stepping-stone to the

---

[1] Monypenny and Buckle, I, 1239.
[2] Memorandum by Prince Albert, 28 November 1852 (*Letters*).
[3] Bell, Palmerston, II, 69.
[4] Memorandum by Stockmar, 27 November 1852 (Royal Archives A.81.39).
[5] Lord Derby to Queen Victoria, 25 November 1852, at 4 p.m. (*Letters*).

premiership. Their fears in this direction became a veritable nightmare under the influence of Baron Stockmar who besides Cobden also saw Aberdeen and Graham.[1] On flimsy evidence the Baron concluded, in a memorandum on 10 December,[2] that "the aim of Palmerston is the leadership of the House of Commons". Having aroused the greatest anxieties on the part of the Queen and the Prince on this score, he proceeded, however, to tell them that the leadership of the House was not a ministerial office and therefore not subject to royal approval:

> Knowing the man [Palmerston] as I do, I should deplore his success as a public misfortune. *To avert it the Queen herself can do very little. The only power to prevent it, is in the House of Commons itself.* The Manchester people, Peel's friends, can frustrate Palmerston's machinations.
>
> My business is to consider beforehand the position the Queen would be in, whenever a combination of circumstances should enable Palmerston to lead the House?
>
> As I read the letter [sic] of the English Constitution, *the Queen has an indisputable right to refuse to such or such person to fill such or such ministerial office, without being constitutionally bound to assign any reason for her refusal. It is of great importance to the Crown* and the well working of the Constitution itself, that though this right is ever to be exercised with the utmost discretion, the Queen nevertheless *should not shrink from making use of it whenever very critical circumstances require it as a Pis aller Remedy* [to prevent something worse].
>
> *But the Constitution says nothing of the Leadership of the House of Commons being a ministerial office.*
>
> In the case in point *therefore*, Palmerston having a chance of a seat in the Cabinet, with the publicly acknowledged Power to lead the Commons, Your Majesty would *find Yourself placed in a dilemma.* Your admitting him as a Minister, You would *constitutionally* not be borne out in refusing him the Leadership. Your doing so would certainly be considered by the Public and by the House as excluding him *from Office altogether in a harsh, ungracious and consequently most unpopular way.* If in such a case Your Majesty was to exclude him from Office altogether *without assigning any reason* for Your resolution, You would, I feel sure, *follow the less offensive mode.*[3]

The Baron's argument deserves close scrutiny. He was certainly right to point out that royal control over the leadership of the House of Commons was far more vague than that over proper government appointments. In the nineteenth century the leadership of the House of Commons was so important that it was a function of the Premiership unless the Prime Minister was disqualified from membership

---

[1] Memorandum by Stockmar, 27 November 1852 (Royal Archives A. 81.39).
[2] Memorandum by Stockmar submitted to the Queen and the Prince (Royal Archives A.81.40).
[3] Ibid.

of the House of Commons by being a Peer. In the second half of the century it became increasingly difficult for a Prime Minister to lead the government from the Lords, although Lord Salisbury managed it for altogether over a decade. It was unsatisfactory to have the leader of the government in the politically more important House subordinate to the Prime Minister. The duality of leadership proved particularly troublesome whenever the Prime Minister in the Lords had difficulty in maintaining his ascendancy over the Leader of the Commons. The Earl of Derby could handle Benjamin Disraeli, but the Earl of Aberdeen was—for a number of reasons—to have a most unhappy experience with Lord John Russell.

The British tradition preventing Peers, even when in high office, from addressing the decisive parliamentary body, was only one of the sources of a problem which has never troubled the standard parliamentary democracies of the continent. Continental legislatures do not know the equivalent of a government leadership of the popular chamber. In Britain the government arranges the business of the House of Commons through the Leader. On the continent, this is normally done by an impartial steering committee of the whole house. The Leader of the House of Commons is thus more than the head of the continental majority parliamentary group.[1]

With his neat continental logic Stockmar created too rigid a distinction between the House of Commons and the government, and thus failed to grasp the essential character of the typically British institution he was analysing. The leadership of the House of Commons in varying degrees formed part of both the executive and the legislature. It was thus erroneous to state that the House of Commons, and indeed the Peelite and Cobdenite opposition, could prevent the appointment of a Leader of the House since this was made by the government. Stockmar had, in fact, completely misunderstood Sir James Graham. According to Stockmar's own minute, Graham had said on 27 November:

> . . . *Now* Palmerston *can*, Gladstone and Herbert *may* join Derby. Newcastle certainly *won't*.
>
> Palmerston from his age, his antecedents and his knowledge of the House of Commons is certainly entitled to its *lead*; and D'Israeli cannot have the slightest hesitation in giving way to him . . . the public will take it [as] a generous and gracious act of D'Israeli's. All D'Israeli will most likely say, will be: on condition that hereafter it will not be forgotten what

---

[1] In Germany, for instance, the head of government does not normally retain the nominal leadership of his parliamentary group while in power.

I have done, since Derby came in, that it was in fact me, who has made Palmerston's present position.

The Tories would hail Palmerston's coming in, who certainly would then set his face *against further reform*. Should afterwards Palmerston and Derby fall out, the chance of becoming Prime Minister would be for Palmerston.[1]

All that Graham said was that, *if* Palmerston joined the Derby government, he would, owing to his standing in the House of Commons, be entitled to its lead, as the Prime Minister was in the Lords. Graham thus inferred correctly that, whenever the head of the government was a Peer the minister with the strongest position in the Lower House had the first refusal of the lead.

His faulty diagnosis led Stockmar straight to a dangerous prognosis. Once more the Baron harped on the Queen's right to veto or end a ministerial appointment on her own authority. This contradicts Stockmar's own—too far reaching—thesis that the Queen is never without a constitutional adviser. While the Sovereign has to make his own decisions in the absence of a government, he will only in rare circumstances be able to oppose the advice of the Prime Minister once appointed. A Premier determined to take Palmerston into his cabinet and to give him the leadership of the House of Commons could have overruled the royal opposition by the threat of resignation.

The Queen and the Prince were wise enough not to attempt to carry out Stockmar's autocratic ideas. The Baron was far more inclined than the Prince to engage in excessive Germanic theorising. The situation Stockmar had in mind when he wrote his memorandum did not correspond to reality and it was not to arise in the form in which he had posed it. Dramatic parliamentary developments upset previous calculations a few days later.

The Budget forced the government to show its hand and offered a sitting target to the most varied criticism from all quarters of the opposition. What finally led to Disraeli's undoing was a brilliant speech by Gladstone. This brought to the fore the rivalry between the two men which was to dominate the political scene after the death of Palmerston in 1865. The government was defeated by a combination of Whigs, Peelites, Radicals and Irish and resigned on 18 December 1852, after an uneasy existence of less than a year. When the outgoing Prime Minister advised the Queen to send for Lord Lansdowne, the Prince pointed out that "constitutionally

[1] Memorandum by Stockmar of 27 November 1852 (Royal Archives A.81.39).

speaking it did not rest with him to give advice and become responsible for it." [1]

(iii)

There was no obvious leader of the opposition on whom the Queen
could call to form the new government. Lord John Russell led the
biggest block of votes which had beaten Lord Derby. But would a
return to his premiership not lead to a repetition of the government
weakness and indecision which the beginning of the year had witnessed? Lord John had still not succeeded in re-establishing the old
co-operation with Palmerston, who stayed away from the division
in which Derby was defeated. In spite of the losses the Peelites had
suffered in the general election, any government without their
support would be in a weak position. The debate over the Budget
had once more underlined the influence of personality which was
the basis of Peelite power. The speech of a Peelite, Gladstone, had
brought down the government; the Peelites still held the key. [2]

Nothing which had happened during 1852 had disproved Lord
John's own admission about his unsuitability for the role of leader
in a coalition government of Whigs and Peelites. It might have been
wise, however, to have gone through the motion of offering him the
government. It is unlikely that he would have been able to form one.

The Queen and the Prince had a further reason for considering
themselves entitled to pass over Lord John. Just before the defeat
of the Government, Lord John had been asked by his brother, the
Duke of Bedford, what course he thought the Queen ought to take
in the event of the resignation of the Ministry. Lord John replied
that the Queen should send for Lord Lansdowne and Lord Aberdeen.
Lord John apparently did not know then that the Duke had asked
him the question at the Queen's desire. When he found out about
this, he thought his brother had not treated him quite fairly. [3] In the
meantime, the Queen had been confirmed in her unwillingness to
call on Lord John by his own reply. This was incidentally the first
government crisis in which the Crown no longer had Wellington's
advice. The Great Duke had died in September 1852 at the age of 83.

The summoning of the two peers virtually meant the first refusal

---

[1] Memorandum by Prince Albert, 18 December 1852 (*Letters*).
[2] But note the view put forward in E. Halévy's "History of the English People"
(IV, 327) that as a result of the 1852 election, "the balance between the Protectionists and Free Traders was held by the Irish brigade" and no longer by the Peelites.
[3] Walpole, Russell, II, 160.

of the premiership of Lord Aberdeen, as it was known that Lord Lansdowne at 72 considered himself too old and ailing to head a government. He was unable to attend the Queen at Osborne because of the gout. Aberdeen secured Lansdowne's support for his own premiership before he left London for the audience, but it still remained to be seen whether he would be able to obtain Lord John's essential support. To the Queen and the Prince Lord Aberdeen emphasised how important it was that only one person should be charged with the task of forming a government. What he had in mind was not simply a return of the Whigs with a few Peelites added, but "a liberal Conservative government in the sense of that of Sir Robert Peel".[1] When the premier-elect had got to this point, the Prince expressed his dislike of coalitions generally. He noted:

> I interrupted by saying that coalitions had always been unpopular and perhaps justly, because often immoral . . . [In the case of coalition governments] two parties divided the spoils of office according to certain proportions, each claiming a vested interest in it . . . The mode of proceeding he proposed obviated these objections, gave a better guarantee against party jobs and was more dignified for the Crown.[2]

Actually, the commissioning of a sole prime minister to head the coalition government did not dispose of all difficulties. It did not prevent a rather undignified fight for the spoils of office between the Peelites and the Whigs. The latter complained with justice about the insistence of the Peelites on a parity of membership in the cabinet, although they provided so little of the parliamentary following. Against this could be set the Peelite wealth of talent, though it may be doubted whether this quality could be claimed by any of their new ministers except for Gladstone, the Chancellor of the Exchequer. Sir James Graham, who became First Lord of the Admiralty, at no stage emerged as more than the second-rate career politician who is as necessary a type as he is uninspiring.[3] The Duke of Newcastle, the Secretary for War and the Colonies, soon found himself completely out of his depth in the troubles ahead. Sidney Herbert, the Secretary at War, disappointed the hopes he had raised. Cardwell, the President of the Board of Trade, perhaps wore better than the rest, securing a place in history with his army reforms during the first Gladstone administration.

The Peelite Prime Minister himself was not considered brilliant

---

[1] Memorandum by Prince Albert, 19 December 1852 (*Letters*).
[2] Memorandum by Prince Albert, 19 December 1852 (Royal Archives C.28.13).
[3] But note Gladstone's praise of Graham (J. Morley, Gladstone, I, 248 and 250; II, 765).

by anybody. Perhaps Palmerston had gone rather far in July 1849, when he had spoken of "antiquated imbecility".[1] Aberdeen had some considerable assets. At the end of a long political life, which had begun during the Napoleonic Wars, he was delighted that he had— after all—reached the highest rung of the ladder. Under a gruff exterior Lord Aberdeen had some warmth and kindness. He worked very hard to keep his heterogeneous cabinet together. As a Peelite, he was able to make greater allowances for the often rather curious and irrational conduct of the other members of his group than a Whig Prime Minister would have done. His main difficulty arose over the Whig component of the coalition and in particular over his relations with Lord John Russell.

It was as unsatisfactory for Lord Aberdeen as Prime Minister to be dependent for his parliamentary majority on a member of his cabinet, as it was for Lord John to accept an inferior position which made a mockery of their respective strengths in the House of Commons. What made it worse in the case of Lord John was his inability to see his own limitations. In spite of his utterances to the contrary, he felt that he should have been Prime Minister after all. He was not content with a vague promise on the part of Lord Aberdeen that he would have the reversion of the premiership on his resignation.[2] He was not convinced that he would have been un-acceptable as the leader of a coalition government. He objected not so much to serving under a Peelite Prime Minister, as to not being Prime Minister himself. A Lansdowne premiership would not have been a solution. It might have sweetened the pill for Lord John. But with an aged and sick premier there would have been constant bickerings in the Cabinet.

Lord John could never get over the "indignity" of his prospective position and was thus constantly changing his mind as to whether he should join the Aberdeen government or stay out.[3] His brother, the Duke of Bedford, was in favour of his coming in, but his wife, Lord Minto's daughter, was not so sure. As Lord John was ruled by his lady, the formation of the government was several times in doubt. According to Stockmar, Clarendon was supposed to have said:

> We shall really be safe only when we have a calm, steady man of our party to sleep in the same room with John and his Lady.[4]

---

[1] Bell, Palmerston, I, 443.   [2] Walpole, Russell, II, 163.
[3] Walpole, Russell, II, 160 ff.; Gooch, II, 114 ff.; Russell's "Recollections and Suggestions", 270 ff.; Letters; (Royal Archives C.28.various).
[4] Memorandum by Stockmar of 27 November 852 (Royal Archives A.81.39).

The Queen made a strong appeal to Lord John to join the new government:

> The Queen thinks the moment to have arrived when a popular, efficient and durable government could be formed by the sincere and united efforts of all parties professing conservative and liberal opinions. The Queen knowing that this can only be effected by the patriotic sacrifice of personal interests and feelings to the public good, trusts that Lord John Russell will as far as he is able, give his valuable and powerful assistance to the realisation of this object.[1]

It was understood that Lord John would be Leader of the House of Commons. It was usual that the Leader should hold some office, though it could be a nominal one. Colonel Phipps, the Keeper of the Queen's Privy Purse, who had gone to London to assist in the formation of the government, reported to the Court on 20 December:

> I hear that Lady John is very much alarmed at Lord John accepting an office of heavy executive business with the Leadership of the House . . .[2]

The compromise reached between Lord and Lady John was the worst possible solution. Lord John was to accept the Foreign Office initially and to yield it to Lord Clarendon in due course and then to lead the House of Commons without office.

The objections to the arrangement proposed by Lord John were not confined to the Queen and the Prince. The first to demur were, indeed, not the Court but the Prime Minister and his colleagues. They were startled to read in Lord John's organ, *The Globe*, in the middle of January that the new Foreign Secretary proposed to give up the seals of his office at the meeting of Parliament and to hand over to Lord Clarendon, while retaining the lead of the House of Commons without office. When questioned about the origin of the announcement Lord John did not deny that he had been responsible for its insertion. The new government had thus not been in power for a month before the first serious differences of opinion between the Premier and his senior Minister arose. The Prime Minister pocketed his annoyance at this attempt to face him with a *fait accompli* and at once took up the whole question of Lord John's position with him in a conciliatory spirit. He reported his conversation to the Queen:

> Lord Aberdeen stated his conviction [to Lord John] that it was fully

---

[1] The Queen to Russell, 19 December 1852 (Royal Archives C.28.14).
[2] Colonel Phipps to Colonel Grey, Prince Albert's Private Secretary, 20 December 1852 (Royal Archives C.28.20).

understood a short trial, after the meeting of Parliament, would be indispensable, in order to enable Lord John with propriety to resign the
office in consequence of the accumulated labour of the various duties.
Lord Aberdeen therefore strongly pressed upon Lord John the necessity
of his continuing to hold the Foreign Office until Easter, when some
arrangement might be made; and as the recess would take place in little
more than a month after the meeting of Parliament, no great degree of
fatigue would be incurred.

Lord Aberdeen did not hold out much hope of success for his
endeavours.[1]

The Prime Minister also questioned the propriety of Lord John's
leading the Commons without government office. He called the
proposed arrangement "in many respects objectionable and scarcely
consistent with constitutional principles". He felt it would be
necessary for Lord John to hold at least a nominal office, such as
the Chancellorship of the Duchy of Lancaster.[2] Like the Court, Lord
Aberdeen probably feared a weakening of control over a leader of
the House of Commons who was not in every sense a member of the
government. Another issue involved was connected with the necessity
for a minister on appointment to a new office to vacate his seat in
the House of Commons and to resubmit himself to the electorate.
If Lord John took a less onerous office than that of the conduct of
foreign affairs, he would again have to face the electors of the City
of London. If he remained as leader without office, there might be
a public outcry about his evading re-election.[3] Against Aberdeen's
views, the precedent of the Duke of Wellington leading the Lords as
a cabinet minister without office after 1841 could be cited.

As so frequently on these occasions when Lord John was proving
difficult, an attempt was made to enlist the services of the Duke of
Bedford. Lord Aberdeen had suggested to the Queen that she should
discuss the situation with him, as he was about to stay at Court.[4]
On 19 January, Prince Albert saw the Duke who agreed to see his
brother and to suggest to him that he should remain at the Foreign
Office until Easter and then take the Chancellorship of the Duchy of
Lancaster.[5]

[1] Aberdeen to the Queen, 18 January 1853 (Royal Archives C.28.89).
[2] Ibid.
[3] Aberdeen to Russell on 19 January 1853: " . . . I fear this question will not be
decided exclusively by the Crown and the Cabinet, and that we may encounter
a formidable judgment of the House of Commons." (Royal Archives C.28.91b.)
[4] Aberdeen to the Queen, 18 January 1853 (Royal Archives C.28.89); also the
Queen to Aberdeen in reply, 18 January 1853 (Royal Archives C.28.90).
[5] Memorandum by Prince Albert, 23 January 1853 (Royal Archives C.28.91).

The Duke did not, however, go to London to see his brother, as the Prince discovered to his annoyance:

> Lord Clarendon had prevented him, saying that *he* ought to see Lord John, as he had been personally so much mixed up with the original arrangement, the Duke should not move till he heard from him.
> I [Prince Albert] was very much vexed at this turn the affairs had taken, not feeling sure at all that Lord Clarendon would be as honest as the Duke would have been.
> Lord Clarendon wrote the following day to the Duke that he had come just in time, finding Lord Aberdeen and Lord John together, nothing was to be done till Parliament met, but Lord John could take no office when he left the Foreign Office.[1]

The Prince realised that Lord Clarendon would not be as disinterested as the Duke, for, in spite of his professed unwillingness to go to the Foreign Office, the late Lord Lieutenant and former diplomat was only too eager to assume control of the department. He was, in fact, following with regard to the Foreign Office the same tactics with which he had been so successful in obtaining the Lord Lieutenancy in 1847. Lord John, as Prime Minister, had initially offered it to his brother. Clarendon helped to dissuade the Duke and eventually only accepted himself with reluctance, because he feared the job would be too much of a burden for Bedford.[2]

Clarendon was not very successful in persuading Lord John to stay at the Foreign Office, and it seems doubtful whether he at heart wished to be. As usual he enjoyed himself in the part of the go-between and exaggerated his own share in the negotiations. The Prince caught him out on little inaccuracies.[3]

Lord John remained adamant. He insisted that he had been promised release from the Foreign Office on the meeting of Parliament, as Lady John's records showed.[4] He was not prepared to "descend" to the Duchy of Lancaster and to vacate his seat in Parliament anew. He rejected the objections of his chief and of some of his colleagues as "frivolous and superficial".[5] He only made a

---

[1] Ibid.

[2] Regarding the disposal of the Lord Lieutenancy in 1847, see Greville's entry for 7 June 1847 (V, 448 ff.).

[3] "Lord Clarendon did not find Lord Aberdeen and Lord John together as he wrote to the Duke of Bedford, but rather Lord Aberdeen found Lord Clarendon and Lord John together." (Memorandum by Prince Albert, 23 January 1853, Royal Archives C.28.91.)

[4] "Lords Aberdeen and Clarendon gave me their words of honour as gentlemen that on the meeting of Parliament J. should leave the F.O. and not be asked to take any other office." (Lady John Russell's Journal for 23 December 1852, published in Gooch, Russell, II, 117.)

[5] Prince Albert's memorandum of 23 January 1853 (Royal Archives C.28.91).

slight admission at the end of an acrimonious correspondence with Lord Aberdeen, that "it may have been owing to my uncertainty of purpose that the misapprehension had arisen".[1] Finally he had his way because he threatened to resign and thus to break up the government.

Shortly before handing over the Foreign Office to Lord Clarendon, Lord John discussed his future position with the Queen and her husband on 17 February.[2] At the beginning of the interview, the Prince gave some ground.

> I said he [Lord John] had proved completely that his course [leading the House of Commons without office] was *theoretically constitutional*; but this did not prevent, that *in practice* it might turn out to carry a *material alteration* into our Constitution. . . . *In practice* the appointment of a Leader of the House of Commons without the responsibility of office might become most dangerous. It might be quite true that he would in fiction bear a share in the collective responsibility of the Cabinet, yet he was properly speaking *not a servant of the Crown* but rather a delegate of the majority of the House of Commons, sitting in the Cabinet, or a retained orator by the Cabinet to smooth matters in Parliament. All his moral ties would be to the House of Commons, none to the Crown.[3]

The Prince to some extent based himself on Stockmar's doctrines, but did not follow him all the way. He feared that a divorce of the parliamentary and governmental aspects in the leadership (whose combination he saw far more clearly than Stockmar) might result in the leader of the House being elected by parliament. Though Palmerston's name was not mentioned, both sides in this discussion realised that he loomed large in the whole issue:

> . . . the majority of the House might elect one member, who was popular with them, as their Leader, to whom would then have to be entrusted the most important functions in the Country without there existing any guarantee either for his moral or public character or for his acquaintance with the details of Departments, his knowledge of business generally etc . . . I instanced Mr. Disraeli, who, if he had not had to submit a Budget, would never have been tested, at all, as a statesman, and would very likely have laughed at the unfortunate Chancellor of the Exchequer and his clumsy Budget, and have remained a great man himself. Mr. Brougham[4] would very likely have preferred that very situation in 1830 to have to

---

[1] Russell to Aberdeen, 22 January 1853 (Royal Archives C.28.94).
[2] Memorandum by Prince Albert, 18 February 1853 (Royal Archives C.28.104).
[3] Ibid.
[4] Actually, while Brougham might have *desired* leading the House of Commons without office this was never seriously considered. Brougham actually wanted an irremovable office compatible with a seat in the House of Commons, i.e. the Mastership of the Rolls.

go as Lord Brougham to the Woolsack and nobody could doubt the danger into which that would have led the Country. . . .

The Leader of the House of Commons [without government office] would merely look to the wishes of the House and to his position there, and might be tempted to push further the establishment of what is called *"parliamentary government"*, which was a gradual transition from the constitutional Monarchy to the Republic, and while he [Lord John] proved that the arrangement was in theory compatible with the constitutional Monarchy, the Democratic Republic might steal a march upon it.

Lord John rejoined that the influence of Parliament upon the conduct of affairs had already been carried so far that it could hardly be extended any further.[1]

The interview showed that Lord John still considered his subordination to Lord Aberdeen an indignity:

. . . of late great efforts had been made to run him down in the world: first the Irish were got from him, then the Radicals, at last he was undermined with the Whigs, and those who had been most active in producing this would have triumphed to see him at last in a low office [such as the Chancellorship of the Duchy of Lancaster] saying: "that is quite what he is fit for."

. . . the Queen . . . said that he stood so high as a public man that he might have taken any office without any fear, but added that if that had been contemplated the better way would have been for him to take two offices at first and when the parliamentary business began to retire upon the easier one: but his taking another office now would entail another election for the City . . .

To the Queen's question: "why nobody had thought of that?" he answered, slyly laughing: "I thought of it, but I would not say it, because I did not wish it." [2]

It was clear to the Queen and her husband that Lord John was likely to prove troublesome in the future and might even endanger the continued existence of the government. This disunity in the Cabinet was not a good omen for its ability to deal with a serious question. The test was to come sooner and more dramatically than anybody anticipated.

[1] Memorandum by Prince Albert, 18 February 1853 (Royal Archives C.28.104).
[2] Ibid.

Chapter Eleven

THE CRIMEAN WAR

(i)

WHEN hostilities between Britain and Russia seemed to be imminent early in 1854, Prince Albert found himself the victim of a violent press campaign. Public opinion was becoming impatient at what it considered to be the weak attitude of the Aberdeen government to Russia's dictatorial handling of Turkey. Newspapers on the extreme Right and the radical Left singled out the Queen's husband as the target for their attacks. To them, the Prince was the very embodiment of a pro-Russian policy. Some of them went so far as to denounce him as a Russian spy. There was vague talk of a Coburg conspiracy with Russia and Austria. Prince Albert was accused of unconstitutional interference in affairs of state and rumours were in circulation that he had been imprisoned in the Tower of London.

The press campaign was the result of a war hysteria which was to cost the country dear. Though the accusations need not be taken seriously, they are of some interest. The charge of unconstitutional interference was only to be expected. The strange feature is the imputation of pro-Russian sentiments which are belied by the whole record of the Prince's diplomatic views.

It has been shown how a coalition such as the Aberdeen administration was inescapable as things stood in British domestic politics at the end of 1852. With their responsibility for the formation of a stable government, the Queen and her husband inevitably became identified to some extent with the new Cabinet. But it did not follow that the Court was agreed in all respects with the foreign policy of the new ministers.

During the whole of 1853 the courts and cabinets of Europe were kept occupied by the intricacies of the Eastern question which Prince Albert, with his flair for diplomacy, followed closely. He read all the relevant despatches from the British diplomatic representatives abroad, from Lord Stratford de Redcliffe in Constantinople, from Sir Hamilton Seymour at St. Petersburg, from the Earl of Westmorland in Vienna and from Lord Cowley at Paris. He had copies of the despatches made for his files, which also included newspaper cuttings and a copious correspondence between the Court and the

Prime Minister, as well as the Foreign Secretary. The Prince himself made extensive summaries of the contents of the files, which number about half a dozen, containing on an average 150 documents each, for the Eastern question in the year of 1853 alone.[1]

To the student of history, reading these files after a century, they are full of the tension of a drama moving inexorably to a tragic conclusion. But it is easy to be wise after the event. As 1853 opened, the basic problem of diplomacy for the coming year could not be detected with certainty. The previous months had still left the heritage of a strong suspicion of the Bonapartist régime in France, hardly allayed by the President's self-proclamation as the Emperor Napoleon III. Prince Albert sympathised with the anti-French group led by Aberdeen which allowed the contacts made by Derby and Malmesbury—an old personal friend of Napoleon—to lapse. Peace was just as likely to be broken by the Emperor of the French as by the Tsar of all the Russias. In the very question which was to be the overture to war, that of the rights of Christians in the Holy Places, France and not Russia took the initiative. The Russian demands for the Greek Orthodox Church were a reaction to privileges granted to the Latins at the request of the French.[2] It only became apparent during the course of 1853 that the Christian power most likely to cause war in the East was not France, but Russia. Britain had always been most jealous of any undue extension of Russian influence at Constantinople, but it was difficult to resist Russia, as the champion of the Christians, without appearing to condone Turkish brutality to her Christian subjects in the Balkans.

The Prime Minister, Lord Aberdeen, and the Chancellor of the Exchequer, Gladstone, saw the question mainly from the point of view of a clash between Christianity and Mohammedanism. The Home Secretary, Lord Palmerston, and the Leader of the Commons, Lord John Russell, put the inter-European balance of power at Constantinople first. The advocates of an anti-Russian policy found themselves driven to a white-washing of the Turkish régime,[3] whereas the

---

[1] Royal Archives, G Series.

[2] Thus Clarendon's despatch to Stratford No. 1 of 25 February 1853 emphasises the dangers arising from Tsarist ambitions, but at the same time sides with the Russians against the French in the question of the Holy Places. The draft of the earlier parts of the despatch is in Russell's handwriting (Public Record Office FO/78/924).

[3] The Foreign Office despatches to Seymour (St. Petersburg) in the early part of 1853 contain frequent denials of reports about Turkish atrocities (Public Record Office FO/65/420).

critics of Turkish brutality to the non-Moslems often went too far
in their defence of the Tsar's honourable intentions.

Prince Albert adopted an intermediate position. He had never
had any illusions about the ultimate expansionism of Russian policy.
At the same time he was fully aware of the bad record of Turkish
rule over the Christians and of the deep gulf which divided the
British constitutional monarchy from the Sultan's régime. To check
the Tsar without letting the Sultan get out of hand, he proposed a
"European" policy towards Turkey. He wanted the European
powers to agree on a common policy with regard to the Sultan
which would secure greater rights for the Christian population
without giving any state, particularly Russia, a controlling influence.
The Prince objected to violent attempts to tamper with the *status
quo*. He was thus opposed to Tsar Nicholas' famous proposals to
Sir Hamilton Seymour early in 1853 that Britain and Russia should
come to some arrangement about the "dying bear". Unfortunately,
Aberdeen was too pro-Russian and Lord John was at the Foreign
Office too short a time to convince the Tsar of the honesty of the
British view "as to the necessity of every power abstaining from
views of aggrandisement".[1] Later British criticism of the Tsar's
honesty was excessive. A long and rambling note[2] by Lord John
towards the end of his few weeks' tenure of the Foreign Office failed
to put over the point which a brief statement would have made
much better.[3]

One also has to allow for the puzzlement of the Tsar with regard
to the policy to be expected from the Aberdeen administration. There
must be some sympathy with Nicholas I for misjudging the situation
in one fatal respect. The Russian autocrat over-estimated the importance of the Prime Minister and was misled by his intimate
knowledge of Aberdeen's past and character. He remembered the
part the Prime Minister had played as a young man in the inter-
Allied negotiations at the end of the Napoleonic wars. He knew him
as friendly towards the Eastern Powers and as basically suspicious
of France. When the Tsar paid a flying visit to London in 1844,
Aberdeen, then Foreign Secretary, had apparently been favourable
to plans for Russian expansion at the expense of Turkey. Nicholas I

---

[1] Undated covering memorandum by Prince Albert (Royal Archives G.2).
[2] To Seymour No. 38, 9 February 1853 (Public Record Office FO/65/420).
H. Temperley's comment in "The Crimea", 274 ff., is more favourable.
[3] The Tsar recurred to the subject the following month and Clarendon had to
issue a damper (to Seymour No. 23 of 23 March 1853, Public Record Office
FO/65/420).

did not realise that the extent of a Prime Minister's influence in Britain depended on his personality, that a head of government who was as conciliatory a man as Aberdeen could easily find himself overruled in his own Cabinet. The Tsar had a fatal belief that Aberdeen would never declare war on him. He was prepared to discount British policy during a critical period because it did not seem to follow any set course. He found it difficult to reconcile the existence of a pro-Russian premier in London with an apparently anti-Russian ambassador in Constantinople. In his inability to see any pattern in British policy, he was all the more infuriated if Britain seemed to check him anywhere, as over the Menshikov mission in Constantinople.

Prince Albert at first favoured the Russian demands which were presented at Constantinople by Prince Menshikov in the spring of 1853. In his opinion Russia was entitled to secure for the Greek Orthodox Church the same privileges in the Holy Places as France had obtained for the Catholics. When it became clear, however, that Russia was at the same time trying to establish a Protectorate over millions of the Sultan's Greek Orthodox subjects, Prince Albert and Queen Victoria at once reacted strongly against St. Petersburg. In the Prince's view the Russian demands were quite inadmissible.[1] The Court became seriously alarmed about the Tsar's intentions and began to find Aberdeen's policy towards Russia too weak. At the beginning of May, the Queen asked the new Foreign Secretary, Lord Clarendon, to draw the attention of the Russian government to the discrepancy between peaceful words at St. Petersburg and Prince Menshikov's threats to the Sultan at Constantinople.

. . . We cannot accept such mysterious proceedings at Constantinople, whilst a boast is made of franchise at St. Petersburg, and we must take care not to become the dupes of Russian policy.[2]

Clarendon, still too much under Aberdeen's influence to oppose his pro-Russian policy, suggested postponing any formal representations until further details about the Russian demands were available. He confined himself to a careful private letter to Sir Hamilton Seymour at St. Petersburg.[3] The Court agreed with this method of proceeding.[4]

The Crown was still wavering in its attitude to Nicholas. When

[1] Undated covering memorandum by Prince Albert (Royal Archives G.2).
[2] The Queen to Clarendon, 4 May 1853 (Clarendon Papers).
[3] Clarendon to the Queen, 5 May 1853 (Royal Archives G.2.65).
[4] The Queen to Clarendon, 6 May 1853 (Clarendon Papers).

at this juncture the Queen received a personal letter from the Tsar, the Prince expressed satisfaction at its "cordial terms".[1] Rather prematurely, the Foreign Secretary congratulated himself on the success of his "judicious" policy achieved by not being suspicious of Russia.[2] Clarendon was never to regain quite the same self-assurance about a peaceful solution of the Eastern question. For within a fortnight, it became clear that the faith of the Prime Minister and the Foreign Secretary in the good intentions of the Tsar was misplaced. Prince Menshikov was not satisfied with the concessions he had obtained—with Stratford's help—in the matter of the Holy Places. He issued an ultimatum to the Porte insisting on the full extent of the Russian demands. The Sultan refused to accept an interference with his sovereignty which public sentiment at Constantinople would have never allowed him to admit. Menshikov thereupon broke off diplomatic relations and withdrew with the staff of the Russian Embassy. When the Russian Ambassador in London, Baron Brunnow, blamed the breakdown of the Menshikov mission entirely on the advice Lord Stratford had given the Porte, the Queen agreed with her Foreign Secretary that the Russian envoy's language was "most uncalled for".[3] In the opinion of the Court, the instructions sent to Sir Hamilton Seymour at St. Petersburg a few days later[4] were too mild.[5] The British historian of the diplomatic prelude to the Crimean War calls the despatch which was to be read to the Russian Chancellor, Count Nesselrode, "argumentative".[6] Actually it was more a historical recapitulation of the conflict and the Crown did not consider it strong enough:

> ... The Draft ... does not fully refer to the systematic want of confidence and openness shown by Prince Menshikov to Lord Stratford, takes no credit for Lord Stratford's assistance in the settlement of the question of the Holy Places, does not refer to the excitement in this country and the pressure made upon the government to take active steps for the protection of Turkey, and takes little credit for the risk which it braves—relying implicitly and entirely on the Emperor's honour.[7]

The Court now found the Prime Minister too weak in his approach to Russia. At the same time the Queen and the Prince were becom-

---

[1] Prince Albert to Clarendon, 5 May 1853 (Clarendon Papers).
[2] Clarendon to Prince Albert, 7 May 1853 (Royal Archives G.2.66).
[3] Clarendon to the Queen, 20 May 1853 (Royal Archives G.2.81); the Queen to Clarendon, 21 May 1853 (Clarendon Papers).
[4] To Seymour Nr. 81, of 31 May 1853 (Public Record Office FO/65/421).
[5] The Queen to Clarendon, 1 June 1853 (Clarendon Papers).
[6] Temperley, "The Crimea", 335.
[7] The Queen to Clarendon, 1 June 1853 Clarendon Papers).

ing aware that Lord Aberdeen was no longer leading a united Cabinet. The Prime Minister himself furnished the Crown with little information on the dissension in the Cabinet during the earlier stages. The Foreign Secretary was more forthcoming. Whereas Lord Aberdeen's report on the important Cabinet meeting held on 28 May was quite formal,[1] Lord Clarendon wrote:

> . . . some difference of opinion existed amongst Your Majesty's Servant's as to whether it would be expedient that the British and French fleets should proceed together to the Turkish waters for the protection of Constantinople in the event of its being attacked, or to wait for more certain information as to the occurrences which immediately preceded the departure of Prince Menshikov and not to close the door against future negotiation by a demonstration that the Emperor of Russia would regard as a threat . . . it is probable that Your Majesty's pleasure will be taken as to giving Lord Stratford conditional authority to send for the Fleet . . .[2]

Read in conjunction with an entry in Lord Malmesbury's diary on 29 May,[3] it is apparent that Lord Palmerston began his opposition to Aberdeen's pro-Russian course earlier than has been thought.[4] The Court knew from now on that in opposing Lord Aberdeen's weak policy, it was playing into the hands of Lord Palmerston who was still *persona non grata*.

The Prince and the Queen realised that in view of the uncertainty of Russia's future intentions, it was no longer possible to keep France in quarantine. The only chance of checking Russia lay in the combination of as many European powers as possible against her. Little reliance could be placed on Austria and Prussia. This left France as the sole potential ally. Napoleon III was only too ready to oblige. Gradually, if slowly, the Queen and the Prince were changing their attitude to the upstart monarch. In May, the Queen expressed to the Foreign Secretary her satisfaction at France's moderation.[5] The Court accepted the necessity of naval collaboration with France, requested by the French Ambassador in London, Walewski.[6] The Queen readily approved the conditional placing of the British Fleet at Malta under Lord Stratford's authority. She sanctioned the Fleet's moving to the Dardanelles,[7] thus assuming that the Ambassador would "call it up", which he only did much later. Actually the

---

[1] Aberdeen to the Queen, 28 May 1853 (Royal Archives G.3.8).
[2] Clarendon to the Queen, 28 May 1853 (Royal Archives G.3.9).
[3] The Earl of Malmesbury, "Memoirs of an Ex-Minister", 401.
[4] By Temperley, "The Crimea", 339.
[5] The Queen to Clarendon, 23 May 1853 (Clarendon Papers).
[6] Clarendon to the Queen, 24 May 1853 (Royal Archives G.3.3); Prince Albert's covering memorandum (Royal Archives G.3).
[7] The Queen to Clarendon, 2 June 1853 (Clarendon Papers).

Fleet remained outside the Hellespont, at Besika Bay. The decision of the Cabinet had all the fatal consequences of a compromise between irreconcilables. Without going far enough to deter the Russians, as Palmerston and Lord John wished, it was sufficient to embitter the Tsar even further and thus frustrated the conciliatory policy that Aberdeen had in mind.

Simultaneously, the Russians gave further evidence of their war-like intentions by occupying the Principalities of Moldavia and Wallachia, which formed part of the Turkish empire (though Russia had certain special treaty rights there). The Western Powers persuaded the Porte not to declare war on Russia, but to be satisfied with a protest and to call upon Europe for redress. The British government contented itself expressing "astonishment and regret" at the occupation.[1]

In view of the allegations about a Coburg conspiracy on behalf of Russia, it is interesting to note that the King of the Belgians and his nephew found themselves in disagreement over the Oriental question in June. King Leopold's prestige was rising with the Eastern Powers and he basked in the sunshine of the favour of his newly found friends. The Belgian monarch was about to marry his son and heir, the later Leopold II, to an Austrian princess. To his uncle's attempts to play down the differences between Russia and the other powers, the Prince replied:

> ... I can assure you that I am doing everything in our power to con-
> tribute to a peaceful solution. You call the complication "a matter mainly
> of *form*". I wish I could see clearly whether this is so, or whether the
> substance of the "transfer of allegiance of 12 Millions of Christians from
> the Sultan to the Emperor of Russia" is the object . . . of the Emperor?
> Up to now, every proposal to change something of this substance has
> excited the most extreme rage of the Russian Diplomacy. In the *form*
> even Menshikov has been conciliatory . . .[2]

The Prince defended Lord Stratford against the accusation of hostility to Russia:

> His steps, as far as we know them, bear witness to moderation, helpfulness
> and indulgence towards Russia; only he could not advise the abdication
> of the sovereignty of the Sultan.[3]

Prince Albert advocated a conference of the powers as soon as the

---

[1] Clarendon to Seymour No. 134 of 16 July 1853 (Public Record Office FO/65/421).
[2] Prince Albert to King Leopold, 14 June 1853 (Royal Archives G.3.72), tr.
[3] Ibid.

Russians had violated Turkish territory by invading the Principalities:

> Austria would be in the best position to be a mediator; but as she has sold herself to the Russians for Hungary, the peace of Europe lacks its best support.[1]

While the Prince took a more realistic view than the Premier of Russia's aims, his attempt to solve the Russo-Turkish problem with the help of the European powers appealed to him. But he had few illusions about Austria:

> Austria *cannot* be honest to the rest of Europe on *any* question in her present position, convinced as she is that her existence as a State depends entirely on her keeping in abject submission not only her own populations, but the whole of Italy and Germany, which she can only hope to accomplish with Russian aid.[2]

Thus, when Russia was increasingly showing her hand in the summer of 1853, Prince Albert once more picked up the threads of his Cracow policy of 1846 and reverted to the ideas he developed after the February Revolution of 1848. He had always looked on Russia as the most dangerous of the Holy Alliance states. To curb her, he wished to detach Austria and Prussia from her. This would at the same time have the advantage of freeing Austria and Prussia from what he considered the pernicious reactionary influence of St. Petersburg. The necessary preconditions for a solution of the German and Italian problems would thus be created. The crisis at Constantinople presented itself to the Prince mainly in the wider setting of the general future of Europe.

Thanks to the impact of the Eastern question, Prince Albert hoped once more for a change of heart in Berlin. The government of Otto von Manteuffel, which had come into power after Olmütz, did not show quite the servility to Russia which might have been expected from it. Strong pressure was brought to bear on Frederick William IV by his Russian brother-in-law to show more solidarity with St. Petersburg. At the end of July, Prince Albert wrote to Lord Clarendon:

> . . . The state of things at Berlin is lamentable. Baron Manteuffel was placed in office by the Russo-Austrian Reactionary mock-religious Cabal and did its dirty work . . .; the moment he shows any zeal for the interests of his country he is to be displaced by it, and I have no doubt that he will be so displaced.[3]

---

[1] Ibid.
[2] Prince Albert to Clarendon, 23 July 1853 (Royal Archives G.4.49).
[3] Prince Albert to Clarendon, 25 July 1853 (Clarendon Papers). Manteuffel reverted to his pro-Russian line and remained in power.

(ii)

In spite of his care and occasional intervention, Prince Albert's contribution to a peaceful solution of the Eastern question is disappointing, particularly when compared with his action over the *Trent* affair when he was dying. He did not have an overall picture of the situation any more than the other statesmen of his day. Conciliatory and peace-loving, he was for a long time in favour of all the attempts made, be it from London or Vienna or Constantinople, to settle outstanding differences. He failed to foresee the unfortunate effect which numerous negotiations and proposals at several centres would have on each other. For all these projects, counter-projects, modifications and counter-modifications were almost as confusing to the contemporary negotiator as they are to the student of the period.

The influence of the British Court on diplomatic negotiations involving several countries was bound to be much more restricted than in the case of bilateral differences. The main reason for the failure of the Crown to intervene effectively lay, however, in the disunity of the Cabinet. All important decisions taken by the Cabinet during the period were made only after long and often heated argument. They usually represented a compromise between contradictory policies and disharmonious personalities. The Court realised that if it proposed even slight alterations of policy, this precarious balance might be upset and the government endangered by a threat of resignation on the part of the leaders of the anti-Russian section, of Lord John or Lord Palmerston or both. Thus ironically, with a friendly government in power, the influence of the Court was smaller than it had been in the days of friction.

There was an additional obstacle. During highly critical weeks in the late summer and autumn the Court was out of reach. There was a state visit to Ireland at the end of August and later a prolonged stay at Balmoral. While the Court was some distance from London, it had to forgo any effective supervision of foreign policy. There were almost daily changes in the general diplomatic situation which was made all the more confusing by the discrepancy between speedy telegraphic news from Paris and Vienna, and the necessity of relying on archaic means of communications for the last lap to Turkey, between Vienna and Constantinople.[1] When the Queen complained

---

[1] After a reform instituted by Lord John in February 1853, it was "hoped . . . that the arrival of despatches from Constantinople in 16 days will be secured" (Public Record Office FO/78/924).

from Balmoral in the middle of September about despatches reaching her late and going off without her sanction, the Prime Minister expressed regret but hardly offered any prospect of improvement.[1] The Court accepted the explanation as reasonable.[2]

Faced with a government to its liking, the Crown was bound to see the situation largely through the ministers' eyes. Although Prince Albert could not go all the way with Lord Aberdeen in his Russophil tendencies, he agreed with the Prime Minister's views on other points. Thus the Prince accepted at their face value the allegations Lord Aberdeen and Lord Clarendon were constantly making about their ambassador at Constantinople. He agreed with the Prime Minister and the Foreign Secretary in thinking that Lord Stratford was sabotaging the efforts to obtain a peaceful solution.[3] But historical research has cast doubt on the old interpretation according to which Stratford was the villain of the piece.[4] The attacks on the ambassador came largely from interested parties, such as the Prime Minister and Foreign Secretary in the search of an alibi. From the information available to the Queen and the Prince, a different inference could more plausibly be drawn about the Constantinople Embassy. The letters of the Prime Minister to the Queen and her husband reflected a lack of control over the Cabinet and foreign policy which could not fail to strike them. It is unfortunate that they were prevented from making searching criticisms at an early stage owing to their confidence in the moral integrity of the Prime Minister. In one respect, the Queen repeatedly asked for action. Accepting the conclusions of her government, she did not see how Lord Stratford could be left at his post in Constantinople and asked for his recall.[5] But she was overruled. Neither Aberdeen nor Clarendon relished the prospect of Stratford focusing his attentions on their Oriental policy from the opposition benches in the House of Lords. So the most vital embassy in these days continued to be held by a man suspected of rank disobedience by his own government. Even if the more recent view of Stratford's policy is accepted, the Queen's demand for his recall was justified by the circumstances. For it was essential that there should be complete confidence between Whitehall and the envoy at the critical centre left to his own devices by the slowness of communications.

[1] Aberdeen to the Queen, 19 September 1853 (Royal Archives G.5.69).
[2] The Queen to Aberdeen, 21 September 1853 (Royal Archives G.5.78).
[3] There are frequent phrases like "Lord Stratford showing eagerness for war" even during the summer of 1853 (Royal Archives G.4).
[4] See Temperley, "The Crimea", Chs. XII–XIV.
[5] Thus 5 November 1853 (see the Queen to Lord Aberdeen in *Letters*).

Prince Albert had a particular reason for dreading Stratford. He thought—wrongly[1]—that he was in regular intimate correspondence with the main protagonist of the anti-Russian policy in the Cabinet, Lord Palmerston. The Court still had no more confidence in Palmerston than during his last years at the Foreign Office. He continued to be cold-shouldered by the Crown, though it was becoming clear that Aberdeen's conciliatory policy towards Russia had failed and that Palmerston's recipe of early resistance to the Tsar might have served better.

By the end of September, Prince Albert's confidence in the ability of the Prime Minister to deal with the crisis had been severely shaken. He wrote to Stockmar:

> . . . I cannot hide from you that the whole course of the [Oriental] affair has done Aberdeen extraordinary harm with the public and that the outcry against him and Clarendon will soon become great, *unjustly*; but the great mass only judges by success and Aberdeen is too courageous in his confidence in the honesty of Russia and Austria, just as he had been in that of Louis Philippe and Guizot,[2] and denies from obstinacy the most obvious facts. He is probably quite right, and is to be honoured and praised for maintaining that one has to treat one's enemies like *honest* people and that one should treat them honestly, but because of that one should not believe that they *are* actually so. . . .
>
> Just imagine Uncle Leopold now preaches *to him* moderation and the necessity of forcing the Porte to give in . . .[3]

But though the Court considered Aberdeen too patient with the Russians, it did not like to see the Prime Minister overawed in his own Cabinet by the section demanding strong naval demonstrations in the Straits and possibly in the Black Sea.

(iii)

Early in October it looked as if a Cabinet crisis would be added to all the intrinsic difficulties of the Eastern question. At one stage Lord Aberdeen feared that both Lord John and Palmerston might secede from the government.[4] Actually the trouble came more from Lord John than from Lord Palmerston. The Leader of the House of Commons wanted to take up the option on the premiership as quickly as possible.

[1] According to S. Lane-Poole, there was no political correspondence between the two statesmen (see his "Life of Stratford Canning", II, 231).

[2] This might be interpreted as criticism of Aberdeen's handling of the early stages of the Spanish marriage question.

[3] Prince Albert to Stockmar, 27 September 1853 (Royal Archives G.5.99), tr.

[4] Aberdeen to Graham, 6 October 1853 (Royal Archives G.6.10), submitted to the Queen.

The domestic crisis was closely connected with the decisive stage which the Oriental question had reached. Russia had, it is true, accepted the "Vienna note" containing the proposals of the Powers, but had at the same time put a "violent interpretation" on it according to which she understood by it more than the Powers meant and the Porte could grant. When it became clear to Stratford at Constantinople that the Porte could never accept the Vienna terms, he proposed modifications which were, however, in turn rejected by the Tsar. In the meantime the mood at Constantinople, encouraged by the proximity of British and French naval forces at Besika Bay, got completely out of control and war was declared on Russia by the Porte. This enabled the Allied Fleet to move into the Sea of Marmara without treaty violation. A meeting of the Tsar with the Emperor of Austria resulted in a new set of proposals, but tension had increased to such an extent that the voice of diplomacy was muted.

Aberdeen was in a most unhappy position. Sympathetic to Russia, abhorring the Porte's persecution of Christians and passionately devoted to the maintenance of peace, he was constantly finding himself overruled in his own Cabinet by the protagonists of a more forward policy. He would have been more consistent if he had resigned. But he strongly believed that his presence constituted a brake on the war-like elements in the Cabinet and thus increased the chances of keeping peace. Rarely was a more fatal opinion held.

The Prime Minister had another consideration in remaining in his place. He wanted to hand over the premiership at some convenient time in the future to a successor who would be able to keep the Whig-Peelite coalition together. Here Lord John proved the stumbling block. For while it was unlikely that he would be able to lead the coalition, he could, if he so desired, prevent anybody else from doing so. In Lord John's own mind, there was no room for doubt about his rights. He considered himself as crown prince and thought that Aberdeen's retirement was overdue. The Prime Minister feared that Lord John was on the point of breaking up the government and that he was being supported in this by Palmerston. Actually, Lord John did not have Palmerston's support. The Home Secretary was biding his time. In consequence of the promptings of Aberdeen and Clarendon he had even been asked to Court at Balmoral.[1] The last thing Palmerston wanted was to help Lord John

[1] Aberdeen to Queen Victoria, 11 September 1853 (*Letters*); Maxwell, Clarendon, II, 21 ff.

back into 10, Downing Street, however much he might agree with
him on foreign policy. Even over the Eastern question, he was finding
that all too often Lord John was trying to outbid him in the Cabinet.
Both wanted Liberal and Radical support and the only safe way
of getting that was to be anti-Russian. Liberalism at home had
disadvantages, but liberalism abroad was highly profitable. For
various reasons hardly anybody was satisfied with Lord John.

The Whig chief was looking for a pretext to resign from the
government and to force the succession question. At the end of
September he threatened to leave the Cabinet owing to another
attempt by Lord Aberdeen to try a peaceful solution at Vienna. But
he did not carry out his threat. The Prime Minister gave one of the
reasons for Lord John's change of mind in a report to Sir James
Graham, who was at that time Minister in attendance at Balmoral:

> . . . the comical part of this affair is, that we caught Palmerston on his
> way to Balmoral, and the proposal which has so much excited Lord John's
> indignation, not only has Palmerston's concurrence, but was in great part
> his own work! ! !¹ [1]

Lord John's second string was his proposal for another reform
bill. The Whig leader felt strongly about the necessity for further
parliamentary reform. At the same time, he used the reform bill to
try and obtain the premiership. His argument was that in order to
bring forward the bill, he ought to be Prime Minister and not
merely Leader of the House of Commons. In the middle of the
Eastern crisis, the timing was certainly unfortunate. He soon saw
himself that he could not press his proposals. The Prime Minister
was convinced, however, that

> Lord John will seek, and of course will find, an opportunity of breaking
> off on a popular ground, instead of one ridiculously untenable.[2]

The domestic and international crisis was so severe, that Lord
Aberdeen wrote to the Queen "pretty strongly to hasten her return" [3]
from Balmoral at the beginning of October. It is unfortunate that
the Queen and the Prince deprived themselves of an opportunity to
influence affairs at a critical time by their absence from the London
area. This would not have mattered so much if they had been satisfied with the government's policy. But they disapproved both of

---

[1] Aberdeen to Graham, 22 September 1853, communicated to Prince Albert on
5 October (Royal Archives G.6.2 & 3).
[2] Aberdeen to Graham, 6 October 1853, communicated to Prince Albert
(Royal Archives G.6.10).
[3] Ibid.

the substance of its measures and of the method by which they were decided. The Court realised from the reports of the Prime Minister and the Foreign Secretary, as well as from conversations with Sir James Graham, that Lord Aberdeen was allowing himself to become responsible for a policy of which he disapproved. The Court agreed with the Prime Minister in judging this policy wrong. In the opinion of the Queen and her husband, Lord Aberdeen should not have agreed to Palmerston's demand for the grant of powers to Lord Stratford to "call up" the Fleet into the Black Sea. The royal couple also criticised the Prime Minister for failing to insist on safeguards to prevent the Turks from using British support for their own ends. The Queen wrote to the Prime Minister:

> ... The state of affairs is not altogether pleasant; nor is the Queen reassured that the course adopted with reference to the oriental difficulty is that which on the whole Lord Aberdeen thinks the wisest and safest to adopt. As the chance of a European war is at stake in the decision now taken or about to be taken with regard to the answer to . . . the instruction to the Admirals, the Queen feels in duty bound, before giving her sanction to these . . . documents (which she has not yet seen) to ask from Lord Aberdeen his deliberate counsel on the spirit and ultimate tendency of the policy which he would recommend the Queen to approve.[1]

The Court put the right foreign policy first and foremost, whereas Lord Aberdeen seemed to be primarily concerned with keeping the Cabinet together. The Queen and the Prince were worried lest they might be involved in a war as a consequence of the policies of the Aberdeen administration which might then break up and leave the Crown without an efficient government.[2] Here the old fear of Palmerston was a factor, though not the only one.

When the Court returned to England in the middle of October, most of the steps which were eventually to lead to war had already been taken. The initiative now lay with the warlike Divan. The Queen's protest about the large powers given to Stratford proved of no avail.[3] On 23 October, Omer Pasha went over to the offensive against the Russians in the Balkans.

The Queen and the Prince were in a difficult position. They realised that it would not be possible for Lord John to take over from Lord Aberdeen. On his way south from Balmoral, Prince Albert had discussed Lord John's position with the Peelite Secretary for

---

[1] The Queen to Aberdeen, 10 October 1853 (Royal Archives G.6.25).
[2] Memorandum by Prince Albert, 10 October 1853 (*Letters*).
[3] Ibid.

War and the Colonies, the Duke of Newcastle. The Duke had told the Prince that:

> ... Lord Palmerston never would serve again under Lord John, none of the Peelites would willingly do so and the Whig members like Sir Ch. Wood and Lord Granville etc would equally regret the necessity. He said the Irish were as bitter against Lord John as ever, the Radicals preferred Lord Aberdeen, only a knot of Elliots, Russells and Romillys could wish for the change, *Lady* John was bent on attaining it and the quiet passing off of the last Cabinet was mainly owing to *her* not having come up to town with Lord John.[1]

Apparently Lady John had told Sir James Graham in June: "I almost begin to become a supporter of the present government." [2]

The Queen disapproved of Lord Aberdeen's discussions with Lord John about the future of the premiership. She wanted to retain her Prime Minister,[3] in spite of her strictures. At the request of the Queen, the Prince drew up a memorandum on the Court's attitude[4] which satisfied neither party in the Cabinet fully, although both Lord Aberdeen and Lord John expressed some agreement.[5] The Prince came down more on the pro-Turkish side as far as the merits of the conflict were concerned than Lord Aberdeen would have wished. On the other hand he also inferred that the foremost objective of British policy, the maintenance of peace, had been jeopardised by the naval precautions. He concluded, however, by admitting that a war to prevent Constantinople from falling into Russian hands "may be right and wise". He then tried to draw a—somewhat artificial—distinction between a war to maintain Turkish rule over a Christian population and one for the maintenance of the European order. The war should not be fought to uphold the integrity of the Ottoman Empire:

> ... It ought to be carried on unshackled by obligations to the Porte and will probably lead, in the Peace which must be the object of that war, to the obtaining of arrangements more consonant with the well-understood interests of Europe, of Christianity, liberty and civilisation, than the reimposition of the ignorant barbarian and despotic yoke of the Mussulman over the most fertile and favoured portion of Europe.[6]

However admirable these sentiments may have been, it should have been apparent even then that a victory of the Anglo-Franco-

---

[1] Memorandum by Prince Albert, 16 October 1853 (Royal Archives G.6.44).
[2] Ibid.
[3] Memorandum by Prince Albert, 16 October 1853 (*Letters*).
[4] Memorandum by Prince Albert, 21 October 1853 (Martin, II, 525 ff.).
[5] See Martin, II, 527.
[6] Memorandum by Prince Albert of 21 October 1853 (Martin, II, 525 ff.).

Turkish alliance over Russia was not likely to prove a propitious moment for a curtailing of Turkish rule. In holding the balance between the Ottoman Empire as a European necessity on the one hand and as the Moslem oppressor of Christians on the other, the Prince came close to the contemporary attitude of Gladstone, then Chancellor of the Exchequer, of whom the Queen's husband thought very highly.[1]

Palmerston decided not to leave the Prince's reasoning un-answered, though the memorandum admitted his main contention, that war on behalf of Turkey might be necessary. The Home Secre-tary argued very forcibly that Britain could no longer draw back. At the same time he tried to deny the truth of reports about Turkish atrocities in the Balkans. He drew attention to the inconsistencies in the Prince's argument and maintained that the time was not yet ripe for creating more independent Christian states in the Balkans. Aberdeen felt it necessary to answer Palmerston's arguments. He still believed that Britain was free to act as she wished:

> If the Turks should reject our advice and should be obstinately bent on war, when we are labouring for peace, I confess that I am not disposed to sacrifice our freedom of action, and to permit ourselves to be dragged into war by a Government which has not the requisite control over its own subjects, and is obliged to act under the pressure of popular dictation.[2]

The Turkish government was not the only one which was subject to the pressure of "popular dictation".

Though from a practical point of view, the Court was closer to Palmerston than to Aberdeen, the Home Secretary was still suspect. Aberdeen, in his desperate straits, used Stratford and Palmerston as whipping-boys and saw fit to keep alive the Court's old mistrust of the Home Secretary. Thus, when the Prime Minister informed the Queen of the Cabinet's rejection of a Turkish proposal for naval co-operation against Russia early in November, he added that the origin of this suggestion became apparent in the course of the dis-cussion.[3] The Prince's footnote explains the meaning of this remark:

> Lord Palmerston having failed to carry this plan formerly in the Cabinet sent it out secretly to Lord Stratford.[4]

---

[1] See Prince Albert's congratulations to the Chancellor on his budget, 19 April 1853 (*Letters*).
[2] Aberdeen to Palmerston, 4 November 1853 (Royal Archives G.6.102).
[3] Aberdeen to the Queen, 8 November 1853 (Royal Archives G.7.1).
[4] Ibid.

(iv)

In the meantime, Palmerston had managed to reinforce the Court's old antagonism to him by interfering in the affairs of the Royal Family. He had supported a scheme for the marriage of Princess Mary of Cambridge—the mother of the late Queen Mary—to Prince Jerome Bonaparte.[1] This prince was a son of the Jerome who was King of Westphalia during the Napoleonic régime, and was thus a first cousin of the Emperor Napoleon III. Palmerston backed the plan in order to strengthen Anglo-French understanding and to forestall an eventual Franco-Russian alliance. In doing so, he only did himself harm without the remotest possibility of achieving anything at all. He also used arguments which were anathema to the Court:

> The young man is said to be good looking, pleasing and intelligent and would be likely to make a better husband than some petty member of a petty German Prince's House . . .[2]

He never bothered to find out, before he took the first steps, whether the idea was agreeable to the Queen and whether the religious difficulties arising out of Prince Jerome's Catholicism could be overcome. He persevered even when he realised the "strong prejudice of the Queen . . . against it".[3] The Queen's and Prince Albert's reaction was a sharply negative one. Prince Albert noted:

> Prince Jerome is the greatest scamp in all France, conspired with the Socialists, is not trusted by his Cousin, lives a life of profligacy, which has even *disgusted* the French.[4]

Lord Aberdeen described the whole affair to Prince Albert as "an instance of the infatuation of Lord Palmerston for the cause of Louis Napoleon".[5] It is odd that a great man like Palmerston at this critical juncture, where his standing at Court might be of considerable importance, prejudiced his position there even further in a hopeless cause, merely accentuating in memory the events with which his dismissal in 1851 had been connected.

Lord Palmerston was not the only person connected with the marriage scheme. It had the backing of the Emperor himself and

---

[1] Memorandum by Prince Albert, 4 November 1853 (Royal Archives A.81.43).
[2] Palmerston to Aberdeen, 5 November 1853 (Royal Archives A.81.46), submitted to Prince Albert by Lord Aberdeen shortly afterwards with a covering note: ". . . I cannot resist laying before Your Royal Highness the inclosed letter . . ." (Royal Archives A.81.45).
[3] Ibid.
[4] Memorandum by Prince Albert of 4 November 1853 (Royal Archives A.81.43).
[5] Ibid.

was actively supported in London by the French Ambassador, Count Walewski, an illegitimate son of Napoleon I. The Bonaparte family went so far as to appeal to Leopold I for his help, though the King of the Belgians had been Louis Philippe's son-in-law. Prince Albert thought that Palmerston had suggested that King Leopold should put the plan to Queen Victoria, so as to by-pass Lord Aberdeen. When King Leopold raised the matter, he was firmly told that there was no possibility of the marriage taking place.[1]

The Bonapartes showed considerable perseverance in pursuing the marriage scheme. For some time, its sponsors maintained that Princess Mary was not disinclined to accept Prince Jerome.[2] Eventually Lord Clarendon got the truth about this from Walewski, who told him:

> Eh bien il serait très naturel qu'une jeune personne de son âge veuille se marier, et le Prince est beau garçon, a une très belle position, qui peut devenir assez brillante un jour. Il y a là assez pour plair à une jeune dame . . .[3]

There seemed, indeed, to be little evidence for a favourable attitude to the proposal on the part of Princess Mary. Prince Albert made painstaking enquiries:

> We thought it right to communicate to the Duchess[4] the whole affair in order to ascertain how far she could have been cognisant of it. She nearly fainted away at the news and could [hardly] bring herself to realise the possibility of such a project having been seriously entertained; she felt *quite certain* that her daughter could not have been spoken to, or got at by anybody who could have been in the intrigue and was very much offended that it should have been thought that she or her daughter could have stooped so low, as to be capable of entering upon such a proposal. She knows the young Jerome by *reputation* from his former stays in London and had during the wars been robbed and persecuted by the father together with her whole family, when they had to fly from Cassel and the whole of Hesse was ransacked and plundered by him.[5]

When the London emissaries had failed, the Emperor Napoleon himself revived the proposal at the end of November in a conversation with the British Ambassador, Lord Cowley, with whom he was on close terms. The Emperor attached great importance to the scheme which would provide evidence of the cordial relations

---

[1] Ibid.
[2] Ibid., Palmerston to Aberdeen, 5 November 1853 (Royal Archives A.81.46).
[3] Memorandum by Prince Albert, 16 November 1853 (Royal Archives A.81.50).
[4] Augusta Duchess of Cambridge belonged to a junior line of the House of Hesse-Cassel.
[5] Memorandum by Prince Albert, 18 November 1853 (Royal Archives A.81.50).

between England and France. Cowley was in a difficulty, from which he extricated himself as best he could, pleading the religious differences.[1]

The incident closed in February 1854, but not without involving a further person, Lord Henry Lennox, a son of the fifth Duke of Richmond. Lennox was a collaborator of Disraeli and actually spent some time in Paris at this juncture as the special correspondent of the Protectionist organ, *The Press*,[2] which was distinguished for its violent attacks on Lord Aberdeen. Lord Henry was suspected at Court of having visited the Duchess of Cambridge and of having discussed the marriage project with Princess Mary without her mother's knowledge. Prince Albert asked the Duchess of Cambridge to forbid Lord Henry her house,[3] but his wife's aunt refused.

Any further action was hardly necessary any more, as the whole marriage project had been dropped. Prince Jerome married a daughter of Victor Emanuel II of Sardinia in 1859. Princess Mary became the wife of Prince Francis of Württemberg-Teck in 1866.

(v)

In the middle of December, the difficulties between Palmerston and Aberdeen came to a head. Palmerston was dissatisfied not only with the Eastern policy of the government, but also with its acceptance of Lord John's proposals for a reform bill. There must remain some mystery as to the exact reasons for Palmerston's sudden resignation on 14 December. But it is unlikely that the reform measure was his primary reason for wishing to leave the government. For months, at least since May, he had had to witness the execution of a foreign policy in a manner of which he largely disapproved. When he seemed to be put in a position of having to swallow domestic measures with which he also disagreed, his patience was exhausted. His old rivalry with Lord John came to the fore once more when he said that "he refused . . . to be dragged through the dirt by John Russell".[4]

Lord Palmerston's resignation was voluntary. The files[5] disprove theories that he had been "extruded" by the Prime Minister[6] and that the Court brought any pressure to bear before Palmerston sent

[1] Private letter from Cowley to Palmerston, 27 November 1853 (Royal Archives A.81.62), submitted to the Queen on 29 November.
[2] Monypenny and Buckle, I, 1340 ff.
[3] Prince Albert to the Duchess of Cambridge, 5 February 1854 in German (Royal Archives A.81.136).
[4] Memorandum by Prince Albert, 16 December 1853 (Royal Archives G.7.106).
[5] Royal Archives, G.7 and A.81 series.
[6] J. K. Laughton, "Memoirs of Henry Reeve", II, 352 ff.

in his resignation. In a letter to his political friend Lord Lansdowne, who like himself disapproved of reform, Lord Palmerston emphasised this issue, but not without referring also to his dissatisfaction with the Eastern policy.[1] When writing to the Prime Minister on 10 December, and enclosing a copy of his letter to Lansdowne, Palmerston began by mentioning his objections to reform but devoted the greater part of his epistle to the Eastern question.[2] On 13 December Lord Aberdeen was still writing to Palmerston in conciliatory and patiently explanatory terms about the Eastern question, though he rejected his proposal for an interdiction of the Black Sea to the Russian Navy.[3] Neither Lord Aberdeen nor the Queen and the Prince were, however, going to let Palmerston force the Cabinet to abandon the reform measure. The Queen pointed out the necessity of having a united government introducing the reform bill.[4] The Court and the Prime Minister agreed that if Lord Palmerston was to resign at all it would do the government less harm if he did so over the Reform Bill than over the Eastern question. When the Prime Minister remained firm about reform, as he had every right to be, the Home Secretary decided to resign.[5] Aberdeen made no immediate effort, as Lord John had done during his government, to prevent the resignation from taking place.

The Court was delighted to be rid of Palmerston. Prince Albert thought that the ex-Home Secretary wished to put himself at the head of the Protectionists and Ultra Tories in the Commons with a view to becoming Premier. He regarded domestic affairs as the primary cause of the resignation, but particularly welcomed Palmerston's withdrawal for its effect on the foreign policy of the Cabinet which he thought and hoped would now become less warlike.[6] He misjudged both the man and the situation.

By a strange coincidence Palmerston's resignation coincided with the receipt of the first news in London of an event which made the outbreak of war between the Western Powers and Russia inevitable. On 30 November a Turkish flotilla was attacked by Russian warships in the Black Sea port of Sinope in Asia Minor and almost totally wiped out. The "massacre" of Sinope had a tremendous effect on public opinion in England which now demanded an end of

[1] 8 December 1853 (*Letters*).
[2] Palmerston to Aberdeen, 10 December 1853 (Royal Archives G.7.82).
[3] Aberdeen to Palmerston, 13 December 1853 (Royal Archives G.7.100).
[4] The Queen to Aberdeen, 9 December 1853 (*Letters*).
[5] Memorandum by Prince Albert, 16 December 1853 (Royal Archives G.7.106).
[6] Prince Albert to his brother, 19 December 1853 (Ernst, II, 99, ff.); Memorandum by Prince Albert, 16 December 1853 (*Letters*).

parleys. In this new constellation Palmerston's resignation became a symbol. The official and literally true explanation that he resigned because of the reform question was disbelieved. With uncanny accuracy, the opposition and radical press detected the real major underlying cause.[1] Palmerston had resigned mainly because he could no longer bear the shilly-shallying of the Russophil Aberdeen.

The protectionist and radical press in its excitement overshot the mark. The Court noted that almost immediately after Palmerston's resignation the non-government newspapers engaged in a violent tirade against the evil influence of the house of Coburg in general and of Prince Albert in particular.[2] There were absurd accusations of Russophil tendencies. The radical newspapers took it for granted that Austria would maintain solidarity with Russia, an assumption which it would have been better to avoid as long as there was any hope of that split between the Eastern Powers which Prince Albert wanted to encourage. The Queen's husband was, in many eyes, the embodiment of this imaginary combination between the Eastern Powers and the House of Coburg. The Court had no doubt about Palmerston's responsibility for the press campaign.[3]

Prince Albert thought the attack on him was part of the onslaught on the government:

> . . . There is probably also a trick in it which the Tory Party applied comprehensively against the Queen before her marriage in order to make her drop Lord Melbourne, viz. that to maintain an unpopular ministry any longer would destroy her popularity, and to use this belief with the public, too, as a weapon against the Minister.[4]

The Prince still hoped that the middle and lower classes were in his favour, in spite of constant efforts to estrange them from him. He blamed the mental inertia [*Denkfaulheit*] of the ordinary public for the success of the campaign.

> This inertia has prevented the nation these 14 years from thinking about the true state of the relations between the constitutional Queen and her husband. . . . The surprise of the stupid about him [the husband] helping his wife with advice and deeds in every way has made it [the nation] believe in the most dreadful consequences as a result of this . . .[5]

The campaign died a natural death both owing to its inherent

[1] See B. Kingsley Martin, "The Triumph of Lord Palmerston", 193 ff.
[2] Thus the Queen to Aberdeen, 4 January 1854 (Royal Archives G.8.39).
[3] Prince Albert's (undated) covering memorandum (Royal Archives G.8).
[4] Prince Albert to Bunsen, 11 January 1854 (Royal Archives G.8.82), tr.
[5] Ibid.

absurdity and thanks to the sensible public explanations made by the ministers at the request of the Queen. There was also a change in Palmerston's position.

In the excited state of public opinion the ex-minister could have hoisted himself into power by rallying all the elements which were dissatisfied with Aberdeen's weak attitude towards Russia. In spite of Prince Albert's prediction, he did not do so, which shows that in resigning he had acted less according to plan than by impulse. Within five days of his resignation, he had begun to make approaches to the government for a return.[1] Something has been made of Lord Lansdowne's refusal to resign with him to account for Palmerston's change of mind. In the crisis following Sinope domestic affairs were, however, entirely overshadowed by the proximity of war. Palmerston returned because he realised that even Aberdeen could now hardly avoid war.

On their part, the ministers were glad to see Palmerston back again. They realised that their position would be weakened if the former Home Secretary crossed the floor. Furthermore, Aberdeen began to doubt whether it was really better to have Lord John as a colleague than Palmerston. After a brief moment of anti-Palmerstonian solidarity with the Prime Minister, the Leader of the Commons again returned to his old tactics of constantly threatening resignation unless he had his way. Lord John's influence seemed to be increasing. He was forcing the government to undertake a reform programme at an awkward moment. He also imposed on the Prime Minister, by the threat of withdrawal, his wish for stronger measures against Russia in the Black Sea. But many members of the cabinet, Peelite and Whig, were straining under his leash. They longed for the return of Palmerston to check Lord John, even if the Home Secretary also favoured a tough attitude to Russia.

The main opposition to Palmerston's return came from the Court. When the Prime Minister informed the Queen that Palmerston's resignation had been cancelled, the Queen only accepted this reluctantly:

> The Queen . . . must remind Lord Aberdeen that, although he may not have officially communicated to Lord Palmerston the Queen's acceptance of his resignation, yet this acceptance has taken place, and the Queen has allowed the seals to be offered to Sir George Grey. If Sir George hesitates,

---

[1] Aberdeen to Graham, 19 December 1853: "There is a strange story of Palmerston being disposed to repent and to look for the possibility of a reconciliation! !" (Royal Archives G.7.121). Submitted to the Queen.

it is but natural to presume that he has, in some manner, been made aware of Lord Palmerston's wish to retain them after all.[1]

The Queen stated her opinion that Palmerston had not given up his attempt to dislodge Lord Aberdeen and to take his place. She judged that he was merely looking for a more favourable opportunity to resign.[2] In spite of the Queen's appeal, Lord Aberdeen proved adamant. Palmerston returned, but had to withdraw his opposition to the Reform Bill. He may well have foreseen that the reform measure would be forgotten in the preoccupation with the war.

(vi)

Britain was at war from March 1854 and in September an Anglo-French force invaded the Crimean Peninsula. However hard the Prince had striven to prevent war, he favoured energetic campaigning once the fighting had begun. Right through the war he made numerous suggestions for its more efficient conduct, which did not endear him to the Commander-in-Chief, Lord Hardinge. Indeed, the Horse Guards was suspected by the Prince of being one of the centres of the press campaign against him.[3]

Paradoxically, the Prince was not popular with the critics of the military machine either. The redoubtable Roebuck, whose motion for a committee of investigation into the conduct of the war brought down the Aberdeen government, apparently turned over in his mind the plan for an impeachment of the Queen's husband for unconstitutional interference in the affairs of the Army. It is impossible, within the scope of this study, to examine in detail the Prince's influence on the development of the Army, which was considerable. It was beyond his power to prevent the Army's lack of preparedness at the outbreak of the war. One obstacle was the traditional British dislike for anything smacking of militarism in peacetime, another the conservatism of the Duke of Wellington and his disciples until the defects revealed in war made reform inevitable. In some respects, however, Prince Albert impeded an indispensable overhaul of the military apparatus. He was extremely jealous of anything like civilian interference.[4] Understandably impatient with the violence and frequent unfairness of the Press attacks made on men in respon-

[1] The Queen to Aberdeen, 21 December 1853 (Royal Archives G.7.126).
[2] Ibid.
[3] See Prince Albert's letter to Stockmar, 24 January 1854 (*Jagow*).
[4] Prince Albert to Hardinge, 26 November 1854 (Royal Archives E.4.57).

sible positions during the war, he failed to realise that public discussion helped to overcome the vested opposition to those reforms which he had himself at heart. The Prince frustrated his own endeavours for innovations by his attachment to the archaic institution of the Commander-in-Chief of the Army which fitted so ill into the constitutional system and obstructed a stream-lining of the military machine. The absurd duplication of ministers for the army—a Secretary of State *for* War and also a Secretary *at* War—was closely connected with the problem of the Commander-in-Chief. In at first opposing the abolition of the Secretaryship *at* War, the Crown realised that its disappearance would only be a preliminary step to the suppression of the office of Commander-in-Chief.[1]

The way the Prince supported the existing army régime disposed him in favour of the Aberdeen government and largely blinded him to its defects as a war administration. He certainly considered a government under Lord Aberdeen to be preferable to any possible alternative. The Prince did not favour a Russell premiership, though he had some sympathy with Lord John's proposals for parliamentary reform which had to be dropped owing to preoccupation with the war in April 1854. He disapproved strongly of the threats Lord John—who had become Lord President of the Council—made to withdraw from the government. Since Lord John and Palmerston were rivals, the discomfiture of one was usually to the advantage of the other. Thus Lord John succeeded in achieving the apparently impossible: he smoothed the path for Lord Palmerston's return to Court favour. Indeed, when Lord John's resignation from the government seemed to be imminent in December 1854, the Queen agreed that Palmerston should replace him as Leader of the House of Commons.[2] This is particularly significant as earlier in the year Prince Albert had still been noting that "Lord Palmerston has been playing a deep game all along" over Lord John's Reform Bill.[3] The Home Secretary did not have to scheme. He could afford to wait. His time was coming.

The appalling errors of the military during the Crimean campaign and the many needless sufferings of the soldiers resulted in ever-growing criticism of the administration and demands for the removal of the Prime Minister, Lord Aberdeen, and the Secretary for War,

[1] The separate office of Secretary at War was abolished at the end of 1854 and that of the Commander-in-Chief of the Army in 1907.
[2] Memorandum by Prince Albert, 9 December 1854 (*Letters*).
[3] Memorandum by Prince Albert, 26 February 1854 (Royal Archives A.81.143).

the Duke of Newcastle. Public opinion in the main regarded Palmerston as the man of the hour. The government's fate was sealed when Lord John resigned after the tabling of Roebuck's motion for a committee of investigation into the conduct of the war.

Lord Aberdeen resigned on 30 January 1855 after his government's defeat over this motion. Reluctantly the Queen and the Prince had to give up their trusted servant and to find a solution to the crisis. Consultations with the various political leaders were begun immediately. Wisely, both Lord Derby and Lord John were offered the premiership so that they could not complain of having been passed over. But as early as 1 February, within 48 hours of Aberdeen's resignation, the Queen and the Prince were fully aware of the key importance of Lord Palmerston and accepted its implications. The Court considered a Derby government a dangerous experiment at that critical stage of the war[1] and was relieved when the Tory leader failed. Lord John was sent for next, but the Court rightly discounted the possibility of his succeeding. That left only two possibilities. The first was a formal premiership of the aged Lansdowne with Palmerston as Leader of the House of Commons and as War Minister. The Queen wrote:

> ... If Lord Lansdowne refuses—there is Lord Palmerston *himself*. I know this would be very objectionable in many respects—and personally not agreeable to me—but *I* think of *nothing* but the Country—and the preservation of its Institutions—and *my own* personal feelings would be sunk if only the efficiency of the Government could be obtained. If the *Peelites* and *Whigs* would serve *under* Lord Palmerston, *I should not* apprehend the consequences—for they would restrain him from mischief, and Palmerston *himself* in *that position* would feel the weight and responsibility of *such a position* in a manner that would make him feel very differently to what he has hitherto done, as a Subordinate.[2]

On Lord Lansdowne's refusal to form a government, Lord Palmerston was commissioned on 4 February. He succeeded after protracted negotiations in forming an administration with the Whigs and Peelites. Lord Aberdeen was dropped, but he persuaded his Peelite colleagues to serve under Palmerston, though they were to resign on 21 February. The Duke of Newcastle was replaced as Secretary for War by Lord Panmure. Clarendon remained Foreign Secretary, while Lord John accepted a commission to go to Vienna as British plenipotentiary in the peace negotiations, which were carried on there while war was raging. On the resignation of the

---

[1] Memorandum by the Queen, 1 February 1855 (Royal Archives G.23.53).
[2] Ibid.

Peelites he became, in addition, a member of the Cabinet, as Colonial Secretary *in absentia*. The Vienna mission had an unhappy ending for Lord John, for he had to resign from the government in July owing to his concessions to Austria over the peace proposals to Russia.

In summoning Lord Palmerston, the Queen had the support of her husband. Prince Albert closed his special files on Palmerston which he had been keeping for the years since 1848.[1] He noted:

> ... Since his [Lord Palmerston's] conducting the government the whole public fall upon him as inefficient, as one impostor in whom they had been entirely mistaken, although he acts with great prudence and moderation. He receives every support from us in his difficult situation.[2]

Understandably, the mistrust of Palmerston bred during at least seven years did not vanish in a moment. This was shown when Lord Palmerston informed the Court of a personal letter he had addressed to the Emperor Napoleon remarking on "le mauvais état de l'Armée Anglaise".[3] The Court disapproved both of a personal correspondence of the Prime Minister with the head of a Foreign State and of the reference to the British Army. Prince Albert noted:

> We had anxiously to consider what answer the Queen could give to Lord Palmerston. It is evident that after his former misdeeds and the public notice which the Queen was obliged to take of them, he is now willing, perhaps even anxious, not to sin in the same manner again and openly to communicate what he is doing, and it is of the highest importance that he should do so. If the Queen were to object to his plan, he would at once both calumniate us for it on the ground of inveterate hostility to the Emperor for family reasons, and trick us by carrying on his correspondence secretly. On the other hand, he may have laid a trap for obtaining the Queen's sanction to a proceeding otherwise very irregular and probably very dangerous.[4]

In the circumstances the Queen merely thanked Lord Palmerston for communicating the letter to her.[5]

Thus Bonapartism continued to affect the relationship between the Court and Palmerston. But both sides were changing their views about Napoleon. Palmerston, who had always supported him, was beginning to discover the Emperor's shortcomings. Under the impact of war and the French alliance, the Queen and the Prince were moving towards a friendly attitude to their fellow-monarch. When

[1] Royal Archives A.79–81.
[2] Memorandum by Prince Albert, dated 1855 (Royal Archives A.81.145).
[3] Palmerston to Napoleon III, 8 February 1855 (*Letters*).
[4] Memorandum by Prince Albert, 11 February 1855 (Royal Archives G.24.14).
[5] The Queen to Palmerston, 11 February 1855 (*Letters*).

the Emperor was at last received at Windsor, the Queen was most impressed by him, though her husband remained somewhat more critical.[1]

Basically the aims of the Court and of the Prime Minister were the same, to bring the war to a speedy victorious conclusion and to obtain a peace which would greatly weaken Russia's influence in the Black Sea. On the diplomatic side, there was naturally room for discussion as to the best methods for achieving these aims. Palmerston and Prince Albert were no longer divided, as in the years after 1848, by a divergence of attitudes to Austria and Prussia. But the Prince had a greater understanding of the limitations of British pressure on continental nations than Palmerston. Even under the Aberdeen régime, early in 1854, the Court had pointed out to the Foreign Secretary the futility of abusing continental powers which "would have to bear the brunt of the war".[2] Under the Palmerston premiership, these warnings by the Prince not to antagonise Austria and Prussia unnecessarily, became intensified. Thus the Court stopped Clarendon from threatening Prussia with the loss of her neutrality in January 1856.[3] With the Premier's propensity to haughtiness towards European governments, particularly of the reactionary brand, Prince Albert was anxious to prevent the war from losing its European character.[4]

Prince Albert had been disappointed that Austria and Prussia had failed to stop the war by a show of solidarity with the Western Powers against Russia. Once war had broken out, he regretted that the German powers prolonged it unnecessarily by staying out. He regarded the issue as a moral one. To him, it was the duty of Austria and Prussia to support Britain and France in their struggle to uphold the public law of Europe.[5] The Crimean War was a Crusade of good against evil. In the dust of battle, the shades, the half-tones, disappeared. Everything was white or black.

While Austria did not go as far in its action against Russia as the Prince would have wished, it did do something. The Austrian government obtained the evacuation of Russian troops from the Principalities by ultimatum. On their withdrawal they were replaced by Austrian forces. Austria participated in the formulation

---

[1] See Martin, IV, particularly 108, 319, 352 ff.
[2] The Queen to Clarendon, 18 January 1854 (*Letters*).
[3] See Queen Victoria to Clarendon, 11 January 1856 (*Letters*).
[4] See also "The Influence of the Crown", in "Crimean War Diplomacy" by G. B. Henderson.
[5] Martin, III, 21; 69.

of the "Four Points", acceptance of which was to be demanded of Russia. It is true that the Austrian Foreign Minister, Buol, succeeded in watering down the Black Sea clauses to the advantage of Russia.[1] But there could be no doubt about the anti-Russian bias of the Four Points. Finally, Austria sent the ultimatum to Russia which ended the war in the spring of 1856.

Thus there could be a reasonable satisfaction with the attitude of Austria. But no allowance could be made for Prussia and the Prince condemned its policy in the most outspoken terms.[2] After toying with the possibility of a more Western policy, King Frederick William IV had come down against the pro-Westerners in April 1854. Bunsen and the War Minister, Bonin, had to take their leave. Prince Albert regretted the motives for the recall of Bunsen and their implications, though he had become increasingly dissatisfied with the Prussian minister's irresponsibility in constantly putting forward new schemes for changing the map of Europe and thus embarrassing everybody.[3] A learned scholar, Bunsen was a poor diplomat.

The Crimean War proved to Prince Albert beyond doubt that Frederick William IV would never carry out a truly German policy as the Prince had hoped. The Russian ties at the Court of Berlin were too strong as long as the present reign continued. Prince Albert's thoughts turned increasingly to the more distant future. He continued to keep in close touch with the Prince of Prussia who had once more, as in 1850 after Olmütz, gone into temporary semi-retirement owing to his dissatisfaction with his brother's policy. Prince Albert's plans went even further, for in the middle of the Crimean War plans were laid for giving a new direction to Prussian policy in the next reign but one.

[1] Lord John's concessions to Buol led to his resignation.
[2] Thus see Queen Victoria's reply to the King of Prussia, 17 March 1854 (*Letters*).
[3] See Martin, III, 62 ff.; Prince Albert to his brother, 2 May 1854 (*Jagow*).

Chapter Twelve

THE PRUSSIAN MARRIAGE

(i)

PRINCE ALBERT did not regard the "Crimean coalition" as a sufficient foundation for the future diplomatic framework of Europe. Even during the war the difficulties of co-operation with France became apparent. Though Austria had begun to emancipate herself from her subordination to Russia, Prussia and the rest of Germany had remained ineffective. Prince Albert's great aim was to mobilise Germany as a force in the future of Europe, for its good as he believed. His main instrument in this great design was the "Prussian Marriage".

Of all his children, it was the eldest, Victoria, the Princess Royal, who seemed destined to perpetuate his ideas in the following generation. Even as an adolescent, the Princess had shown great aptitude for learning the political lessons her father taught her. Prince Albert was confident that she would prove a powerful emissary for the ideas of constitutional government in Germany. Thus the Queen and her husband formed the plan to marry her to Prince Frederick William of Prussia, the only son of the Prince of Prussia and a nephew of King Frederick William IV. When young "Fritz", who was later to ascend the throne as the Emperor Frederick III, and "Vicky" were immediately attracted to each other, the engagement was concluded in 1855. The marriage was to take place as soon as the Princess—who was born in 1840—was old enough.

The match was an arranged marriage of the best kind. There was a close friendship between the parents of bride and bridegroom, consolidated by the troublesome days of 1848. Young Fritz was very fond of his future father-in-law and imbibed his political principles. His mother, the Princess of Prussia, who had always advocated a Prussian constitutional development along English lines, was happy to see the strengthening of these ideas. She hoped that with all the help from Windsor, a relapse of her husband into his reactionary pre-1848 outlook could be prevented. It seemed to be entirely a matter of time until, on the death of Frederick William IV, a more liberal course would replace the reactionary régime of the Minister-President Otto von Manteuffel and of the Court Camarilla.

It was hard for public opinion in Britain to judge the reasons which led Prince Albert to marry his daughter to the eventual heir to the Prussian throne. *The Times* published a bitter leader in October 1855, giving vent to its contempt for the vacillations of Prussian policy, particularly during the Crimean War:

> What sympathy can exist between a Court supported like ours on the solid basis of popular freedom and national respect, and a camarilla just engaged in the interests of a foreign patron in trampling out the last embers of popular government which a revolution resisted with perfidy, yielded to with cowardice, and quelled with insolence, had left behind?

It was, indeed, to dislodge the ultra-conservative influences at the Court of Berlin that Prince Albert planned the union. It took courage to make the first moves at a time when the prestige of Prussia in this country had reached its lowest ebb. Unlike the British government and public opinion, the Queen's husband regarded every reverse in the Crimean War as an additional reason for not losing patience with Prussia. In his view this became even more necessary when the weakness of the links between Britain and France was revealed in 1856 at the Paris peace conference. France refused to support Britain in the full extent of her demands against Russia. The "Crimean Coalition" proved a temporary phenomenon, for the Russians were determined to undo the neutralisation of the Black Sea which had been imposed on them at the Paris conference. They thus joined the ranks of the revisionist powers which threw them into the arms of Bonapartist France, eager to undo the Vienna settlement of 1815. Unforeseen by Prince Albert, the very success of the war against Russia proved an element of instability in Europe for the future.

(ii)

In 1856 Palmerston seemed to be firmly in the saddle. His prestige stood high with Court and people. Yet, within two years, he was out of office. He was defeated in 1858 because he did not stand up to a foreign government—that of his old friend, the Emperor Napoleon. This time his fall was not, as in 1851, due to the Court, but to public opinion. He was criticised for not having sufficiently resisted French pressure to tighten up the conspiracy laws following Orsini's attempt on the life of the Emperor. The Italian revolutionist Orsini had planned the assassination attempt in England. The French government demanded stronger English measures to prevent a recurrence of this kind of plotting. During the debate on the new government conspiracy bill in the House of Commons, Lord Palmerston was defeated when it became clear that he had left unanswered a French note making peremptory demands on the British government. Palmerston's fall was the last thing Napoleon wished. For Orsini's attempt on his life fulfilled its purpose of reminding him forcibly of his old Italian conspiratorial associations and of his promise in younger days to further the cause of Italian unity and liberty. When the armed conflict between Austria and the Franco-Sardinian coalition began in Northern Italy the following year, Napoleon was to hope and pray for a Palmerston government.

The Court took the inevitable return of a Tory ministry under Lord Derby more quietly than the earlier attempts of the Protectionists to form an administration. Prince Albert—who had been granted the title of Prince Consort by the Queen in 1857—considered the new government, though it also did not command a parliamentary majority, to be a stronger one than its predecessor in 1852. The main offices were held by the same people. Disraeli returned to the Treasury and Lord Malmesbury to the Foreign Office. The Prince Consort could never forgive what he considered Disraeli's indifference to principle. He thought that this was as apparent in the Chancellor's attitude to the question of parliamentary reform as it had been earlier over Protection. He told his uncle:

> We have great difficulties with the question of Reform. The irresponsibility of Derby and the complete lack of character and the untruthfulness of Disraeli put all the weapons in the hands of the Democrats, for they undermine the confidence of the moderates of all parties.[1]

But in spite of these strictures, the Court was reluctant to revert to Lord Palmerston. When Lord Derby asked for a dissolution in April 1859 to enable the government to stay in power, the Queen granted it readily, though the House was still relatively new, having been elected in 1857. The reason for the Court's preference for Lord Derby at this stage lay mainly in its dislike of Palmerston's and Lord John Russell's ideas over the Italian question, which had become of overriding importance. The Prince Consort summed up the Court's attitude in a letter to his uncle:

> . . . The dissolution has much in it that is questionable and may lead to great excitement in the country, *must* lead to a large number of members of the new Parliament committing themselves at the elections to the most extreme measures of democratic reform. . . . Yet the ministers thought they

---

[1] The Prince Consort to King Leopold, 14 March 1859 (Royal Archives J.16.59), tr.

hardly had any choice. Lord Palmerston's insolent speech had made a modification of their own bill in the present House impossible, resignation at this moment would have been a European disaster and Victoria was reconciled against resignation and to a certain extent with the dissolution by the probable circumstance that Lord John Russell would . . . have demanded a dissolution in order . . . to put into effect a democratic measure. . . . We would then have had a general election in by far still more unfavourable circumstances, the Crown and Government in the same *boat with Democracy*.[1]

To the Prince Consort the Italian policy of Lord Malmesbury was only acceptable because it was bound to be less anti-Austrian than that of Palmerston and Russell. But unlike public opinion, he found the Tory Foreign Secretary not sufficiently pro-Austrian. He thought early in May 1859 that Malmesbury was not doing enough to deter France from invading Lombardy in company with Sardinia, and he criticised him for trying to restrain Germany from coming to the aid of Austria. Commenting on some drafts submitted to the Queen, the Prince wrote to the Foreign Secretary:

> . . . The Queen takes . . . exception to the expression that a participation in the war against France "on the part of Germany without casus foederis" would be morally and politically unjustifiable. Impartiality on our part will be our strength and only safeguard. We never declared it unjustifiable when France came to the assistance of Sardinia (who is not bound to her in any way acknowledged by Europe) against Austria. The connection of Germany with Austria is of a totally different kind and is both national and political, and what was not unjustifiable in France, we can still less call so in Germany.[2]

The Prince was sorry for the poor way in which the Austrians handled an apparently strong diplomatic and military position. He regretted that they allowed themselves to be manœuvred into an unfavourable diplomatic situation at the outset by presenting an ultimatum to Sardinia and by invading Sardinian territory on its rejection. The Prince Consort saw eye to eye with King Leopold once more. He wrote to him on 9 May:

> . . . I can imagine your dissatisfaction with the diplomatic audacity and the inexplicable military dilatoriness of the Austrians. . . . I hardly want to read any more despatches. At last Lord Malmesbury has stopped giving good advice, to make proposals etc. . . . as was time; for the stage of diplomacy is over for the moment. . . .
> Malakoff [the French Ambassador] has said goodbye to us with tears in his eyes, the Emperor is sending Persigny as his successor, although he knows that the government does not wish it. The purpose is to work for

---

[1] The Prince Consort to King Leopold, 5 April 1859 (Royal Archives J.17.27), tr.
[2] The Prince Consort to Malmesbury, 4 May 1859 (Royal Archives J.19.28).

its downfall with Palmerston. The Emperor absolutely relies on Palmerston, who finds his whole plan justified and would give its success every possible support.[1]

(iii)

Though the Tories increased their representation in the general election, they still fell short of a majority and were beaten in June 1859 following an understanding being reached between Palmerston and Lord John. The Italian war was now at its height and the last thing the Crown wanted was Ministers who like the two Whig leaders believed in solving the Italian question in alliance with France. To avoid recourse to them, the Queen tried Lord Granville, under whom neither wished to serve. Palmerston, unlike Lord John, succeeded in evading responsibility for causing the failure of Granville's mission. This was one of the reasons why he was preferred to his old rival in the choice of the Premiership. During his second administration, Palmerston was much more dependent on the Radicals than previously and formed the first government which has been called liberal. Gladstone returned to the Chancellorship of the Exchequer which he had resigned during the Crimean War. Lord John became Foreign Secretary, in spite of the Court's preference for Lord Clarendon. When the Italian question once more reached a critical stage, the British Court was thus faced with the old combination of Palmerston and Lord John, though with their roles of 1848 reversed. It is curious now to see the Queen and the Prince Consort appealing to Viscount Palmerston against Lord John.[2] This was of little avail. For there was a unity of views regarding foreign policy between the two men which had been lacking during Lord John's administration. Together with Gladstone, who was with them in the Italian question if in very little else, they imposed their views on the rest of the Cabinet and on the Court.

Before Palmerston came in, the important Austrian defeat at Magenta had already taken place. The first stage of the war, on which they could have little effect, ended with the Armistice of Villafranca which Napoleon surprisingly concluded with the Austrian Emperor in July 1859 soon after his victory at Solferino. Austria yielded Lombardy to Sardinia, but retained Venetia. The English pro-Italians like Lord Palmerston and Lord John regretted that Napoleon had not fulfilled his pledge of freeing Northern Italy up to the Adriatic. They were not the only ones who were caught out.

[1] The Prince Consort to King Leopold, 9 May 1859 (Royal Archives J.19.45), tr.
[2] Thus the Queen to Palmerston, 10 February 1860 (*Letters*).

It was Prussia which was left in the weakest position by the Peace of Villafranca, an event for which the Prince Consort is not entirely blameless. For the first time the advice he was asked to give played its part in shaping Prussian policy in an important international crisis. This had become possible by far-reaching changes which had taken place at Berlin.

The mind of King Frederick William IV, whose brilliance always verged on the abnormal, gave way completely in 1858 and his brother William, Prince Albert's old friend, and his eldest daughter's father-in-law, became Regent with full powers in October 1858, after having acted for a year merely as his brother's deputy. As a result of the grant of the Regency, the Prince of Prussia was able to take measures against that part of the King's policy which he considered mistaken. He lost no time in dismissing the reactionary Manteuffel ministry and in opening the "New Era" with the appointment of a government representing moderate liberal opinion. Prince Anton of Hohenzollern-Sigmaringen, whose son Charles was to become King of Rumania, headed the ministry which included the Prince Consort's old teacher at Bonn, Bethmann-Hollweg. Schleinitz was the Foreign Minister. The Prince Consort was delighted about the change on which he congratulated the Regent.[1] He was pleased about the "effect on Germany of Prussia identifying herself with liberal constitutional government",[2] and did his best to stiffen the Regent against the influence of the reactionary party. He tried to reassure him:

> I do not think that you need fear to be driven to the left against your better insight, and . . . the elections . . . seem to prove . . . that the party of lawful progress does not have anything in common with the Democrats and that the people relies on the former and does not want to have anything to do with the latter.[3]

Foreign policy was not forgotten:

> I am particularly glad of the prospect of henceforth seeing among the five Powers one on the Continent which wants to base itself on fair play . . . and will thus be a corrective element in the great policy of intrigue on the continent. . . .[4]

While the Prince Consort hoped that the development of Prussia

[1] The Prince Consort to the Prince of Prussia, 9 November 1858 (Royal Archives I.31.24).
[2] Undated memorandum by Prince Albert (Royal Archives I.31).
[3] The Prince Consort to the Prince of Prussia, 26 November 1858 (Royal Archives I.31.30), tr.
[4] Ibid.

would be turned into fruitful channels by a transition from reactionary influence to a proper constitutional régime, he was by no means blind to the defects of the State in general or of the dynasty in particular. His correspondence is full of references to the unfortunate way in which the country seemed to be dominated by its bureaucracy and its officer corps, of the arrogance of Prussians towards other Germans, of the spirit of isolation prevailing in Berlin. He regretted the preoccupation of the Hohenzollern family with military affairs which was to provoke a dangerous constitutional conflict shortly afterwards. He was scathing in this respect even of his own son-in-law, however much he trusted him otherwise:

> . . . That Vicky's husband has lapsed into his family's and his country's playing at soldiers is to be regretted, though it is not to be wondered at. . . .[1]

Unfortunately, Fritz's father was little inclined to entrust him with political functions, even after he had become Regent.

The Italian question was a test for the Regent, as well as for the Prince Consort. Prussia had to decide whether to come to the aid of Austria, a fellow-member of the German Confederation, or to remain neutral. Public opinion in Germany, particularly in the South, was sympathetic to Austria and hostile to France, apart from the comparatively small band of liberals and radicals who saw in the Habsburg Monarchy an engine of oppression and in the fate of Italy the prototype for Germany.[2] The Prince Consort developed his programme in reply to a memorandum by the Regent's wife, the Princess Augusta,[3] before the outbreak of hostilities:

> . . . I understand, and Lord Malmesbury, too, understands completely the difficulty . . . of Prussia's position. Austria naturally seeks protection through Germany; on Prussia falls the odium of either having provoked France through threats of war and of having attracted her [unfavourable] attentions towards Germany, or of having by her reserve prevented the patriotic unanimity in Germany against France, which it is hoped would keep France in check. But in spite of that Prussia *must* in my view maintain for herself this waiting position, if it does not want to expose itself and Europe to great dangers. For one could in Vienna very easily be led astray into a most dangerous obstinacy precisely by being sure that Germany and Prussia would draw the blows of France on *themselves*. . . .[4]

---

[1] The Prince Consort to his brother, 22 April 1858 (Coburg Archives), tr.

[2] Thus Ludwig Bamberger in Juchhe nach Italia (Politische Schriften von 1848 bis 1868, III, 159 ff.).

[3] Ernst, II, 476 ff. According to the Duke of Coburg, the Princess of Prussia often wrote to the Prince Consort to elicit the views of the British government (Ernst, II, 461).

[4] The Prince Consort to the Princess of Prussia, 1 March 1859 (Royal Archives I.16.1), tr.

The Prince Consort advocated that the Ministry should make a public statement of its policy in the Chamber. He suggested that Prussia should declare that it would come to the assistance of an Austria unjustly attacked, but that it was not prepared to provoke France or to encourage Austria to resist just demands in Italy.[1] A few days later, he criticised a Prussian circular to the German courts for committing Prussia to neutrality and thus encouraging France too much.[2]

While the Prince Consort welcomed the reiterated Prussian desire for British co-operation, he criticised the authorities in Berlin for always making their actions dependent on an outside power. He attributed this to an unfortunate dualism in Prussian policy:

> ... If Prussia wants to pursue two points of view, one as a German power, the other as a Great Power, it will fall between two stools. Prussia is not a Great Power apart from Germany. ... Prussia as a Great Power thus always first seeks an ally abroad, in order to make up for this weakness of which it is conscious; thus the strong point of its policy falls to the outside (formerly to Russia or to Austria) and as there are no two powers which have exactly the same interests, Prussian interests have to be sacrificed to foreign ones.
>
> Prussia *is*, however, a Great Power in connection with and at the head of Germany, does not need an ally if it is identified with Germany. ...[3]

The policy advocated by the Prince Consort left Prussia isolated when the Peace of Villafranca was concluded. Still, though neutrality did not bring any prestige, it kept Prussia and Germany proper out of a conflict with which it had little direct concern. It was, however, unfortunate that the government of the New Era was so soon involved in a major diplomatic problem which hardly gave it an opportunity to shine. The episode did not help to strengthen the Regent's confidence in the Ministry. William had shown himself excessively preoccupied with the question whether Austria would agree to his becoming Supreme Commander of the German Confederation (*Bundesfeldherr*). His military hobbies were to lead him into still greater difficulties.

(iv)

In his synopsis of the German correspondence for 1860, the Prince Consort noted a

> ... dangerous conflict of the Prince Regent of Prussia with his Cabinet

---

[1] Ibid.

[2] The Prince Consort to the Princess of Prussia, 4 March 1859 (Royal Archives I.16.13 and 14).

[3] Memorandum by the Prince Consort, forwarded to Berlin, 4 May 1859 (Royal Archives J.19.27), tr.

and Chambers on the question of the reorganisation of the Prussian Landwehr and Army.[1]

It was tragic for the Prince Consort that his hopes of his old friend William were so quickly to be disappointed, at the very moment when the disappearance of Frederick William IV from the political scene seemed to clear the path for constitutional progress. After a promising start William was beginning to revert to many of the ideas he had held before 1848, of which Prince Albert had tried to cure him. The Prince Regent of Prussia was prepared to subordinate the whole political situation to his overriding military interests. He insisted on an extension of the period of conscription to three years in the teeth of the opposition of a loyal Landtag. His plan for military reform also alienated moderate opinion at a sensitive point, by demanding a sharp reduction of the Landwehr, a kind of citizen "Territorial Army" and its integration in the army proper. The Regent felt that the men of the Landwehr were not sufficiently reliable, particularly in case of internal difficulties. He recalled his own experience during the crushing of the revolution in Baden and the Palatinate in 1849 when he had come to the conclusion that a somewhat stricter discipline was necessary than the Landwehr provided. The far-reaching political implications of the reorganisation of the Landwehr were as clear to the Prussian Chamber as they were to the Regent. The reactionary circles at Court, ever active, used the question to widen the gulf between the Regent and his liberal government and parliament. With the appointment of Roon as War Minister in December 1859, they succeeded in planting a mine in the heart of the Cabinet which was soon to explode it.

The Prince Consort was deeply troubled by the possible consequences of a head-on clash between the Regent and the Chamber. William insisted on the three-year period of conscription and the integration of the Landwehr. Would he be prepared to use unconstitutional methods to achieve his aims? What would be the position of young Fritz and Vicky if the Regent subverted the constitution? Prince Albert had no doubt what attitude his daughter and son-in-law should adopt. It was a bitter stroke of fate which now once more made topical the advice he had given to Fritz in 1855 when Frederick William IV was threatening to use unconstitutional methods. Then the guidance was given to William as much as to Fritz. Prince Albert had advised his future son-in-law to consider himself the trustee of

Undated (Royal Archives I.31).

the next generation, not to remain an inactive spectator of the murder of a sworn constitution, that he should

> make a solemn protest . . . not in the sense of an opposition against the government, but in that of a reservation of the rights of the nation. . . .[1]

When the Regent was drifting into dangerous waters in 1860 and 1861, Prince Albert strained every nerve to make him adhere to constitutional methods, so that Prussia would not endanger all the —albeit limited—progress she had made after 1848 in moving away from arbitrary methods of royal government. The Regent himself was at a loss to know how to deal with the situation and remained in close touch with Prince Albert to whom he sent confidential reports of his meetings with various crowned heads, such as the French, Austrian and Russian Emperors.[2]

The death of Frederick William IV and the Regent's succession as King William I in January 1861 only made the situation worse. The Prince Consort was worried about the increasing gulf between the new sovereign and his people:

> . . . The King has been deliberately irritated . . . by those who do not wish him well and thus shaken in his confidence in his people. This is the usual game of those people of whom the General Gerlach (whom Heaven has fortunately summoned) was typical. Once proper mistrust has been established between the rulers and the ruled, they become apparently important and necessary as the only loyal ones who gather round the throne for its defence.[3]

Although the Prince Consort wrote in the same letter that he had stopped giving advice to the King of Prussia because it was discredited,[4] he never in fact ceased his activities as a mentor to the King of Prussia. He wrote to him in March:

> . . . Let no one succeed in shaking your confidence in your own people and the German nation! There are so many who consider it their business to make princes *afraid* of their peoples. From this source of fear have arisen most of the mistakes of the governments, as well as the most shameful atrocities of history.[5]

He added another remark to make constitutionalism and German unity more palatable to the King:

> Should liberally-minded [freisinnige] systems of government have been

---

[1] Prince Albert to Prince Frederick William, 6 November 1855 (*Jagow*), tr.
[2] Martin, V, 124, 225, etc.
[3] The Prince Consort to his daughter, now Crown Princess of Prussia, 16 January 1861 (Royal Archives I.34.42), tr.   [4] Ibid.
[5] The Prince Consort to King William I, 12 March 1861 (Royal Archives I.35.22), tr.

developed in Austria, Germany and Italy, then the role of Napoleonism will be played out, for then he can no longer direct the French people's urge of freedom to other states, to gain satisfaction for it there. . . .[1]

To the end the Prince Consort never abandoned his belief that Prussia could only assume the leadership of Germany if she became a truly constitutional state and broke with the narrow, militarist and bureaucratic tradition of Frederick William I and Frederick II. In May 1861, he wrote to King Leopold of

> . . . the . . . hypocritical feelings . . . of the Prussian Government, which makes an immoral "convenience" of the Holstein question, lays stress in Denmark upon the maintenance of the rights of the Estates to control their own budget, and at home raises money for the augmentation of the army without the knowledge of the Chambers. . . .[2]

He rejected any idea that German unity might be achieved by seeking martial laurels abroad and that this might be the way out of the Prussian constitutional deadlock. He wrote to his son-in-law in Berlin:

> . . . An *external* war for the elimination of *internal* dissension and evils is always a morally unjustified undertaking. . . . [Also] the very evils, personal weaknesses, internal contradictions etc. which form the obstacles to the solution of internal difficulties are . . . just the ones which would most impede success in war. . . . Prussia, with its broken territory, which is only a part of Germany and whose other members are hostile to it, with a policy which has not yet found its own principle, entangled with alliances and treaties of all kinds, and vulnerable at all corners, is not in a position to risk a daring undertaking without perishing. The altogether exceptional case of Frederick the Great misleads and blinds many a Prussian. . . .[3]

The Prince made it clear that Prussia still had a long way to go before it could hope for the success Sardinia had just had in Italy:

> It was the *liberally-minded* [freisinnige] government of Sardinia from 1850 to 1858 which enabled that country to count on the sentiments of the inhabitants of the rest of Italy when the great clash came, which won it the sympathy of England to such an extent that even its crimes are pardoned, nay not even noticed. The internal weakness vis à vis the liberal system of government, the demonstrated, unfortunately well-known antipathy of the higher classes and government to popular rights and representative government, etc., made it *impossible* for Prussia to be the champion of popular rights. The local seclusion of Berlin from the

---

[1] The Prince Consort to King William I, 12 March 1861 (Royal Archives I.35.22), tr.
[2] The Prince Consort to King Leopold, 3 May 1861 (Martin, V, 344–5), tr.
[3] The Prince Consort to the Crown Prince of Prussia, 1 May 1861 (Royal Archives I.36.1), tr.

remaining Germans prevented Prussia from becoming at once the representative of Germany in a major question.[1]

One of the last important letters by the Prince Consort on German affairs, in July 1861, revealed his deep anxiety about the reactionary policy of William I:

> ... There exists in Prussia a great Junker and bureaucrats' party which comes together in the Army and particularly in the Guards, which is determined not to allow the constitution and constitutional government to develop, and which for this purpose does not shrink from cunning, fraud, and violence for the provocation of a revolution or of a coup d'état, and ... the King *himself* belongs to this party by sympathy and by tradition....[2]

Thus the first year of William's reign proved a deep disappointment to the Prince Consort. Although the King had broken the constitution over his army reorganisation, Prince Albert did not consider that the time had yet come for his son-in-law to implement the advice he had given him in 1855, to make a solemn protest. However, the Prince's loathing for these unconstitutional methods is beyond doubt.

(v)

It was galling for the Prince Consort that Italian unification was going from strength to strength while little progress was being made in Germany. His disappointment did not merely spring from a preference for Germany. He disapproved of the methods employed to unite the rest of Italy under the Sardinian banner, of the use of force to remove established rights laid down in treaties. He considered the cession of Savoy and Nice to France as a reward for French support in the Italian war disgraceful for both parties. It is only fair to add that he condemned the application of similar methods to Germany in his correspondence with the Court of Berlin.

It would be easy to argue that if Prussia had renounced all the methods condemned by the Prince, Germany would never have been united. The Prince can certainly be charged with an excessive legalism and an undue reliance on the *status quo*, though recent international organisations which have adopted similar principles could be criticised on the same grounds. The Foreign Secretary, Lord John Russell, considered that the British Court could hardly make a stand on the irremovability of Princes—in Italy—in view

[1] Ibid.
[2] The Prince Consort to King Leopold, 4 July 1861 (Royal Archives I.36.57), tr.

of the debt of the Hanoverian dynasty to the Glorious Revolution
of 1688. That this shaft came home is clear from a reference to this
argument in a letter from the Prince Consort to an Austrian correspondent in August 1859:

> . . . The comparison with the glorious revolution of 1688 is not historically
> conclusive, but is much talked about here just now and has had an effect
> on national sentiment . . .[1]

Palmerston and Russell had an unanswerable case when they held
that the expelled petty princes could not be restored by force and
that England had always recognised de facto changes, at any rate
after a time.

It is regrettable that the Italian question strained, once more, the
relationship with Palmerston which had improved so much during
his first premiership. Prince Albert talked about all Palmerston's old
tricks being revived again, and was also scathing about Lord John's
"inefficiency" at the Foreign Office.[2] Constitutionally, the Court had
some justification in resisting Palmerston's and Russell's Italian
policy, as the majority of the Cabinet was frequently not consulted
and was hardly enthusiastic. Prince Albert, however, misjudged the
aim of Palmerston's policy when he regarded it as one "of revenge
against Austria and to bind us to the Emperor Napoleon more than
ever".[3] The strongest argument of the Prime Minister and of the
Foreign Secretary was, on the contrary, that England might as well
cash in on the Italian enterprise to make the new Kingdom less
dependent on France. The difference of opinion was thus far more
one of methods rather than aims. From a practical point of view,
Palmerston and Russell had a better case than the Queen and the
Prince.

Though there were some signs of discord reminiscent of the years
round 1848, Palmerston's position was so immensely stronger that
the comparison falls short of reality. Palmerston was recognised as
an able Prime Minister and the Court sympathised with him in all
the personal difficulties he encountered in his Cabinet, particularly
with Mr. Gladstone. What made the relationship most difficult from
the Court's point of view, perhaps, was its feeling of powerlessness
to resist the mighty premier if he chose to be adamant. There was
an instance of this when Lord Palmerston overrode the Court's

---

[1] The Prince Consort to Prince Esterhazy, 20 August 1859 (Royal Archives
J.22.53), tr.
[2] Memorandum by the Prince Consort, 31 December 1859 (Bell, Palmerston,
II, 230).
[3] Ibid.

objections to the appointment of the archaeologist Layard as Under-
Secretary at the Foreign Office. Lord Granville, the favourite
mediator, was called in and the Prince Consort wrote to him when
enclosing the Layard correspondence:

> ... You will not fail to perceive with how little candour Lord Palmerston
> meets that of the Queen and how little real consideration he shows her,
> which is rendered still more offensive to delicate feeling by the flattery
> which accompanies it.[1]

(vi)

Greville records how smoothly the Court's supervision of government business generally functioned just after the Crimean War,
thanks to Prince Albert.[2] The time of intense personal friction was
over, though differences of opinion over policy naturally remained.
The closing episode of the Prince Consort's life is typical of his
essentially constructive conception of Crown control. On the evening
of 30 November 1861, when the Prince lay on the sick-bed from which
he was never to rise again, a critical draft reached Windsor Castle
from Whitehall. At the beginning of the American Civil War Lord
Palmerston's government favoured the South against the North.
Feeling ran high when an American warship stopped an English
steamer, the *Trent*, on the High Seas, and forcibly removed two
Envoys from the Southern Confederacy on their way to Europe.
Following the powerful lead of the Prime Minister, the Cabinet
decided to send a strong note to Washington demanding reparation
and to instruct the British Ambassador to withdraw in case of
refusal. The Foreign Secretary accordingly drafted instructions,
which were sent to Windsor for the Queen's approval. The Prince
Consort, though already very ill, saw at once that the Foreign
Secretary's wording closed any avenue of withdrawal of which the
United States Government might wish to avail itself. He suggested
a more conciliatory phrasing and proposed the insertion of a passage
expressing the hope that the American Captain did not act under
instructions.[3] These suggestions were adopted to the delight of those
ministers, like Gladstone, whose advocacy of mildness had been
overruled. War with the United States was avoided. The American
Government took the chance presented by the amended note of

[1] The Prince Consort to Granville, 27 July 1861 (Royal Archives A.29.116).
[2] Entry of 8 October 1857 (Greville, VII, 304).
[3] Martin, V, 418 ff.; Morley, Gladstone, I, 708, etc.

yielding with honour and the whole matter was referred to arbitration.

Thus, the last political act of the Prince Consort is—like so much of his life—one of conciliation. It shows his love of peace, his dislike of any excessive appeal to feelings of national honour. It reflects once more, at the end of the road, his never relenting, never relaxing vigilance. Within a fortnight of his intervention in the *Trent* affair, on 14 December 1861, he died at Windsor Castle from what seems to have been typhoid fever. He was only in his forty-third year, but his activity during two decades as the Queen's husband has left its mark on British history.

EPILOGUE

THE Prince Consort's prestige has suffered from being damned with too much praise. It has been affected even more adversely by his widow's claim of perfection for him than by all the ridicule which has been heaped on him for his often rather pedantic methods. In the inevitable reaction against this premature canonisation—and for a number of political and personal reasons—the significance of the Prince Consort's achievement was missed during the early decades of the twentieth century.

It was not only the widow whose excessive praise harmed the Prince. Disraeli, whom the Prince mistrusted during the last years of his life perhaps more than any other leading politician, paid the Queen's husband a highly dubious compliment. The Saxon Minister at the Court of St. James reports the Tory leader as saying to him early in 1862 that if the Prince Consort

... had outlived some of our "old stagers", he would have given us, while retaining our constitutional guarantees, the blessings of absolute government. ...[1]

Closely examined, Disraeli's extravagance yields little sense. The reference to absolute government made a far greater impact on posterity than the neutralising clause about the constitutional guarantees. Unwittingly the favourite Prime Minister of Queen Victoria's widowhood threw later generations off their scent. They missed the Prince's most important achievement on the domestic scene, his contribution to the theory and practice of the constitutional monarchy. In spite of the Queen's opposition, he checked the essentially personal approach of Hanoverian royalty as early as 1841. The Crown was to be kept free of a permanent attachment to one political party and was to act largely impersonally, according to certain recognised rules. This still left a large sphere of influence to the Crown. The border-line dispute with Lord Palmerston from 1848 to 1851 should not be allowed to overshadow the fact that the new system generally worked well. Similarly, it would be absurd to criticise the Court's influence at this time as "excessive", because it went further than democratic notions will allow in the twentieth century.

[1] Count Charles Frederick Vitzthum v. Eckstädt, St. Petersburg and London, ed. H. Reeve, II, 176.

From 1841 to 1861, Prince Albert played a prominent and often decisive part in all the political decisions of the Crown. As he himself had no constitutional standing, not even after the title of "Prince Consort" had been bestowed on him by his wife in 1857, he could only act in the name of the Queen who naturally retained the limelight. Accustomed to this close co-operation with her husband, the Queen attempted, after his death, to act as she thought her husband would have advised. But a state cannot be ruled from the grave. Four decades brought new personalities, new problems. The changed situation created by the death of Palmerston in 1865 and the resignation of Russell in 1866 brought a radical shift in the opinions of the Court, and the Prince Consort's views might well have undergone some adjustment had he lived. The Queen's approach to politics returned to some extent to the personal one she had adopted early in her reign. In the long run the Prince Consort's conception of the role of the Sovereign prevailed and his son King Edward VII reverted to it.

This does not mean that the new King approved all his father's ideas. His reign marked a turning away from much for which his father had stood. Father and son had clashed temperamentally during their lifetime and the father seemed to haunt his son from the grave. For the widowed Queen had attributed her husband's fatal illness partly to his worry over their eldest son and to the strain of his last visit to him at Cambridge.

There were also marked political differences between father and son. The Prince of Wales reacted against his father's apparent overestimation of Germany. His marriage with the daughter of the future King Christian IX of Denmark, which the Prince Consort had helped to plan,[1] was bound to draw the Prince of Wales into the anti-German camp owing to the Schleswig-Holstein war of 1864. In the following decades his sympathies lay with France rather than with Germany.

It is, indeed, the course of later German history and an apparent association of Prince Albert with some of this development which has threatened to deny him his rightful place in British history. Some writers in this country have gone so far as to establish a link between him and the National Socialist régime. Thus the British translator of the letters of the Prince Consort from the Hohenzollern Archives, E. T. S. Dugdale, makes the following comment on the

[1] Thus the Prince Consort to the Crown Princess of Prussia, 24 April 1861 (Royal Archives Z.462.27).

Prince's letter to the Bishop of Oxford, Dr. Wilberforce, in October 1845.[1]

> This letter is remarkable as defining the German view of the duties of the Churches in relation to the State—a view which Bismarck tried in vain to enforce, and which Herr Hitler in our own day is attempting to carry out to its bitterest extreme.[2]

This statement, published in 1938, is perhaps the culmination of the anti-German campaign against the Prince Consort.

Perhaps the time has come for a more dispassionate assessment, free from the passion of current political events. It is quite untenable historically to make the Prince Consort, who died in 1861, responsible for the wars in which Prussia and Germany engaged after his death and to associate him with the National Socialist régime. Indeed, there is considerable evidence that he would have disapproved strongly of the way Germany was united by Bismarck. All the Prince's advice to King William I of Prussia was in favour of his liberal ministers and against the reactionary circles. The King realised that Prince Albert would never have approved of the nomination of Bismarck to the Premiership and it is worth noting that he did not appoint him until 1862. As early as 1855 Prince Albert had advised his son-in-law to protest against any violation of the constitution, a precept which the Crown Prince was to follow in his famous Danzig speech against Bismarck's press ordinance in 1863. The Prince Consort emphasised, with almost wearying repetitiveness, that Prussia should only lead Germany if she became truly liberal and if she used her *moral* influence over her neighbours. He had gone on record as condemning unity through a foreign war. He was thus opposed to everything which critics have found objectionable in the Bismarckian solution.

The Prince Consort's tragically early death had an even greater impact on German and thus on world history than on the development of the British constitutional monarchy. In Britain he had largely established his ideas on government. In Germany, matters were still in a state of flux when he died. The political task to which the Prince had looked forward above any other was to act as the mentor of his daughter and son-in-law in Berlin when they ascended the throne. His death left them exposed in a weak position, deprived of the

---

[1] See p. 169.
[2] Letters of the Prince Consort 1831–1861, edited by K. Jagow, translated by E. T. S. Dugdale (London 1938). The letter to the Bishop is given on page 97 in that edition.

support on which they had counted. King William's offer to abdicate
in 1862, as he could not deal with his constitutional crisis, found the
young couple without the help of their paternal adviser at Windsor.
The Crown Prince's decision to persuade his father to remain on the
throne condemned him and his wife to frustration and bitterness. For
shortly afterwards William called on Bismarck who succeeded in
eliminating the influence of the heir of the throne and of his English
wife, as well as that of Queen Augusta. The old King—who became
German Emperor in 1871—breathed his last when his son was
himself dying, unable to do more than make a few gestures to
vindicate his liberal ideas. On his accession, the Emperor Frederick
III was aware not only that Bismarck would outlive him, in office,
but also that his heir was bitterly opposed to his parents' principles.
William II considered the ninety-nine days of his father's reign as
an unfortunate interlude. He had little in common with his maternal
grandfather, Prince Albert, beyond some slight superficial re-
semblances. The later German Chancellor Hohenlohe in August
1888 actually thought that he detected a similarity in voice and
seriousness. He added:

> If he develops like his grandfather, then we can be content.[1]

The young Emperor identified himself with the prevailing mili-
tant Germanism, perhaps all the more strongly to compensate for his
English mother. In the new climate of opinion, dynasties could no
longer be links between nations, as in Prince Albert's day. The
historian Treitschke made this quite clear in his "History of Germany" by attacking the supra-national ideals of the Coburg family.[2]
Fate was perhaps kind to Prince Albert in not allowing him to
experience this new intolerance—should he have been unable to
prevent it.

Queen Victoria, who was preoccupied with British problems, did
not possess her husband's mastery of the intricacies of German affairs
and was thus unable to help her daughter and son-in-law in Berlin,
except occasionally. Her German sympathies were rudely shaken
when Prussia and Austria pocketed Schleswig-Holstein, instead of
giving it to the Duke of Augustenburg, as she had supposed they
would. The Queen condemned Prussia's action against Austria in
1866. Though she regretted Prussia's annexation of Hanover, she
eventually welcomed the foundation of the German Reich in 1871.

[1] "Die Denkwürdigkeiten des Fürsten Chlodwig zu Hohenlohe-Schillingsfürst",
II, 445.
[2] Heinrich von Treitschke, "Deutsche Geschichte", IV, 82 ff.

While the Queen was not an entirely uncritical admirer of everything German, it was sometimes felt that her sponsorship of German princes for the hands of English princesses was excessive. It was sad that these outward trappings were almost all that remained of Prince Albert's far-reaching German policy.

The British constitutional monarchy remains a memorial to the Prince Consort's achievement. Though his influence on the development of Germany was in the end largely frustrated, it is no longer possible to criticise him for a preoccupation with the future of his native country. He realised the importance of a healthy solution of the German question for the future of Europe.

Two world wars, National Socialism and the consequent division of Germany have only served to emphasise this and to help keep many of his ideas remarkably fresh.

SOURCES

I UNPUBLISHED

Britain
The Royal Archives
The Clarendon Papers
British Foreign Office Papers at the Public Record Office
Germany
The Ducal Archives, Coburg
The Leiningen Archives, Amorbach
The Bonn University Archives

II PUBLISHED

Abbreviations (for full titles see below):
Bolitho = *The Prince Consort and his brother.*
Ernst = Ernst II., *Aus meinem Leben.*
Grey = C. Grey, *The Early Years of the Prince Consort.*
Jagow = *Prinzgemahl Albert* (Letters of the Prince Consort).
Letters = *Letters of Queen Victoria.*
Martin = T. Martin: *Life of the Prince Consort.*

ANSCHÜTZ, GERHARD and THOMAS, RICHARD: *Handbuch des Deutschen Staatsrechts* (I). (Tübingen 1930.)
ARGYLL, 8TH DUKE OF: *Autobiography.* (London 1906.)
ASHLEY, EVELYN: *The Life and Correspondence of Henry John Temple, Viscount Palmerston.* (London 1879.)
BAILLEU, P. and SCHUSTER, G.: *Aus dem literarischen Nachlass der Kaiserin Augusta.* (Berlin 1912.)
BALFOUR, FRANCES: *The Life of George, 4th Earl of Aberdeen.* (London 1923.)
BAMBERGER, LUDWIG: *Politische Schriften 1848–68, III.* (Berlin 1895.)
BARKELEY, RICHARD: *The Empress Frederick.* (London 1956.)
BELL, HERBERT C. F.: *Lord Palmerston.* (London 1936.)
BINDING, KARL: *Zum Werden und Leben der Staaten.* (München 1920.)
BISMARCK'S *Briefe an den General Leopold von Gerlach.* Ed. H. Kohl. (Berlin 1896.)

BOLITHO, H.: *The Prince Consort and his brother; 200 new Letters.* (London 1933.)

>*Further Letters of Queen Victoria.* (London 1938.)

>*A Biographer's Notebook.* (London 1950.)

BONJOUR, E., OFFLER, H. S. and POTTER, P. R.: *A short History of Switzerland.* (Oxford 1952.)

BONJOUR, EDGAR: *Englands Anteil an der Lösung des Neuenburger Konflikts, 1856–57.* (Basel 1943.)

>*Der Neuenburger Konflikt, 1856–57.* (Basel 1957.)

Bonn, the University of: . . . with a concise account of the College Life of H.R.H. Prince Albert . . ., by a member of the Middle Temple. (London 1845.)

BRANDENBURG, E.: *Briefe Kaiser Wilhelm I.* (Leipzig 1911.)

>*Die Reichsgründung.* (Leipzig 1922.)

>*König Friedrich Wilhelm IV. Briefwechsel mit Ludolf Camphausen.* (Berlin 1906.)

BRIGGS, A.: *Victorian People.* (London 1954.)

BRILIOTH, REV. YNGE: *The Anglican Revival.* (London 1925.)

BROUGHTON: *Recollections of a Long Life.* (London 1911.)

BRUNNO, C. (Ed.): *Lettres de Leopold Ier.* (Brussels 1943.)

BUNSEN, FRANCES: *A Memoir of Baron Bunsen.* (London 1868.)

CECIL, A.: *Queen Victoria and Her Prime Ministers.* (London 1953.)

CECIL, D.: *Lord Melbourne.* (London 1955.)

CLARKE, F. L.: *The Childhood of the Prince Consort.* (London 1884.)

CORTI, E. C.: *Wenn . . . Sendung und Schicksal einer Kaiserin.* (Graz 1954.)

>*Leopold I. von Belgien.* (München 1922.)

DOHME, R.: *Unter fünf preussischen Königen.* (Berlin 1901.)

EHRICH, S.: *Persönliche und politische Beziehungen der Königin Victoria von England zum Prinzgemahl Albert.* (Leipzig 1935.)

EMDEN, P. H.: *Behind the Throne.* (London 1934.)

ERNST II, Herzog von Sachsen-Coburg-Gotha: *Aus meinem Leben.* (Berlin 1887.)

EYCK, ERICH: *Bismarck.* (Zürich 1941–44.)

FAY, C. R.: *A Study of the Great Exhibition.* (Cambridge 1951.)

FISCHER-AUE, H. R.: *Die Deutschlandpolitik des Prinzgemahl Albert von England, 1848–1852.* (Coburg 1953.)

FITZMAURICE, E.: *Second Earl Granville.* (London 1905.)

FRENCH, YVONNE: *The Great Exhibition: 1851.* (London 1950.)

FREYTAG, GUSTAV: *Gesammelte Werke (Essay on Stockmar).* (Leipzig 1887–8.)

FRIEDJUNG, HEINRICH: *Der Krimkrieg und die österreichische Politik.*
(Stuttgart 1911.)
FULFORD, ROGER: *The Prince Consort.* (London 1949.)
GASH, NORMAN: *Politics in the Age of Peel.* (London 1953.)
GERLACH, LEOPOLD VON: *Denkwürdigkeiten.* (Berlin 1891–2.)
GILL, C.: *History of Birmingham.* Vol. I. (Oxford 1952.)
GOOCH, G. P.: *The Later Correspondence of Lord John Russell 1840–78.*
(London 1925.)
GREVILLE, CHARLES: *Memoirs.* Ed. by L. Strachey and R. Fulford.
(London 1938.)
GREY, C.: *The Early Years of the Prince Consort.* (London 1867.)
GUEDALLA, P.: *Palmerston.* (London 1926.)
GUICHEN, VICOMTE DE: *Les Grandes Questions Européennes et la Diplomatie des Puissances sous la seconde République Française.* (Paris
1925.)
HAENCHEN, K. (Ed.): *Revolutionsbriefe 1848. Ungedrucktes aus dem
Nachlass von König Friedrich Wilhelm IV. von Preussen.* (Leipzig 1930.)
HALÉVY, E.: *History of the English People.* (London 1924–34.)
HAMMOND, J. L. and B.: *(7th Earl) Lord Shaftesbury.* (London 1923.)
HARDIE, F. M.: *The Political Influence of Queen Victoria.* (Oxford 1935.)
HARTUNG, FRITZ: *Deutsche Verfassungsgeschichte.* (Stuttgart 1950.)
HENDERSON, G. B.: *Crimean War Diplomacy . . .* (Glasgow 1947.)
HEUSS, THEODOR: *1848. Ein Vermächtnis. Werk und Erbe.* (Stuttgart
1954.)
HÖCKER, WILMA: *Der Gesandte Bunsen als Vermittler zwischen Deutschland und England.* (Göttingen 1951.)
HODDER, EDWIN: *The Life and Work of the 7th Earl of Shaftesbury.*
(London 1886.)
HOHENLOHE-SCHILLINGSFÜRST, FÜRST CHLODWIG ZU: *Denkwürdigkeiten.* (Stuttgart 1907.)
JAGOW, KURT: *Prinzgemahl Albert. Ein Leben am Throne.* (Berlin 1937.)
Letters of the Prince Consort 1831–1861. Tr. E. T. S. Dugdale.
(London 1938.)
JONES, W. D.: *Lord Derby and Victorian Conservatism.* (Oxford 1956.)
KINGLAKE, A. W.: *The Invasion of the Crimea.* (Edinburgh and
London 1877.)
KÜNTZEL, G. (Ed.): *Briefwechsel zwischen König Friedrich Wilhelm IV.
und dem Reichsverweser Erzherzog Johann von Österreich 1848/50.*
(Frankfurter Monatshefte 1924.)
KUTSCH, RUTH: *Queen Victoria und die deutsche Einigung.* (Historische
Studien—Heft 330.) (Berlin 1938.)

LANE-POOLE, S.: *Life of Stratford Canning.* (London 1888.)

LAUGHTON, J. K.: *Memoirs of the Life and Correspondence of Henry Reeve.* (London 1898.)

LEE, SIDNEY: *King Edward VII.* (London 1925.)

Letters of Queen Victoria. First series 1837–1861. Ed. A. C. Benson and Viscount Esher. (London 1908.)

LIVERMORE, H. V.: *A History of Portugal.* (Cambridge 1947.)

LUCAS, R.: *Lord Glenesk and the "Morning Post".* (London 1910.)

LUCKHURST, KENNETH W.: *The Story of Exhibitions.* (Cambridge 1951.)

MALMESBURY, EARL OF: *Memoirs of an Ex-Minister.* (London 1884.)

MARCKS, ERICH: *Kaiser Wilhelm I.* (Leipzig 1900.)
    Bismarck und die deutsche Revolution 1848–1851. (Stuttgart 1939.)
    Männer und Zeiten, I. (Leipzig 1911.)

MARTIN, THEODORE: *Life of the Prince Consort.* (London 1875–80.)

MARTIN, B. KINGSLEY: *The Triumph of Lord Palmerston.* (London 1924.)

MAXWELL, H.: *Life and Letters of the 4th Earl of Clarendon.* (London 1913.)

MEINECKE, FRIEDRICH: *Weltbürgertum und Nationalstaat.* (München 1915.)
    Radowitz und die deutsche Revolution. (Berlin 1913.)

MEYENDORFF, PETER VON: *Politischer und Privater Briefwechsel.* Ed. O. Hoetzsch. (Berlin 1923.)

MONYPENNY, W. F. and BUCKLE, G. E.: *The Life of Benjamin Disraeli.* (London 1929.)

MORLEY, J.: *The Life of William Ewart Gladstone.* (London 1905.)

MOTTRAM, R. H.: *"Town Life"* in *"Early Victorian England".* Ed. G. M. Young. (Oxford 1934.)

MÜLLER, MAX: *Die Stammutter des englischen Königshauses.* (Kusel undated.)

NAMIER, LEWIS: *1848: The Revolution of the Intellectuals.* British Academy Proceedings Vol. XXX—1944.

NIPPOLD, F.: *Aus dem Leben der beiden ersten deutschen Kaiser und ihrer Frauen.* (Berlin 1906.)

PARKER, C. S.: *Sir Robert Peel, from his private papers.* (London 1899.)
    Life and Letters of Sir James Graham. (London 1907.)

PARRY, E. JONES: *The Spanish Marriages 1841/46.* (London 1936.)

PASTOR, LUDWIG VON: *Das Leben des Freiherrn Max von Gagern.* (München 1912.)

PONSONBY, ARTHUR: *Henry Ponsonby.* (London 1942.)

PONSONBY, F.: *Letters of the Empress Frederick.* (London 1928.)

PRECHT, H.: *Englands Stellung zur deutschen Einheit 1848–50.* (München 1925.)

RANKE, LEOPOLD VON: *Aus dem Briefwechsel Friedrich Wilhelm IV. von Preussen.* (Leipzig 1873.)

RAY, G. N. (Ed.): *The Letters of W. M. Thackeray.* (London 1945.)

REUMONT, A. VON: *Aus König Friedrich Wilhelm IV. gesunden und kranken Tagen.* (Leipzig 1885.)

RITTER, GERHARD: *Staatskunst und Kriegshandwerk.* (München 1945.)

RUSSELL, JOHN EARL: *Recollections and Suggestions 1813–1873.* (London 1875.)

SCHÄFFER, HANS: *Die auswärtigen Hoheitsrechte der deutschen Einzelstaaten.* (Leipzig 1908.)

SCHARFF, ALEXANDER: *Schicksalsfragen schleswig-holsteinischer Geschichte.* (Neumünster 1951.)

Die Europäischen Grossmächte und die deutsche Revolution 1848–1851. (Leipzig 1942.)

SCHNABEL, FRANZ: *Deutsche Geschichte im 19. Jahrhundert.* (Freiburg 1947–51.)

SCHULTZE, JOHANNES (Ed.): *Die Briefe Kaiser Wilhelm I.* Herausgegeben vom Kaiser-Wilhelm-Institut: Weimarer Briefe. (Berlin 1924.)

SMITH, CECIL WOODHAM-: *The Reason Why.* (London 1953.)

Florence Nightingale. (London 1956.)

STADELMANN, RUDOLF: *Soziale und Politische Geschichte der Revolution von 1848.* (München 1948.)

STANMORE, BARON: *The Earl of Aberdeen.* (London 1893.)

Stenographischer Bericht über die Verhandlungen der deutschen constituierenden Nationalversammlung. Ed. F. Wigard. (Frankfurt am Main 1848–9.)

STERN, ALFRED: *Geschichte Europas.* (Vols. III and IV.)

STOCKMAR, ERNST FREIHERR VON: *Denkwürdigkeiten aus den Papieren des Freiherrn Christian Friedrich von Stockmar.* (Braunschweig 1872.)

STRACHEY, LYTTON: *Queen Victoria.* (London 1921.)

TAYLOR, A. J. P.: *The Italian Problem in European Diplomacy.* (Manchester 1934.)

The Struggle for Mastery in Europe 1848–1918. (Oxford 1954.)

TEMPERLEY, H.: *The Crimea.* (London 1936.)

TEMPERLEY, HAROLD and PENSON, L. (Ed.): *Foundations of British Foreign Policy.* (Cambridge 1938.)

THACKERAY, W. M.: *Vanity Fair.* (First published, London 1847.)

Times, The History of The . . . (Vol. II, 1841–84). (London 1939.)

TREITSCHKE, HEINRICH VON: *Deutsche Geschichte im 19. Jahrhundert.* (Leipzig 1923.)

    Historische und Politische Aufsätze. Vol. I. (Leipzig 1867.)

TÜMPLING, W. VON: *Erinnerungen aus dem Leben des Generaladjutanten Kaiser Wilhelm I. Hermann von Boyen.* (Berlin 1898.)

VALENTIN, VEIT: *Geschichte der deutschen Revolution von 1848–49.* (Berlin 1930.)

VALENTIN, VEIT: *Fürst Karl Leiningen und das Deutsche Einheitsproblem.* (Stuttgart 1910.)

    Bismarcks Reichsgründung im Urteil englischer Diplomaten. (Amsterdam 1937.)

Victoria, Queen: The Girlhood of Queen Victoria. Ed. Viscount Esher. (London 1912.)

    Journal of Life in the Highlands. (London 1868.)

    More Leaves from the Journal 1862/82. (London 1884.)

VITZTHUM, COUNT CHARLES FREDERICK VON ECKSTÄDT: *St. Petersburg und London.* Ed. H. Reeve. (London 1887.)

WALPOLE, SPENCER: *The Life of Lord John Russell.* (London 1889.)

WEBSTER, C.: *Foreign Policy of Palmerston 1830/41.* (London 1951.)

WOODWARD, LLEWELLYN: *Three Studies in European Conservatism.* (London 1929.)

    The Age of Reform (1815–1870). (Oxford 1938.)

INDEX OF PERSONS

(Does not include Prince Albert and Queen Victoria)